THE LINE

BATTLES AND CAMPAIGNS

The Battles and Campaigns series examines the military and strategic results of particular combat techniques, strategies, and methods used by soldiers, sailors, and airmen throughout history. Focusing on different nations and branches of the armed services, this series aims to educate readers by detailed analysis of military engagements.

SERIES EDITOR: Roger Cirillo

AN AUSA BOOK

THE LINE

COMBAT IN KOREA
January–February 1951

Edited by
William T. Bowers

THE UNIVERSITY PRESS OF KENTUCKY

Published by The University Press of Kentucky
Scholarly publisher for the Commonwealth,
serving Bellarmine University, Berea College, Centre
College of Kentucky, Eastern Kentucky University,
The Filson Historical Society, Georgetown College,
Kentucky Historical Society, Kentucky State University,
Morehead State University, Murray State University,
Northern Kentucky University, Transylvania University,
University of Kentucky, University of Louisville,
and Western Kentucky University.
All rights reserved.

Editorial and Sales Offices: The University Press of Kentucky
663 South Limestone Street, Lexington, Kentucky 40508-4008
www.kentuckypress.com

12 11 10 09 08   5 4 3 2 1

All photographs courtesy of the U.S. Army.

Library of Congress Cataloging-in-Publication Data

Bowers, William T., 1946–
  The line : combat in Korea, January–February 1951 / William T.
Bowers.
    p. cm. — (Battles and campaigns)
  Includes bibliographical references and index.
  ISBN 978-0-8131-2508-4 (hardcover : alk. paper)
  1. Korean War, 1950–1953—Participation, American. 2. United States.
Army—History—Korean War, 1950–1953. 3. Korean War, 1950–1953—
Korea (South)—Wonju-si Region. I. Title. II. Title: Combat in Korea,
January–February 1951.
  DS919.B69 2008
  951.904'24—dc22
                                        2008024093

This book is printed on acid-free recycled paper meeting
the requirements of the American National Standard
for Permanence in Paper for Printed Library Materials.

Manufactured in the United States of America.

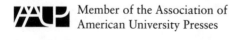 Member of the Association of
American University Presses

CONTENTS

Photo gallery follows page 168

PREFACE

Much can be learned about combat from studying the thirty-eight months of fighting in Korea from June 1950 to July 1953. Military operations ranged from rapid advances and withdrawals and amphibious landings and evacuations, all reminiscent of World War II, to static operations interrupted by set-piece battles and vicious raids that recall the battles on the Western Front during World War I. The weather was often as brutal as the fighting: summers hot and humid, winters frigid with icy Siberian winds. The rugged terrain challenged even those who thought they were in good physical condition. Before Korea, American strategic planners, and indeed most people in the United States, believed that such a war would never be fought again, and certainly not in Korea. Consequently, preparations were few, and the individuals who had to fight the battles paid the price.

This book takes a close look at some of the fighting that occurred over a two-month period during the first winter of the war. It is part of a series about the Korean War that will focus on combat at the lowest levels: battalion, company, platoon, squad, and individual soldiers. Although the spotlight is on tactical operations and frontline fighting, each combat action is placed in its own unique context, so that the reader is aware of the way in which events and decisions, both in Korea and elsewhere, influenced what happened on the battlefield.

Most of the material for this book is drawn from interviews conducted by Army historians soon after a combat action occurred, in some cases within hours or a few days. Additional information comes from official records, such as unit journals and periodic reports, and from unit and individual award recommendations, which include eyewitness accounts of heroic actions.

Army historians had to overcome many problems to collect the combat interviews that form the basis for this book. They worked on tight deadlines, because the interviews and action summaries were needed not only to capture the historical record while events were still fresh, but also to provide information to other American units about enemy and friendly operations, namely, what tactics and methods the enemy was using and what procedures and tactics seemed to be effective or were failures in fighting the enemy. There were many combat actions, and little time was available to conduct interviews and compile the reports, which in most cases included maps, photographs, and a summary. Sometimes historians could not visit units until long after a battle had ended. On occasion the key individuals necessary to provide a complete understanding of the fight were not available for interviews due to death, illness, wounds, leave, or other reasons. The ideal was for the historian to walk the battlefield with the participants so that the resulting interviews, maps, and photographs brought the action alive. But this could not always be accomplished because of time or because the battlefield now was in enemy territory. Accounts by different participants were sometimes contradictory, even about routine matters such as orders, indicating that the confusion of combat remained after the fighting ended. Other statements were vague about the most recent actions or seemed to focus on one specific incident, indicating perhaps that the trauma produced by the immediate presence of danger and death in combat was still present.

Despite occasional shortcomings, this group of interviews provides a unique picture of the fighting in Korea. When soldiers described what they saw and heard, it becomes clear that many narrative histories of the war fail to capture the confusion, uncertainty, fear, hardships, incompetence, dedication, professional skill, determination, and heroism that were everyday occurrences in combat. When the interviews are compared with unit records, it appears that on occasion, higher headquarters had an incomplete and erroneous understanding of what had actually happened. Taken as a whole, the interviews explain why the UN forces prevailed in the difficult war that was fought in Korea. In most cases soldiers and their leaders found a way eventually to overcome all problems and to succeed on the battlefield.

Chapter 1 provides the context needed to understand the fighting that took place during January and February 1951. Problems remaining from peacetime neglect were still present and exerting their influence. The effects of the recent defeats in North Korea were obvious. The 2d Infantry Division, which would play the key role in the fighting in January and February, had been gravely wounded in the fighting in North Korea in late November and early December. It entered combat in early January without adequate recovery time and suffered as a result. The interviews in the first few chapters focus on units of the 2d Division in the fighting around Wonju, a key crossroads town. Because of success in stopping the enemy's New Year's Offensive, General Ridgway directed a limited advance. This led to actions at Hill 312 and Twin Tunnels, the interviews about each being the subject of a chapter. Chapters 7 and 8 look at the special problems involved in supporting allies and show how a plan that looks good on paper can quickly collapse under the realistic conditions of combat. Heavy fighting at Chip'yong-ni and around Wonju again halted a renewal of the enemy offensive, allowing the UN forces to continue moving slowly back to the north. By the end of February, definite changes were noticeable on the battlefield; these are summarized in the concluding chapter.

With the exception of the first and last chapters, the narrative is carried by the interviews, set off by brief remarks in italics to set the stage and link the interviews together. The interviews have undergone minor editing to remove repetitious and extraneous material not key to understanding the action, to correct obvious typographical and grammatical errors so that the reader is not constantly distracted, and to make the interviews more readable by putting them in the form of a statement and changing map coordinates to recognizable locations. Under no circumstances has the meaning been changed. Notes at the end provide information for further research and study.

A number of individuals were of great assistance during the preparation of this book. Roger Cirillo, of the Association of the United States Army, initially proposed the project as a way not only to preserve the Korean War combat interviews, but also to provide an opportunity for a wider audience to become acquainted with their worth as a valuable source for the history of the Korean War and for understanding combat in general. Bob Wright, Mary Haynes, and Jim Knight provided expert assistance and cheerful encouragement and support while I conducted research in the archives and library of the U.S. Army Center of Military History. John Elsberg, Steve Hardyman, Sherry Dowdy, and Beth Mackenzie helped me to gain a better understanding of the cartographic support needed so that the combat interviews could be understood. David Rennie turned my sketches into maps. At the National Archives, Tim Nenninger, Rich Boylan, and Mitch Yockelson, all of the Modern Military Records, provided invaluable assistance as I tracked down unit records and award recommendations, as did Richard Sommers and Dave Keough of the U.S. Army Military History Institute as I searched for additional material. Finally, Stephen M. Wrinn, Anne Dean Watkins, and Ila McEntire of the University Press of Kentucky and copyeditor Stacey Lynn have been instrumental in turning the idea of this project into a book. While all these individuals contributed immeasurably to this book, I alone am responsible for any errors in fact or omission that might appear.

NOTE ON MAPS

A number of the maps used in this work were rough sketches drawn by soldiers as they recounted their experiences during the Korean War. As such, the maps employ a variety of symbols for terrain and military operations. To ensure clarity, notations have been added to some sketches. Whenever possible, the standard military and topographical symbols shown below have been used, along with common abbreviations. Numbers on all contours are in meters.

▭	Unit symbol (enemy shown in gray or labeled)
⊓	Headquarters or command post
△	Observation post (OP)
⬭	Position area
•→	Machine gun or automatic weapon
♠ ♣	Mortar or gun
◇	Tank, self-propelled weapon
▥ ──	Front lines
──→	Route or direction of attack
⨯	Road block
⊓⊔⊓	Trenches, fortified positions

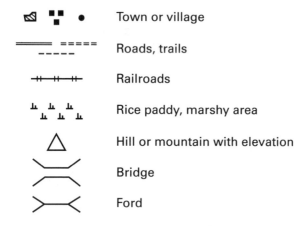

Town or village

Roads, trails

Railroads

Rice paddy, marshy area

Hill or mountain with elevation

Bridge

Ford

The following symbols placed in boundary lines or position area ovals or above the rectangle, triangle, or circle enclosing the identifying arm or service symbol indicate the size of military organizations.

●	Squad
●●	Section
●●●	Platoon
I	Company, troop, battery
II	Battalion, cavalry squadron
III	Regiment, group, combat team
X	Brigade
XX	Division
XXX	Corps
XXXX	Army
XXXXX	Army Group

Examples are given below. The letter or number to the left of the symbol indicates the unit designation; that to the right, the designation of the parent unit to which it belongs. Letters or numbers above or below boundary lines designate the units separated by the lines. Unit designations sometimes are shown as 3/A/9 (3d Platoon, Company A, 9th Infantry Regiment) or as 1–9 (1st Battalion, 9th Infantry Regiment).

A ⊠ 137	Company A, 137th Infantry
⊡ 8	8th Field Artillery Battalion
⊠ 5	Command post, 5th Infantry Division
137 — ||| — 138	Boundary between 137th and 138th Infantry

ABBREVIATIONS

AA	Antiaircraft
AAA	Antiaircraft Artillery
AAA AW	Antiaircraft Artillery Automatic Weapons
A&P	Ammunition and Pioneer
ARCT	Airborne Regimental Combat Team
BAR	Browning Automatic Rifle
BCT	Battalion Combat Team
CCF	Chinese Communist Forces
CG	Commanding General
CO	Commanding Officer
CP	Command Post
DivArty	Division Artillery
DUKW	Amphibious Truck
FA	Field Artillery
FAC	Forward Air Controller
FM	Frequency Modulation
FO	Forward Observer
G-1/S-1	Personnel Officer
G-2/S-2	Intelligence Officer
G-3/S-3	Operations Officer
G-4/S-4	Supply Officer
HE	High Explosive
HEAT	High Explosive Antitank
HMG	Heavy Machine Gun
HQ	Headquarters

I&R	Intelligence and Reconnaissance
JCS	Joint Chiefs of Staff
KATUSA	Korean Augmentation Troops for the U.S. Army
KIA	Killed in Action
KMAG	Korean Military Advisory Group
LD	Line of Departure
MG	Machine Gun
MIA	Missing in Action
MLR	Main Line of Resistance
MSR	Main Supply Road
NCO	Noncommissioned Officer
NK	North Korea
OP	Observation Post; Outpost
OPL	Outpost Line
OPLR	Outpost Line of Resistance
P&A	Pioneer and Ammunition
PLA	People's Liberation Army (Chinese Communist)
POW	Prisoner of War
RCT	Regimental Combat Team
Recon	Reconnaissance
ROK	Republic of Korea (South Korean)
R&R	Rest and Recreation
SCR	Signal Corps Radio
SOP	Standard Operating Procedure
SP	Self-propelled
TACP	Tactical Air Control Party
TF	Task Force
T/O&E	Table of Organization and Equipment
UN	United Nations
WIA	Wounded in Action
WP	White Phosphorous

RANKS

Pvt.	Private
PFC	Private 1st Class
Cpl.	Corporal
Sgt.	Sergeant

S. Sgt.	Staff Sergeant
SFC	Sergeant 1st Class
M. Sgt.	Master Sergeant
1st Sgt.	First Sergeant
Lt.	Lieutenant
2d Lt.	2d Lieutenant
1st Lt.	1st Lieutenant
Capt.	Captain
Maj.	Major
Lt. Col.	Lieutenant Colonel
Col.	Colonel
Gen.	General
Brig. Gen.	Brigadier General
Maj. Gen.	Major General
Lt. Gen.	Lieutenant General

Chapter 1

WAR COMES TO KOREA

The First Six Months

In the predawn darkness of Sunday, 25 June 1950, North Korean artillery and mortar shells began to fall on scattered South Korean army positions along the 38th parallel. Violence was no stranger to the area dividing North and South Korea. Artillery bombardments, minor infantry engagements, and guerrilla incursions were frequent. As the shelling continued and grew in intensity, South Korean soldiers and their American advisors realized that this was something new. As dawn broke, the North Korean army attacked in force all along the border. In many areas strong attacks quickly overran surprised and scattered frontline Republic of Korea (ROK) forces. Some ROK units held for a time but were eventually overwhelmed as more North Koreans poured across the border. Ten to twenty miles below the border, ROK commanders hastily concentrated their reserves, many of whom had been on weekend passes, and moved them into defensive positions. Soon they too were under attack. Messages from the field to ROK army headquarters and to American headquarters in Korea, Japan, and Washington spread the word that a major invasion was in progress.[1]

The North Korean attack achieved complete surprise, although South Korea and the United States had recognized for some time the potential for war on the Korean peninsula. North Korea, under its leader Kim Il Sung, had built a strong military force of 135,000 men organized into ten infantry divisions with a full complement of artillery, a tank brigade of 120 T-34 tanks, and an air force of about 180 aircraft. The army was well equipped and trained by the Soviet

Union, which had provided advisors and a constant influx of supplies, weapons, and equipment. Many of the soldiers, although Korean, had been transferred from the Chinese Communist army and were combat veterans of World War II and the Chinese civil war. The North Korean attack plan was developed with the assistance of Soviet military advisors and took advantage of significant weaknesses of the ROK and American forces in South Korea and the Far East. North Korea had convinced its strategic partners, the Soviet Union and Communist China, that its forces could overwhelm the South Koreans and occupy the country before the United States could intervene. Moreover, there was a belief that the United States did not have the capability or willingness to go to war in South Korea.[2]

South Korea and American Policy

At the end of World War II, Korea, which had been a colony of the Japanese empire, was divided along the 38th parallel for ease in accepting the surrender of the Japanese forces. After occupying Manchuria, the Soviet Union moved into the more developed and industrialized northern part of Korea, while U.S. troops occupied the mainly agricultural southern section of the peninsula. Over the next few years efforts to unite the country under one government failed, and the United States came to accept the fact that the area would remain divided. A South Korean government was formed under Syngman Rhee, who advocated unification by force of the Korean peninsula under one government. Consequently, the United States did not trust or totally support Rhee, particularly in his requests for a buildup of the ROK army.

Initially the ROK army was organized, trained, and equipped as a constabulary or police force. It was designed to fight guerrillas and maintain order in the cities and countryside in the presence of many strikes and protests, all of which Rhee claimed were instigated by the Communists. As part of the overall drawdown of U.S. forces in the years following World War II, the American occupation troops in Korea, consisting of a corps headquarters and two infantry divisions, departed Korea in late 1948 and early 1949. Left behind was a 500-man Korean Military Advisory Group (KMAG) with the job of converting the South Korean constabulary force into an army capable of fighting a modern war with a full range of weapons. When North Korea invaded in June 1950, the process was incomplete. The ROK army on paper was strong, consisting of some 154,000 men organized into eight divisions with mortars and light artillery. However, many weaknesses were present: only small unit training through company level had been completed; shortages existed in medium artillery and antitank weapons as well as all types of ammunition and spare parts; a substantial number of army troops were tied down in internal security missions in the southern part of the country; and perhaps most important, there were serious doubts as to the competence of many of the ROK army commanders and staff officers. The ROK air force was a token organization with only about twenty aircraft for liaison and training and an additional ten World War II–era fighter aircraft for which South Korean pilots were still undergoing flight instruction.[3]

American strategic planning in early 1950 did not include a clear concept for the defense of South Korea. The withdrawal of American combat forces signaled that the United States military with limited resources did not want to fight a major war in an area considered insignificant and difficult to support. Instead, the United States focused on nation building in South Korea through economic assistance, as well as military aid, stationing in the country 2,500 civilian and military advisors, the largest number in any of its world outposts. Plans for responding to a major attack against South Korea before it was prepared to defend itself were vague, although there was an underlying assumption that the United States would not let South Korea fall. Secretary of State Dean Acheson, in a public speech on 12 January 1950, outlined U.S. defense strategy in the Far East. Acheson appeared to exclude South Korea and Formosa, the island to which the Nationalist Chinese government of Chiang Kai-shek had withdrawn after their defeat by the Chinese Communists in 1949, from American defense plans by stating that no one could guarantee the security of these areas against attack and that reliance initially should be placed on the efforts of the people under attack and then on the United Nations.[4]

The surprise attack against South Korea came as a genuine shock to President Truman and his advisors, who were incensed at the action of North Korea, as well as their Soviet and Chinese Communist backers. As the North Korean army continued to push into South Korea, gradually wearing down the resistance of those ROK units holding out in forward positions, Truman saw not only a need to respond to naked aggression, but also an opportunity to mobilize the United States and the free world to meet the larger challenge of Communist worldwide expansion.

At the end of World War II, the United States had quickly demobilized its massive military forces, comprising 12 million men and women, including 95 divisions, 92,000 aircraft, and 1,307 ships. But the hope for world peace did not materialize. The Soviet Union rapidly gained control of Eastern Europe, and Communist supporters appeared to be gaining strength in many areas of the world. President Truman responded with the Truman Doctrine, which promised to aid countries threatened by Communism, but the means were generally limited to economic assistance and military advisors and equipment. The United States relied on airpower and the atomic bomb for its own security. In 1949, however, the Soviet Union detonated its own atomic bomb, completely changing U.S. strategic planning assumptions.

In early 1950 Truman directed a thorough review of U.S. national security policy, which concluded that the Soviet Union and its Communist allies were an aggressive threat and recommended an immediate and large-scale buildup of U.S. and allied military forces as a balance to Soviet power. The security review presented Truman with a difficult problem: how to mobilize and gain the support of the American people for a massive and costly military expansion. The United States as a whole was focused on domestic concerns, and there was strong political support for lower taxes and a reduction in the federal budget. It was doubtful that the American people would support the financial and other sacrifices needed for a renewed effort in the Cold War with vague and open-ended goals. To Truman, the surprise attack of North Korea offered a possible solution.[5]

The United States Responds

Truman began an immediate diplomatic offensive. On 27 June 1950 the United Nations Security Council condemned the North Korean attack and called on all members to go to the assistance of South Korea. Truman ordered General of the Army Douglas MacArthur, the commander of U.S. forces in the Far East, to use American air and naval forces against the North Korean invaders. Air attacks began on 27 June but had little effect in slowing the enemy. On 30 June, one day after Seoul fell, Truman authorized MacArthur to commit American ground troops.

The U.S. Army was unprepared for war. The deep reductions following World War II, and the subsequent personnel turmoil and tight budgets of the late 1940s produced a weak force with severe problems. At the end of demobilization in 1947, the Army strength was 684,000. The expiration of the Selective Service Act in March 1947, the subsequent decline in volunteers, and the exit of the last draftees all combined to reduce the Army to 538,000 within a year. Hoping that Congress would pass legislation for Universal Military Training (UMT) that would provide for a large standing army, the Truman administration delayed asking Congress for passage of a new Selective Service Act. Congress, however, refused to act on UMT, both because of its cost (estimated at $2 billion) and the widespread belief that large armies were not needed in an age of airpower and nuclear weapons.

With no legislation forthcoming for UMT, Selective Service, or funding of recruiting incentives, the Army was forced to cut in order to meet its worldwide commitments. Basic training was reduced from seventeen weeks to eight weeks. Many units were inactivated. The strength of remaining troop units was either reduced across the board, or subunits were reduced to zero strength and their equipment placed in storage. Budget restrictions on procurement and lack of manpower to perform routine maintenance combined over time to produce widespread equipment shortages and unserviceability.

Units were constrained in their training due to the equipment and manpower shortages and tight budgets. Military readiness was severely affected in almost every area.

Although the Truman administration finally acted, and Congress passed a new Selective Service Act in 1948, the damage was done. As the new draft was put into effect, Army strength slowly increased and stood at 591,000 in June 1950, but funding declined, and in fact the 1950 budget of $4.27 billion was almost a one-third reduction from the $6.02 billion of 1949.

At the beginning of the Korean War, the U.S. Army had 591,000 men organized in ten combat divisions and several independent regiments. The bulk, some 360,000 troops (5 divisions), was in the United States. Overseas, about 98,000 men (1 division) were stationed in Europe, while MacArthur's Far East Command had 108,500 men in 4 divisions in Japan.* The divisions in Japan were assigned to Eighth Army and performed occupation duties until the late spring of 1949, when General MacArthur directed that more responsibilities be turned over to the Japanese.

Lt. Gen. Walton H. Walker, the Eighth Army commander, immediately initiated an intensive training program for his soldiers. Company-level training, including a limited amount of basic training for new arrivals, was to be completed by December 1949 and battalion-level by May 1950. June and July 1950 would be spent on regimental exercises followed by full division training from July to December. Provisions were also made for training in amphibious operations with the Navy and in air movements with the Air Force. Walker, a corps commander under General Patton in World War II, was an experienced and capable leader, and he knew how to train soldiers for combat. However, his program was ambitious, and there were severe challenges to fully implementing it.

---

* During this period, Army infantry divisions on paper consisted of three infantry regiments, each with three infantry battalions (numbered 1–3). Each infantry battalion consisted of five companies—Headquarters Company, 3 rifle companies (lettered A, B, C, E, F, G, I, K, L), and a heavy weapons company (lettered D, H, M).

The underlying assumption of the unit training program was that before it began all soldiers would have completed basic training in fundamental soldier skills. Unfortunately, this was not the situation. When basic training had been reduced from seventeen to eight weeks, the portion of instruction that was dropped was the bulk of the tactical field training, including night operations, and a major portion of marksmanship, weapons familiarization, and physical fitness. Because of safety concerns, basic training in the peacetime Army did not include realistic live fire exercises: the infiltration course with overhead machine-gun fire, the overhead artillery fire exercise, the close combat course with units using fire and maneuver, and the combat-in-cities course with flamethrowers and hand grenades. When these partially trained soldiers arrived at their units in Japan after basic training, they did not participate in field training to acquire the missing skills, but instead performed occupation duties such as police and guard functions, civilian relief, and refugee assistance. Even those soldiers who had completed the longer basic training course suffered a loss of those learned skills over time while performing nontactical duties. Moreover, junior officers who had completed their school training did not have an opportunity to hone and further develop their skills in occupation units. The limited amount of basic training that was given to new arrivals in the summer of 1949 in Japan did not fill the gap.

The training of companies and battalions proceeded more or less as scheduled in the limited maneuver areas available in Japan. Units were under strength, and a number of assigned soldiers could not participate because they were on special duty in administrative and support jobs throughout Eighth Army. Personnel turbulence remained high, with some units experiencing a 50 percent annual turnover. This meant that many of those who began the training in 1949 were not in the units at the end of the cycle in 1950, and new arrivals in early 1950 had to pick up the training program in midstream. The quality of the training varied from unit to unit depending on several factors, such as the competence of unit leaders, who would conduct the training, and the number of World War II combat veterans who could introduce the right note of realism and urgency into the instruction. For many units, the training was physically demanding, and the instruction in small unit tactics and basic soldier skills was thorough. Other units merely went through the motions, with soldiers little realizing that their lives might soon depend on what a boring instructor might be saying or the unimaginative, unrealistic tactical exercise that they were walking through.

Most soldiers in Japan in 1950 had few thoughts of war, for life was good in the occupied country. The pay of a private went a long way in the civilian economy. Many soldiers had Japanese girlfriends, and there were many opportunities for recreation or to continue civilian education, a goal for which many had enlisted. When the news of fighting in Korea reached Eighth Army, the prospect of war was viewed by some as a welcome break to the peacetime routine, but to others it was an unwanted disruption, for they enjoyed and were comfortable with Army life in Japan.

Larger unit exercises were interrupted by the outbreak of the Korean War, but would have been severely hampered in any case because of the lack of adequate space in Japan to allow an entire division to train as a whole. Although with one exception the infantry regiments in Japan had two instead of three battalions and two instead of three firing batteries in artillery battalions, even a reduced-strength regiment with its complement of artillery and other support would have been unable to deploy and maneuver in a realistic manner. Because of the lack of opportunities to train larger units, much would depend on the experience of their commanders. Although some were combat veterans of World War II and had commanded divisions and regiments in battle, others had been staff officers and were lacking in the knowledge they would soon need in Korea. In World War II it had taken a full year to train a division for combat, and senior commanders and their staffs were experienced in regimental and divisional field operations. Even then, it was recognized that an unbloodied unit would have a steep learning curve when it entered battle, and if conditions were not favorable in its first fight, it could suffer heavy casualties and possibly defeat. The four divisions in Japan did not have the advantage of the complete one-year training program that most World War II divisions enjoyed, and they would enter combat under the most unfavorable of circumstances.

Equipment was also a problem. Of World War II vintage, old and worn, the condition of the weapons, vehicles, radios, and other equipment posed a daunting challenge. A unit was fortunate if its commander and maintenance personnel recognized that paperwork showing an item was on order or in a repair facility would not be an adequate substitute for weapons and equipment needed in combat. Many units, through hard work, initiative, and ingenuity, ensured that everything was in working order, even if old. Others were plagued with shortages and large numbers of unserviceable or marginal equipment. One regiment reported that it had only 60 percent of its authorized radios and that 80 percent of those were inoperable. A battalion in another regiment reported that most of its rifles and mortars were not serviceable. Weapons such as recoilless rifles, 4.2-inch mortars, and medium tanks were almost nonexistent throughout the command. For example, of 226 recoilless rifles authorized in Eighth Army, only 21 were present. Although ammunition was generally adequate, with a forty-five-day supply in depots in addition to unit basic loads for training, there were critical shortages of certain items, such as trip flares, grenades, antitank mines, antitank artillery shells, and 60mm mortar illuminating shells. These would soon be needed to fight an enemy who frequently used tanks and attacked at night.

The news of the North Korean attack came as a surprise in Japan. Although the intelligence assessments of the Far East Command recognized the buildup of Kim Il Sung's forces, and the clashes along the 38th parallel were no secret, existing war plans were focused on the potential threat of a Soviet invasion of the northern islands of Japan. South Korea was not part of General MacArthur's Far East Command, and he had no responsibility for the area except to provide logistic support for KMAG. This changed on 26 June when President Truman directed MacArthur to assess the situation. Initially it was hoped that the South Koreans, with the assistance of U.S. air support, could hold the enemy, but on 30 June, with the North Koreans still advancing unchecked, President Truman directed the commitment of American ground troops.

There was a widespread belief that the mere presence of American troops, with their reputation of military superiority from World

War II, would be enough to stop the North Koreans. The choice of the term "police action" as a description of the conflict caused a number of soldiers to view the impending deployment to Korea as little more than what they had experienced during riot duty in the cities of Japan during labor or political unrest. Initial optimistic reports from the battlefield carried in the local soldier newspaper, the *Stars and Stripes,* reinforced the impression among many that their task would be easy. The soldiers of Eighth Army soon learned how mistaken they were.[6]

First Battle

On 30 June General MacArthur ordered the 24th Infantry Division to deploy to Korea, with a small delaying force moving immediately by air and the rest of the division following by water. The 24th Infantry Division, which consisted of the 19th, 21st, and 34th Infantry Regiments, each having only two battalions, was the nearest division to Japan, and its commander, Maj. Gen. William F. Dean, was experienced, having commanded a division in combat in World War II and having served in Korea with the occupation forces. The division was quickly brought up to strength by the transfer of 2,108 men from other divisions in Japan, and began moving to ports, where an assortment of transport vessels was rapidly being assembled. By 5 July the bulk of the division had landed at Pusan and was moving north to meet the enemy.

The delaying force from the 1st Battalion, 21st Infantry Regiment, which had recently satisfactorily completed its battalion training test and had undergone air movement training with the U.S. Air Force, flew to Korea on 1 July and moved by rail to Taejon, arriving the morning of 2 July. There its commander, Lt. Col. Charles B. Smith, met Brig. Gen. John H. Church, General MacArthur's representative in Korea. Church could provide little information about the situation to the north. Pointing to the map, he told Smith, "We have a little action up here. All we need is some men up there who won't run when they see tanks. We're going to move you up to support the ROKs and give them moral support."[7]

Early on the morning of 5 July, Smith was in position north of Osan, digging in along a ridge overlooking the main road to the

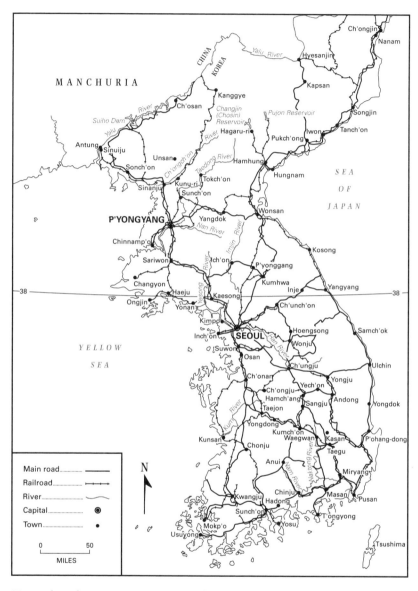

Korea (based on U.S. Army Center of Military History map).

north that penetrated the ridge through a cut. His small force, which became known as Task Force Smith, consisted of 540 men from Companies B and C of the 1st Battalion, 21st Infantry, two composite weapons platoons of recoilless rifles and 60mm and 4.2-inch mortars, and Battery A, 52d Field Artillery Battalion, under Lt. Col. Miller O. Perry. Although it was raining, the site offered good observation and fields of fire to the north. The defensive position, however, could easily be turned by a move around either flank. There were no mines, and the artillery had only six rounds of high explosive antitank (HEAT) ammunition. The nearest American ground support was a battalion of the 34th Infantry Regiment, 24th Division, moving into position about twelve miles to the south. No air support was available, and Smith had no contact with any ROK forces that might be in the area.

About 0700 Smith saw movement to the north and soon identified a North Korean tank column advancing along the road. When the column was a little more than a mile from the position, the artillery opened fire. When the tanks were about 700 yards away, the recoilless rifles began firing, and the 2.36-inch rocket launchers (bazookas) opened when the tanks reached the infantry position. The artillery fire had no effect on the tanks, and although the tanks sustained direct hits from the recoilless rifles and bazookas, there was no damage. The tanks, with only a few accompanying infantry riding aboard, stayed on the road and advanced quickly through Smith's infantry position.

To the rear, two tanks were knocked out by a 105mm howitzer firing HEAT shells, and two others were damaged. When the HEAT rounds were gone, the other artillery pieces opened with regular high explosive shells, and bazooka teams continued firing. This fire had little effect on the enemy tanks. The remaining tanks, numbering about thirty, all from the North Korean 107th Tank Regiment, continued south along the road. They had knocked out the artillery piece that had fired the antitank rounds, destroyed all of the vehicles that had brought the infantry forward, cut the telephone wire connecting the artillery with the infantry, and inflicted about twenty casualties.

As the rain continued, the Americans continued to improve their position. Communications between the infantry and the artillery in the rear remained out, with the cut wire still unrepaired and radios malfunctioning in the rain. Shortly before noon, Smith again saw movement to the north, and soon a column of infantry, estimated to be six miles long, moving by truck and on foot, approached. The North Koreans, consisting of two infantry regiments from the North Korean 4th Division, apparently without communications with the advance force of tanks, was unaware that American combat forces were in Korea. Assuming that the force on the ridge to their front was South Korean, they continued to approach until taken under fire by the Americans. Firing all available weapons except for artillery, which remained out of communications in the rear, Smith's men stopped the advance of the enemy and forced them to deploy. Bringing artillery and mortar fire to bear on the ridge, the North Koreans began to move around both flanks.

By 1430, with ammunition running low, an enemy double envelopment in progress, and tanks roaming somewhere to his rear, Smith gave the order to conduct a fighting withdrawal by leapfrogging his two companies through successive positions, a difficult maneuver in broad daylight for even the most seasoned units. Under heavy enemy pressure, with almost no internal communications except by runner, the movement soon disintegrated into several small groups attempting to escape across country as best they could. Heavy weapons and the dead and most seriously wounded had to be left behind. Task Force Smith suffered its heaviest casualties during the withdrawal, and the next day Smith could account for only about 250 men of the original 406 from the 1st Battalion, 21st Infantry. The artillery suffered about 31 casualties among the 134 men present at the battle. North Korean losses were reportedly 42 killed and 85 wounded.[8]

Task Force Smith's battle set the pattern for the next few days, as other American units were committed to combat under similar circumstances. While the remnants of Task Force Smith were collected and reorganized at Ch'onan, the two battalions of the 34th Infantry occupied delaying positions about ten miles south of Osan. On 6 July one of these battalions quickly withdrew when a North Korean force of tanks and infantry appeared and began moving around its flanks. General Dean concentrated both battalions of the 34th Infantry near Ch'onan and replaced the regimental commander, who himself was new to the unit, having taken over after the previous commander was fired for poor performance on unit training tests in Japan. Dean's hope of achieving sufficient delay at Ch'onan for the rest of his division to arrive quickly collapsed. The North Koreans attacked with tanks the night of 7–8 July, and in sharp fighting the next day forced the regiment back. The new commander, Col. Robert R. Martin, a proven combat veteran of World War II, was killed fighting tanks with a bazooka in the streets of the village.

Dean now planned for the 21st Infantry Regiment (the unit's 3d Battalion had arrived to join Smith's much depleted 1st Battalion), commanded by Col. Richard W. Stephens, to conduct a fighting withdrawal down the main road to the southeast toward Taejon, a major city whose prewar population of 130,000 was swollen with refugees. Dean ordered the battered 34th Infantry to withdraw directly south along a secondary road. Behind the Kum River, which runs in a generally east-west direction north of Taejon, Dean intended to concentrate his division and establish a defensive position. However, the availability of recently arrived American M24 light tanks, antitank mines, additional artillery (including 155mm howitzers), and tactical air control parties, which made close air support much more effective, did little to halt the North Korean advance.

Early on 11 July, after a day of fighting involving both battalions of the 21st Infantry, the enemy hit the 3d Battalion of the regiment in a carefully coordinated and powerful attack about fifteen miles north of the Kum. Under a heavy mortar bombardment, tanks ripped through the 3d Battalion position while infantry moved rapidly around its flanks to establish roadblocks in the rear. By noon the unit was surrounded and being overrun; it disintegrated into small groups, which fought their way out. The 3d Battalion lost 60 percent of its men, including the battalion commander and the bulk of his staff; most of those who escaped were without weapons.

The North Korean advance was slowed by air strikes on the roads that hit troops and vehicles, forcing the enemy in clear weather to move and attack at night. On 12 July the survivors of the 21st and 34th Infantry crossed the Kum River and joined the 19th Infantry Regiment. However, the North Koreans did not allow Dean's men time to recover and establish a solid defense. On 14 July, the

North Korean 4th Division attacked the 34th Infantry, now under Lt. Col. Robert L. Wadlington. Wadlington, with insufficient forces to defend all of the crossing sites over the Kum, had planned to leave a screen of troops from the 3d Battalion and the Intelligence and Reconnaissance (I&R) Platoon along the river and use the 1st Battalion as a counterattack force. The North Koreans, once again showing the ability for rapid reconnaissance and speedy development of a coordinated attack plan, crossed the river in the weak I&R Platoon sector, overran the firing batteries of the 63d Field Artillery, and established strong blocking positions between the river and Wadlington's 1st Battalion. A counterattack by the 1st Battalion failed, and the 3d Battalion positions along the river collapsed. The 34th Infantry was forced to withdraw with heavy losses.

To the east along the Kum, the 19th Infantry under Col. Guy S. Meloy Jr. was about to experience its first combat. On its own because of the 34th Infantry collapse to the west and the much depleted 21st Infantry's withdrawal toward Taejon to reorganize and recover, the 19th Infantry had two battalions to cover a front of thirty miles, an impossible task. Meloy chose to concentrate against the North Korean 3d Division to his front, while sending one company to screen against a possible advance of the North Korean 4th Division from the west. The North Koreans probed along the Kum on 14 and 15 July, developing intelligence of American positions while preparing their plan of attack. Before dawn on 16 July, the enemy struck with heavy fixing attacks while other forces moved through gaps into rear areas. The North Koreans then began attacking artillery and mortar positions and reserves in the American rear, while establishing blocking positions on main roads and cutting routes of withdrawal. Attacks to eliminate the North Korean roadblocks failed; Meloy was wounded, and the 19th Infantry disintegrated into small groups that fought their way out with heavy casualties.

General Dean now had few choices. All of his regiments had been severely mauled without imposing any significant delay on the North Koreans. The remnants were exhausted from constantly moving and fighting in the rough terrain amid the humid summer heat of Korea. With the likelihood of facing two North Korean divisions with his depleted force, Dean planned to continue the withdrawal before his units were decisively engaged.

On 18 July, General Walker, the Eighth Army commander, visited Dean and requested that the 24th Division provide at least two days of delay at Taejon to allow another division from Japan, the 1st Cavalry, to move into position. Dean reluctantly agreed; it was understood that he might be forced to pull back earlier in order to save his units. One hopeful sign was the arrival by air from the United States of the more effective 3.5-inch rocket launchers, which were immediately issued to units of the 24th Infantry Division.

Despite air attacks, by noon on 19 July, the North Korean 4th Division partially repaired a destroyed bridge over the Kum River, crossed tanks and artillery, and moved forward against Dean's men with one infantry regiment, sending the other two infantry regiments with the bulk of the tanks to the south and then east to outflank the American position. The Americans stopped the initial enemy advance, but positions were driven in, and American artillery was hit with heavy counterbattery fire. Dean's position was too extensive for the number of available forces.

That night the North Korean 4th Division took advantage of the dispersed Americans by penetrating through gaps and establishing blocking positions on the roads running from Taejon to the south and to the east. Before dawn on 20 July, the enemy attacked in force with infantry and tanks cutting through and around the flank of the Americans and moving directly east toward Taejon. The North Korean 3d Division closed on the city from the north. The enemy then went to cover, apparently to avoid American air strikes, but also, likely, to wait for the Americans to react and start withdrawing into the roadblocks south and east of Taejon.

Using a captured radio, the enemy sent a false report that one American battalion was holding on, when in fact it had disintegrated as an effective force with elements generally withdrawing to the southeast. In Taejon, because of the loss of communications with frontline units and the false report from one battalion, the situation across the front did not appear serious. However, unknown to the headquarters and support elements in the city, enemy tanks

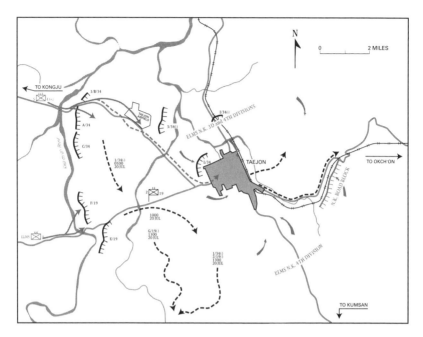

The fall of Taejon, 20 July 1950 (based on U.S. Army Center of Military History map).

from the North Korean 4th Division had entered the town soon after dawn and were roaming the streets attacking American positions wherever found. By 0900 American bazooka teams using the new 3.5-inch rocket launcher moved through the city, stalking the tanks and knocking out four of the five tanks in the town. About noon, other tanks entered the town, most likely from the North Korean 3d Division, and bazooka teams, including one led by General Dean, destroyed them. American air attacks hit additional tanks; overall the North Koreans around and in Taejon lost at least fifteen tanks, with about ten of them being destroyed by 3.5-inch rocket fire.

About 1400, still under the impression that all was well with his units, Dean ordered a daylight withdrawal under the belief that it would be much easier to control than one at night. In response to the withdrawal order, movement out of the city began about 1700 hours. By this time, the North Koreans had closed on the city from almost every direction, and troops and vehicles attempting to leave were met with heavy fire. Forced to abandon vehicles, soldiers moved cross-country as best they could to escape the trap. The survivors wandered back to American lines for several days. An accounting showed that of the 4,000 Americans around Taejon, about 30 percent were casualties, including General Dean, who was captured after evading the North Koreans for thirty-six days.

On 22 July the 1st Cavalry Division arrived to relieve the 24th Infantry Division. In seventeen days of almost constant fighting and moving, the 24th Division had lost most of its heavy equipment and suffered 30 percent casualties. But it had slowed the North Korean advance enough to allow other divisions from Japan to arrive and take up the fight. It had accomplished this despite fighting outnumbered and with little support, with equipment and personnel shortages, and with partially trained soldiers and units. The 24th Division had learned rapidly and had accomplished its mission, but the cost had been high.[9]

The Retreat Continues

While the 24th Division was fighting south from Osan, the rest of Eighth Army mobilized and began to move to Korea to join the ROK army in fighting the North Koreans. The 25th Infantry Division, commanded by Maj. Gen. William B. Kean and consisting of the 24th, 27th, and 35th Infantry Regiments, began arriving at Pusan on 10 July and was ashore by 15 July. Kean's division moved north to Andong and Hamch'ang to support the remnants of ROK divisions attempting to stop the North Korean advance through the central mountains. Meanwhile, based on a United Nations Security Council resolution, General MacArthur had taken command of all UN forces in Korea. On 13 July General Walker assumed command of U.S. troops in Korea, and on 17 July, he took charge of all ROK ground forces.

By this time, the outline of a front had formed across the Korean peninsula. The remnants of the ROK 7th Division were in the west near the coast facing the North Korean (NK) 6th Division; the U.S. 24th Infantry Division was along the Kum River blocking the main road and rail line from Seoul to Pusan against the NK 3d and 4th

Divisions; elements of the ROK 1st, 2d, 6th, 8th, and Capital Divisions were in the central mountains backed up by the U.S. 25th Infantry Division and fighting the NK 2d, 15th, 1st, and 12th Divisions; and the ROK 23d Regiment, part of the ROK 3d Division, held the coastal road in the east against the NK 5th Division. The U.S. 1st Cavalry Division was scheduled to begin landing on 18 July and would move forward to support the 24th Division in holding the main road to Pusan.

As Walker assessed the situation, the immediate problem was holding the enemy long enough for the 1st Cavalry to get into position. If this could be accomplished, then it would be possible to establish a much stronger line and conduct an orderly withdrawal behind the Naktong River, where a stable defensive position could be established and forces could be built up for a counterattack. The 24th Division's delay of the enemy at Taejon allowed the 1st Cavalry, commanded by Maj. Gen. Hobart R. Gay and consisting of the 5th, 7th, and 8th Cavalry Regiments, to move forward to Yongdong, where it relieved the 24th Division on 22 July.

About the same time, the 25th Infantry Division met the North Koreans on the roads leading through the central mountains. On 20 July a battalion of the 24th Infantry Regiment fought an engagement at Yech'on, east of Hamch'ang, and two days later Company F, 35th Infantry, was hit hard as it supported a ROK defensive position near Hamch'ang. The entire 24th Infantry Regiment was shifted into the valleys west of Sangju to stop the North Korean 15th Division, but was forced back in a series of actions. The 35th Infantry moved from Hamch'ang to Sangju to help hold the sector. To the south, the 27th Infantry fought in front of Hwanggang-ni (about ten miles northwest of Kumch'on) to stop the North Korean 2d Division. The three regiments of the 25th Division managed to hold their lines in front of Sangju and Hwanggang-ni, but pressure was building to their front and on the northern flank, where ROK units were still under heavy attack.

Meanwhile on 23 July the North Korean 3d Division at Yongdong attacked the 1st Cavalry Division. Over the next two days the fighting was severe, and by 25 July the 1st Cavalry's positions had become untenable due to flanking movements, infiltration, and pen-

etrations into rear areas, essentially the same tactics that had worked
so well for the North Koreans against the 24th Infantry Division.
Forced to conduct a fighting withdrawal, the 1st Cavalry Division
pulled back to Kumch'on along with the 27th Infantry Regiment.

An observation team arrived from the United States on 24 July and
spent the next few days visiting all American divisions and regiments in Korea to assess the problems that had developed during
combat. Their final report began by noting the difficult conditions
under which the units fought:

> having been . . . committed more or less piecemeal, after incom-
> plete training, and at reduced strength, with much of their equip-
> ment of marginal serviceability . . . Our troops were opposed by
> an enemy who vastly outnumbered them, and who was well
> trained, well equipped, skillfully led and inspired by a fanatical
> determination to attack. . . . The frontages were enormous and
> precluded a continuous line of defense. This facilitated outflank-
> ing and penetrating operations by the enemy and forced a con-
> tinuous withdrawal.

But the report went on to identify disturbing and serious problems not only in fundamental soldier skills, but also in discipline
and leadership:

> The absolute discipline and automatic obedience to command that
> is vital for control in combat is lacking. All troops were deficient in
> measures for cover and concealment, and in maintaining signal
> communications. The troops were disinclined to leave the roads,
> and were unskilled in use of mines and in night operations. Like all
> green troops, they magnified the strength of the enemy, and tended
> to become panicky and stampede when small hostile groups got in
> their rear. . . . Infantry troops were specifically deficient in aggres-
> siveness in counter-attack, steadiness under fire, [and] confidence
> in their own weapons. . . . Lack of leadership in regimental and
> subordinate echelons was often evident, in both field and company
> grades, and among the noncommissioned officers.[10]

As the American divisions took over much of the fighting against
North Korean forces advancing to the southeast toward Pusan, the

ROK army reorganized into two corps, combining and consolidating fragments of units to form more effective combat formations. The reorganized ROK forces were shifted to the right of the Americans. The II Corps with the ROK Capital and 8th Divisions was at Hamchang; to the east was I Corps with the ROK 1st and 6th Divisions. Separated from these troops by mountains, the ROK 3d Division continued to hold the east coast. The ROK tactical forces by now had been reduced to about 40,000 men, although additional soldiers were in training camps or were reforming in rear areas.

Hampering the operations of both American and ROK forces were hundreds of thousands of refugees fleeing south in front of the North Koreans. They clogged the roads, slowing the movement of troops and supplies. On several occasions North Korean soldiers infiltrated through American or ROK lines disguised as refugees, or used civilians to shield movements of their own forces. In the areas of South Korea overrun by the North, the enemy systematically eliminated political enemies and forcibly took South Korean men as sources of labor or as soldiers for the army. Caught in a war zone, sometimes between tactical forces engaged in battle, many civilians became casualties. Other civilians were lost to disease. Initially regarded as a military problem, the refugees soon became a social and medical problem of huge proportions.

To General Walker the refugee problem seemed minor compared to the North Korean army, which continued to drive back his forces all along the front and now appeared to be slipping around his southern flank. Air observation reports indicated that strong enemy forces, later identified as the North Korean 4th and 6th Divisions, were moving south along the west coast of Korea and across the Kum River and were poised to turn east. Such a move would not only threaten the flank of his frontline forces, but more important, could lead to the capture of the critical port of Pusan, the lifeline of Eighth Army through which supplies and reinforcements flowed. Walker requested that the Air Force attack the enemy columns and ordered the 24th Division to move from reserve at Kumch'on to blocking positions in front of the two North Korean divisions.

This was a desperate measure. The 24th Division, now under General Church, had been in reserve only one day. It urgently needed time to reorganize and recover from the hard fighting over the last two weeks and to be brought back up to strength in men and equipment. Nonetheless, Church immediately moved his unit south, where it joined the two battalions of the 29th Infantry Regiment, newly arrived from Okinawa.

The 29th Infantry was in even worse condition than the units of Eighth Army that deployed from Japan. Their prewar mission had been to guard airbases on Okinawa, and they had no training as a field unit. The two battalions, with no regimental staff or commander as such, were brought up to strength with the addition of 400 recruits from a troop transport that arrived the day before the battalions departed Okinawa. The plan for six weeks of training in Japan was scrapped, and the battalions sailed directly to Pusan, where they were to have three days to clean and test fire newly issued weapons. Instead, upon landing at Pusan on 24 July, the 29th Infantry soldiers moved directly into battle without zeroing their rifles, test firing their mortars, or cleaning their machine guns, which had been packed in Cosmoline for storage. Both battalions suffered heavy casualties in their first engagements on 27 July, the 3d Battalion near Hadong with about 400 casualties and the 1st Battalion near Anui with more than 100 casualties.

General Walker realized that a stronger force was needed to stop the North Koreans advancing on Pusan. Air attacks had only slowed but not stopped the two North Korean divisions; the battalions of the 29th Infantry had been roughly handled; and the units of the 24th Division were too weak to have much impact on the enemy forces. One of the best ROK army units, the 17th Infantry Regiment, was sent to reinforce units of General Church's division east of Anui. General Kean's 25th Infantry Division was ordered to move to Masan on 1 August and relieve the 24th Division units in that area. Kean picked up the 5th Regimental Combat Team, a full strength and relatively well trained unit that had just arrived from Hawaii, and attacked west from Masan toward Chinju. The 24th Division units in the south shifted north so that Church could consolidate his scattered forces. In hard fighting over the next few days, the 24th and 25th Divisions stopped the advance of the North Koreans.[11]

The Pusan Perimeter

At the same time that General Walker ordered the 25th Division to move south from the Sangju-Kumch'on area to Masan, he had also directed the rest of Eighth Army and the ROK forces to pull back to better defensive positions behind the Naktong River. This line became known as the Pusan Perimeter. On maps the line appeared to be a solid defensive line, but this was far from the case. About 140 miles in length and running over extremely rough terrain, the line was two to three times longer than American defensive doctrine stated should have been held by the number of available troops. However, the United States was mobilizing its forces and reinforcements were on the way.

When the Joint Chiefs of Staff asked General MacArthur for an estimate of the number of forces he would need to defeat the North Korean invasion, he replied that he would need the four divisions in Japan, brought up to full wartime strength, plus an additional four divisions. The remaining division in Japan, the 7th Infantry, had been cannibalized to provide soldiers for the other three divisions that deployed to Korea; moreover, all elements of the Far East Command had been stripped of administrative and support personnel to find replacements for Korea. No other men or units were available in Japan, and the 7th Division could not be used until it received a massive influx of personnel. Reinforcements must come from the United States, but the five divisions there were also under strength. Additional forces could be raised through call up of reserves or National Guards or through expansion of the draft, but this would take time.

To solve the immediate problem, all bases in the United States were searched for soldiers who could be sent immediately to Korea as replacements. The first replacements began flying to Japan on 18 July. The 2d Infantry Division at Fort Lewis, Washington, was alerted for movement on 8 July. The division was 45 percent below its authorized manning level, but was quickly brought up to strength with filler personnel pulled from all over the United States, many with poor attitudes. It was apparent that a number of commanders had used this as an opportunity to get rid of their worst soldiers. The 2d

Division shipped out for Korea nine days after being alerted and began arriving in Pusan on 1 August. To bring the divisions that deployed to Korea from Japan up to their complete wartime organizational structure of a medium tank battalion per division, one tank company and three infantry battalions per infantry regiment, and three firing batteries in each artillery battalion, individual infantry and tank battalions and artillery batteries were taken from the 3d Infantry Division and the 2d Armored Division.

In August, because of the continued seriousness of the Korean situation, it was decided that the 3d Infantry Division would also deploy to Korea. This unit had not only been greatly reduced by levies for individual replacements, but it had lost three artillery batteries, two complete infantry battalions, and the cadres—key officers and noncommissioned officers (NCOs)—for three other infantry battalions. The Army brought it quickly up to strength by stripping soldiers from elsewhere. Only one division, the 82d Airborne, was relatively untouched in the process. Four National Guard divisions were called into federal service on 1 September, but they would require several months of training before they could be used. In effect this meant that the Army's ability to respond to a crisis in other areas of the world was practically eliminated for at least a year until the call-up of reserves and expansion of the draft allowed the rebuilding of depleted formations and brought new units into the force.

The Joint Chiefs of Staff had done all in their power to satisfy General MacArthur's estimate of the forces required to defeat the North Koreans. Individual soldiers had been airlifted as replacements; a number of battalions and artillery batteries were being shipped to bring divisions deployed from Japan up to their proper wartime organization, and two Army infantry divisions and a Marine division were on the way as reinforcements. The units that deployed were not fully trained or cohesive, but given the choice, MacArthur decided that less-than-perfect units now were much better than no reinforcements at all.

The 2d Infantry Division and the 1st Provisional Marine Brigade had barely arrived in early August when the North Koreans launched their first attack on the Pusan Perimeter. The North Korean 4th Division crossed the Naktong west of Miryang in the sector of the 24th Infantry Division. Eventually, elements of the 2d Infantry Division and the Marine Brigade were sent to the area, and General Church was able to mount a counterattack in mid-August that inflicted severe casualties on the enemy and pushed them back across the Naktong. Meanwhile, North Korean forces mounted other attacks on ROK units holding the northern shoulder of the line, and against the 1st Cavalry Division in the center near Waegwan. In heavy fighting, although the ROK troops were forced back, the line finally held after reinforcements from the 2d and 25th Infantry Divisions were rushed north. On the last day of August, the North Koreans launched a strong attack against the 2d and 25th Infantry Divisions in the southern section of the perimeter. In severe fighting, the North Koreans were in time driven back, once again with high losses.

The battle conditions in the Pusan Perimeter during August and early September were harsh. General Walker fought the battle skillfully, shifting his few reserves to bolster segments of the line and to mount counterattacks to throw back the enemy. Other factors also contributed to UN success. Although unknown to Walker, by early August with the arrival of the 2d Division and the Marine Brigade, UN forces outnumbered the North Koreans by about 92,000 to 70,000. The disparity in numbers continued to grow as more UN troops arrived and attrition affected the North Koreans. Air attacks became more effective as the front line stabilized and pilots and forward air controllers became more experienced. Large numbers of tanks, artillery, and other weapons were now available. Combat veterans from World War II began to arrive in increasing numbers as replacements, many hand selected to command units because of the experience and skill they had demonstrated in other wartime assignments. To bolster the strength of American units, a number of South Korean civilians were assigned to most tactical units to help transport supplies in the rugged Korean terrain. Additionally as part of the Korean Augmentation Troops for the U.S. Army (KATUSA) program, 100 South Korean army recruits were assigned to each U.S. company-size unit.

While UN forces were gaining in strength, ground combat and air attacks were having a severe effect on the North Koreans. With extreme difficulty, the enemy was able to move new units south from North Korea and forcibly conscript enough South Koreans to replace most losses. These measures brought their strength up to an estimated 98,000 men for the major offensive launched at the end of August. This force, although led by ruthless and highly motivated North Koreans, was composed of a large number of soldiers of doubtful ability and low morale and suffered from shortages of food and ammunition. Even so, heavy fighting, resulting in numerous casualties, was necessary in order to halt and throw back the North Korean offensive. The enemy remained formidable, and the hastily assembled UN force, numbering about 180,000 men by the end of August, had a number of problems.

With the exception of some units, the ROK army remained poorly trained, ill equipped, and plagued with fundamental leadership problems that would take considerable time and effort to remedy. U.S. Army forces still suffered from the same training problems that existed at the beginning of the war. Many of those who had learned basic soldier and tactical skills the hard way, through combat experience, were casualties; others had learned the wrong lessons from combat and were unable to recognize the differences. Many of the replacements either suffered from poor training during peacetime or were rusty on the skills they had learned during World War II combat. A number of units had not yet had time to develop strong cohesion because of the number of new soldiers that arrived just prior to deployment, the constant turbulence caused by loss of casualties and arrival of replacements, and the rapid turnover in leaders. The assignment of South Korean recruits under the KATUSA program, mostly young and untrained with little or no understanding of the English language, did little to help and instead hampered American units, who were now burdened with the responsibility of feeding, caring for, and training them. Many of these problems were difficult to attend to in the middle of combat. Events in mid-September soon produced a major change in the war, and as a result, for a time the problems became unimportant and were ignored.[12]

Inch'on and the Collapse of North Korea

Since the beginning of the North Korean attack, General MacArthur focused on an amphibious landing in the enemy rear as the quickest and most effective way in which to defeat the North Koreans. MacArthur's original idea of using the 1st Cavalry Division for the landing had to be scrapped, as the momentum and strength of the enemy attack continued to draw in all available units and personnel from Japan in an attempt to stop them. During August, with the mobilization and deployment of resources from the United States, the shape of a landing plan began to form. Two divisions would be available: the 1st Marine Division, to include the Marine Brigade that would be withdrawn from Eighth Army for the invasion, and the 7th Infantry Division, currently in the process of absorbing and training almost 6,000 American replacements and 8,600 KATUSAs. Both divisions would operate under X Corps, a newly activated headquarters commanded by MacArthur's chief of staff, Maj. Gen. Edward M. Almond. The location selected for the landing was the west coast seaport of Inch'on, only a short distance from Seoul and close to the main supply route of the North Koreans.

The operation was considered risky. From a naval standpoint, tidal conditions and sea approaches made the operation extremely difficult and hazardous; additionally, there were tactical concerns about landing in an urban area protected by a high seawall. MacArthur insisted on proceeding, arguing that the psychological and strategic shock of landing in the enemy rear and cutting their supply lines, combined with an Eighth Army attack in the south, had the potential of destroying the North Korean forces, and that this goal was well worth the risks. D-Day for the invasion, code-named Operation Chromite, was set for 15 September.

From the beginning, the Inch'on invasion went well. An early morning attack by a battalion of the 5th Marine Regiment, supported by tanks, quickly captured Wolmi Island, which guarded the Inch'on harbor. The North Koreans had few forces in the immediate area, and in the afternoon, the 1st and 5th Marines landed at Inch'on. In fighting that continued into the night, the Marines secured their objectives at the cost of some 200 casualties.

Early the next morning the advance inland began against light resistance. Kimpo Airfield was secured on 17 September, and the next day the troops of the 7th Infantry Division began landing. The Marines continued to advance on the large Seoul suburb of Yongdungp'o south of the Han River, while the 7th Division covered their right flank. North Korean resistance stiffened in front of Seoul, as the enemy moved some 20,000 soldiers into the area to hold the city. The Marines crossed the Han west of Seoul and mounted attacks on the city from the south and the west. On 24 September General Almond, dissatisfied with Marine progress in capturing Seoul, directed the 7th Division to cross the Han and attack the southeast section of the city. Under attack from two directions, the North Korean commander on 25 September decided to save the bulk of his troops and withdrew to the north, leaving a small force to delay the Americans. The North Koreans in the city held out until the night of 27–28 September. Casualties in X Corps were about 3,500; 7,000 North Koreans were captured, and an estimated 14,000 were killed.

The capture of Seoul and severing of the North Korean supply line undoubtedly had a disturbing effect on the North Korean leadership, but word of the American victory was not announced to the North Korean units along the Pusan Perimeter, who continued to launch powerful attacks and to offer strong resistance. General Walker had planned to attack on 16 September to break through the North Korean lines, with the main effort in the Waegwan area, where the 1st Cavalry and 24th Infantry Divisions, along with the ROK 1st Division, were to move directly toward Seoul some 180 miles away. In the south the North Koreans continued to attack, and the American advance stalled. The main effort in the center around Waegwan managed to break through the NK 3d Division in five days of hard fighting. About the same time, the 25th Division in the south collapsed the defenses of the NK 6th and 7th Divisions. On the north side of the Pusan Perimeter, ROK divisions attacked successfully, destroying the NK 8th and 15th Divisions as effective combat forces. By 22 September, the bulk of the North Korean formations had either disintegrated entirely or were in full retreat. This rapid collapse of the enemy was a result of several factors: the strong attacks by UN forces along the perimeter in mid-September, the cumulative effect of equipment and personnel losses over the preceding weeks, and the psychological impact of the Inch'on landing in their rear, news of which eventually filtered down to many enemy soldiers.

The move of Eighth Army to link up with X Corps around Seoul proceeded rapidly against relatively light and scattered resistance. By the morning of 27 September, the advance troops of the 1st Cavalry Division met elements of the 7th Infantry Division near Osan. On the same day, acting on a decision by President Truman after considerable debate, the Joint Chiefs of Staff directed General MacArthur to cross the 38th parallel to complete the destruction of the North Korean forces. Threats from the Chinese Communists to intervene if UN forces moved into North Korea were discounted in both Washington and Tokyo, and MacArthur continued with preparations for the advance.

United Nations strength in Korea by the end of September stood at 229,000 ground troops, including about 103,000 U.S. Army, 21,500 U.S. Marines, 101,500 ROK troops (including almost 19,000 attached to U.S. Army units), a 1,700-man British brigade, and 1,300 men in a Philippine battalion. Eighth Army under General Walker was now organized into two U.S. corps: I Corps with the 1st Cavalry and 24th Infantry Divisions, and ROK 1st Division, and IX Corps with the 2d and 25th Infantry Divisions. Eighth Army also contained the ROK I and II Corps. X Corps, consisting of the 1st Marine and 7th Infantry Divisions under General Almond, remained directly under the control of MacArthur.

The primary considerations in planning to use these forces in North Korea were the remaining enemy strength, logistics, and terrain. It was estimated that only about 30,000 North Koreans had escaped to the north across the 38th parallel to join possibly 30,000 enemy troops remaining in North Korea. Potentially this left a sizable number of bypassed enemy forces in the south that could conduct guerrilla operations. The roads and railways in the south were in poor condition, with many bridges and tunnels destroyed during the fighting. Considerable time would be required to rebuild the lines of communication in order to supply forces operating in the north through the main port of Pusan. Inch'on could handle some supplies, but it was doubtful whether the entire force that would operate in the north could be supplied through that port. Moreover, the terrain in the northern part of North Korea, generally north of a line from P'yongyang, the capital, to Wonsan, was such that east-west movement was greatly restricted, with the main routes running generally north-south.

MacArthur planned for X Corps to make an amphibious landing at Wonsan and advance into the rugged terrain of northeast Korea toward the Yalu River, the border between North Korea and Communist China, using the ports of Wonsan and Hungnam for supply. The ROK I Corps would press forward on the eastern flank of X Corps. Eighth Army was to cross the 38th parallel on a broad front with the U.S. I Corps and the ROK II Corps and advance along the western side of the peninsula through P'yongyang to the Yalu River. Eighth Army would be supplied through Inch'on, while the U.S. IX Corps remained in South Korea to clear it of bypassed enemy forces and provide protection for the rebuilding effort on the roads and rail lines between Seoul and Pusan.

South Korean forces crossed the 38th parallel at the end of September, and the U.S. I Corps followed on 9 October. There was heavy fighting in the west above Kaesong, but by 14 October the 1st Cavalry Division had overcome the resistance. On 19 October elements of the 1st ROK and U.S. 1st Cavalry Divisions entered the North Korean capital of P'yongyang. On the east coast, the ROK I Corps captured Wonsan on 10 October and met the 1st Marine Division that arrived there on the 26th. Three days later the U.S. 7th Division landed at Iwon, some seventy miles northeast of Hungnam. After some initial resistance near the border, North Korean forces offered little opposition. There appeared to be nothing to prevent UN troops from reaching the Yalu River.

In Washington and Tokyo, it appeared that victory was certain and that the fighting would soon end. Planning began for the new conditions, including reductions in the flow of supplies and personnel to the Far East and redeployment of forces already there. The X Corps with one American division, the newly arrived 3d Infantry, would remain in North Korea along with several ROK units, as occupation forces. One American division, the 2d Infantry, would be sent to bolster Western Europe, the area regarded as the top strategic priority for the United States. Additional divisions now training in the United States would also be sent to Europe, along with two corps headquarters. Considerable time was spent in discussions between MacArthur and the Joint Chiefs of Staff as to how long the 3d Infantry Division would remain in Korea; MacArthur was finally told that it would be sent to Europe no later than May 1951. By late October 1950 there were 9,000 men from five nations serving alongside American and ROK units, and additional UN forces totaling some 27,000 men were scheduled to arrive. Inquiries were made by several countries about canceling movement of their forces to Korea, and the United States was debating what policy to adopt in this matter. Little thought was given, either in Washington or at MacArthur's headquarters in Tokyo, about other possible outcomes of the fighting in Korea.[13]

The Chinese Attack

In late October, Chinese Communist Forces (CCF) launched surprise attacks against the overextended ROK II Corps and the ROK 1st Division, part of the U.S. I Corps.* General Walker rushed the 1st Cavalry Division north from P'yongyang to assist the ROK 1st Division. As the powerful and skillful CCF attacks near Unsan continued into the night of 1 November and the following day, the ROK 15th and the U.S. 8th Cavalry Regiments were surrounded and overrun. The 15th Regiment was largely destroyed, and the 8th Cavalry could account for only 45 percent of its men two days later. Walker pulled the Eighth Army back to the Ch'ongch'on River, which runs roughly parallel to the Yalu some fifty miles to the south,

---

*A number of sources use the term Chinese People's Volunteer Army (CPVA) instead of CCF. CCF will be used throughout this work because it was the term in common use in the U.S. Army during the Korean War.

to take up defensive positions and regroup. To the east in the X Corps sector, elements of the 7th Infantry Division reached the Chinese border along the Yalu near Hyesanjin, but to their west the 1st Marine Division was slowed by CCF forces in its advance north from Hungnam toward the Chosin Reservoir.

At the same time as CCF ground troops made their appearance in Korea, Soviet-built MIG fighter planes began to challenge the U.S. Air Force along the Yalu River. General MacArthur was alarmed that Chinese Communist Forces could have crossed the Yalu without detection and in such strength as to launch powerful attacks on UN ground troops. After sharp discussions with Washington, MacArthur received permission to destroy the bridges over the Yalu River, as long as the air strikes were on the Korean end of the bridges and American planes did not cross into Chinese or Soviet territory, even if in "hot pursuit" of enemy aircraft that had attacked them. Under these restrictions, the bombing of the bridges began on 8 November and continued on a daily basis for most of the rest of the month. Meanwhile, the CCF troops melted back into the hills of North Korea.

Intelligence, primarily based on prisoner interrogations, began to accumulate that identified six Chinese armies with eighteen divisions in North Korea. Other information indicated that the Chinese had moved their forces that had been concentrated for the invasion of Formosa into Manchuria, and that some 300,000 men in forty-four divisions were now immediately north of the Yalu. But the information was fragmentary and frequently conflicting. Air observation could not confirm the presence of any large numbers of Chinese in North Korea. As a result, intelligence officials concluded that possibly 35,000 to 70,000 Chinese had entered Korea to reinforce the North Koreans.

Eighth Army and X Corps continued planning for a renewed offensive in late November to complete the destruction of enemy forces south of the Yalu River. MacArthur's headquarters stated that the opportunity for massive Chinese intervention had passed and that if the Chinese did intervene, American airpower would destroy them. General Walker was uncertain and decided that before Eighth Army moved forward it must have all available troops and adequate supplies to support the advance. IX Corps traveled north and was inserted into the line along the Ch'ongch'on between the U.S. I Corps to the west and the ROK II Corps to the east. To the east of the ROK II Corps, separated by some fifty miles of difficult, almost impassable, terrain, was the U.S. X Corps with the ROK I Corps operating on the far right flank. Eighth Army was to advance on 24 November, followed by X Corps three days later.

The UN forces completely misjudged the situation. When the United States decisively intervened to assist South Korea in July 1950, Communist China decided to redeploy its forces opposite Formosa to Manchuria. Diplomatic warnings of intervention were issued, and in early October when UN forces ignored the warnings and crossed the 38th parallel, Chinese troops moved into North Korea. Chinese leaders were concerned that war with the United States, with its airpower and nuclear weapons, could be potentially devastating, resulting in the loss of Chinese provinces and the possible collapse of Communist rule. They reasoned that if a war were to be fought, it would be best to fight outside of China.

In October about 180,000 Chinese moved into North Korea, and by late November, there were more than 300,000. The Chinese soldiers were experienced, highly trained, and well disciplined, accustomed to hardship through almost constant warfare for twenty years against the Nationalist Chinese and the Japanese. Although lacking heavy weapons or an elaborate supply system, their tactics took advantage of their strengths: rapid mobility, camouflage and concealment, night operations, and attacks designed to disrupt enemy operations and in the ensuing confusion encircle and destroy enemy forces. After the initial attacks in late October and early November, the Chinese evaluated their experience with their new American enemy. American firepower, especially artillery, received high marks, but American infantry was regarded as vulnerable. The conclusion was that when Americans were cut off by attacks in the rear, they

> abandoned all their heavy weapons, leaving them all over the place, and play opossum. . . .Their infantrymen are weak, afraid to die, and haven't the courage to attack or defend. They depend

on their planes, tanks, and artillery. At the same time, they are afraid of our firepower. They will cringe when, if on the advance, they hear firing. They are afraid to advance farther. . . . They specialize in day fighting. They are not familiar with night fighting or hand-to-hand combat. . . . If defeated, they have no orderly formation. Without the use of their mortars, they become completely lost . . . they become dazed and completely demoralized.[14]

Committed against the advancing UN forces in late October after lengthy marches from Manchuria, the Chinese were initially victorious against the scattered UN forces, but did not have the strength to attack the Eighth Army defensive positions along the Ch'ongch'on River and near the Chosin Reservoir. When the Eighth Army advanced on 24 November in extended formations, the Chinese were prepared. On the night of 25 November, the Chinese launched strong holding attacks against the U.S. I and IX Corps, while the main blow fell on the ROK II Corps. The effect was immediate.

By noon on 26 November, the UN offensive was halted in its tracks with elements of the ROK 1st and U.S. 2d and 25th Divisions fighting for their lives. Of critical concern, the ROK II Corps completely collapsed. The Chinese rapidly exploited their advantage by driving forward against the Eighth Army rear, seeking to cut off and destroy the UN forces. Walker reacted by ordering his reserves, the Turkish Brigade and the 1st Cavalry Division, to block the Chinese flowing through the ROK II Corps sector, while the I and IX Corps immediately retreated.

The 2d Infantry Division, located on the eastern flank of IX Corps and adjacent to the destroyed ROK corps, was especially vulnerable. On 30 November as they withdrew south from Kunu-ri toward Sunch'on along a valley, the so-called gauntlet, they encountered Chinese roadblocks and strong forces on the hills to either side. Unable to completely break through on the road or to clear the enemy from the high ground, the 2d Division suffered heavy casualties and lost much of its equipment. The only formation to withdraw intact was the 23d Infantry Regiment under Col. Paul L. Freeman Jr., who took his regiment out along another route instead of following the rest of the division through the gauntlet. The 2d Division sustained about 5,000 casualties, one-third of their strength, and most of their equipment, including hundreds of trucks, sixty-four artillery pieces, and between 20 and 40 percent of their communications gear. No longer combat effective, Walker ordered the remnants of the division to move south out of the combat zone.

East of Eighth Army in the X Corps sector, the Chinese attack was equally devastating. The blow fell on 27 November in the Chosin Reservoir area, where the 1st Marine Division was located on the western and southern sides of the reservoir and Task Force MacLean (two infantry battalions with artillery of the 7th Infantry Division) was positioned along the eastern shore. Taking advantage of superior numbers and the scattered American positions, the Chinese attacks overran the 7th Infantry Division task force east of the reservoir. Colonel MacLean was killed, as was Lt. Col. Donald C. Faith Jr., who had taken command of the survivors, called Task Force Faith. Suffering about 40 percent casualties, only about 500 men were able to join the Marines south of the reservoir to continue the fight.

Maj. Gen. Oliver P. Smith, commander of the 1st Marine Division, had moved forward carefully and kept his division relatively concentrated, resisting General Almond's demands for a faster advance that would have strained supply lines and strung his men out over the countryside. After repulsing the initial enemy attacks, Smith was able through hard fighting to concentrate all of his forces around the reservoir at the Hagaru-ri airfield by 4 December. There they regrouped and prepared to continue their withdrawal to Hungnam along a narrow, mountainous fifty-mile-long road that had been cut in several places by the Chinese.

Meanwhile in the west, General Walker continued to withdraw Eighth Army. P'yongyang was abandoned on 5 December, along with massive stockpiles of supplies that were only partially destroyed. Intelligence reports continued to arrive indicating that the enemy was threatening the right rear of Eighth Army, and thus the retreat continued. With X Corps tied down in northeastern Korea, Walker took steps to prevent an envelopment of his open right flank by deploying troops across the Korean peninsula just north of the 38th parallel, a distance of roughly 150 miles. The eastern portion of this line would be held by the ROK II Corps, which was reforming, along with three other ROK divisions drawn from the southern part of the peninsula; the U.S. I and IX Corps would hold the western section of the line. This line was reached on 23 December, and the Eighth Army retreat ended.

In northeast Korea the 1st Marine Division began its move from Hagaru-ri to the coast on 6 December. Over the next few days, using concentrated air and artillery, the Marines and Army elements fought their way south. A task force from the 3d Infantry Division advanced thirty miles north from Hungnam to keep the route open, and by 10 December the linkup was accomplished. General MacArthur ordered X Corps withdrawn. The carefully coordinated evacuation began on 9 December, and by the 24th, 105,000 troops, including the 1st Marine, 7th Infantry, and 3d Infantry Divisions, and the ROK I Corps, had been withdrawn, along with 98,100 refugees.[15]

The New War

A new chapter in the Korean War had opened with the decisive intervention of the Chinese Communists and the withdrawal of Eighth Army and X Corps from most of North Korea. General Walker was killed in a traffic accident on 23 December, and the new commander, Lt. Gen. Matthew B. Ridgway, faced immediate and difficult challenges. Ridgway was a proven combat commander and was knowledgeable about the situation in Korea because of his job as chief of operations on the Army staff in Washington. Ridgway participated in the policy debate in Washington after the Chinese intervention and was well aware of the overall global and national military considerations that affected what was possible in Korea.

In early December after the successful Chinese attacks, MacArthur had requested massive reinforcements, without which he might be forced to withdraw to a beachhead around Pusan. After wide-ranging discussions in Washington of possible options, MacArthur was told that there would be no reinforcements. Policy makers concluded that the priority must be the defense of Western Europe and that the United States could not become engaged in a general war with China that might spread to war with the Soviet Union, one that the United States could not win. Assessments concluded that the threat of Soviet aggression loomed over Europe and Japan, that our Western European allies were weak, that there were no immediately available U.S. forces that could be sent to reinforce either Europe or the Far East, and that the Army could not even replace all of the combat casualties in Korea. Equipment and weapons were a different matter, and actions were undertaken to rapidly replace the massive numbers that had been lost in North Korea. With UN forces in retreat and uncertainty as to their ability to withstand renewed Chinese attacks, a number of options were considered: requesting a cease-fire on the 38th parallel, continued withdrawal into South Korea to the port of Pusan, and immediate, voluntary evacuation of the Korean peninsula. These were all rejected, and for the time being, the decision was to defend and delay along the 38th parallel and continue secret planning for the worst case, retreat to Pusan and emergency evacuation. Rumors of the possible abandonment of South Korea had spread through UN forces and the South Korean government, resulting in widespread uncertainty and low morale. This was the situation when Ridgway arrived in the Far East.

General Ridgway first stopped in Tokyo on 25 December and was briefed by General MacArthur. Gone was any talk of reunification of Korea or even any sign of optimism. MacArthur expressed his concerns about the UN ability to defend Korea. He believed that Walker's defensive line across the peninsula was impracticable because of the lack of troops and the extent of the line over difficult terrain. MacArthur told Ridgway that airpower was exaggerated and that he could not count on airpower to stop the flow of enemy supplies and reinforcements or even to stop any future attacks. Ridgway was told that he must not underestimate the Chinese and that they were expected to renew their attacks at any time. MacArthur then proceeded to give Ridgway what he had never provided for Walker: control of all ground forces in Korea, to include X Corps, and complete freedom to act as he saw fit. As MacArthur summed it up, "Eighth Army is yours."

Ridgway arrived in Korea on 26 December. Scattered enemy attacks were already under way, a prelude to an all-out offensive that was expected at any time. The initial briefing at Eighth Army headquarters was disturbing: information as to enemy locations and strength was almost nonexistent. After a meeting with President Rhee to assure him that South Korea would not be abandoned, Ridgway began a four-day tour of the front line to visit all corps and division commanders. The results were unsettling. Signs of exhaustion, low morale, and defeatism existed throughout the command. Moreover, the operational and tactical situation was bleak. ROK units that were largely untrained and unreliable held two-thirds of the UN line. ROK forces manned the critical central corridor through which led the most direct route to Pusan, the port that was necessary not only for the sustainment of UN forces but also for their survival if evacuation became necessary. The only reserves that existed were untrained levies of South Koreans and the U.S. 2d Infantry Division and X Corps, both of which had been mauled and had suffered heavy losses in their retreats from North Korea. General Almond, whose X Corps was now assigned to Eighth Army and was just arriving at Pusan after its evacuation from North Korea, remained alone in his aggressiveness and willingness to engage the enemy. But there was some evidence that Almond's aggressiveness verged on recklessness, and the Marines were especially insistent that they not serve under him in the future.

Ridgway was confident that he could restore the fighting spirit of the commanders and soldiers of Eighth Army, and that with time the ROK units would become effective. The problem was that there was no time. As suspected, the enemy had succeeded in moving forward some 170,000 Chinese and North Korean troops, along with sufficient stockpiles of ammunition and supplies with which to mount powerful attacks. The North Korean forces had been reorganized and refitted and once again were prepared for action on ground they knew well. Additional reserves were positioned to the north, and Korean guerrilla forces were ready to strike behind UN lines. On the night of 31 December, the enemy opened what came to be known as their New Year's Offensive, with the main blow falling on the U.S. I and IX Corps north of Seoul, but with potentially devastating pressure building up on the ROK front in the center above the key crossroads town of Wonju.[16]

In the final analysis, there was little that Ridgway immediately could do. The outcome of the fighting would depend on the soldiers and their leaders on the battlefield. They had been dealt a hand: poor training and inadequate resources in peacetime; hastily thrown together units, intelligence failures, unrealistic planning, a skillful and powerful enemy, harsh terrain and weather, defeats, and disastrous retreats in wartime. Now the soldiers and their leaders must play the cards they had, relying on common sense, dedication, determination, courage, and heroism.

Chapter 2

RETREAT TO WONJU

2d Infantry Division, 1–6 January 1951

The Chinese New Year's Offensive pushed the U.S. I and IX Corps south of the Han River, forcing the abandonment once again of Seoul. In the mountainous center, rejuvenated North Korean divisions attacked the ROK II and III Corps. General Ridgway believed that if the hard-pressed South Koreans gave way in the center, not only would the flank of the American forces to the west be in peril, but also their lifeline to the critical logistical base at Pusan would be endangered. The only force that was available to move into the central mountains to support the ROK army was the 2d Infantry Division, still recovering from its serious losses at the end of November in North Korea.

The 2d Infantry Division's Command Report for December 1950 describes its activities following the late November disaster at Kunu-ri as it regained its strength, trained new replacements, and moved into the center of the UN line to backstop the ROK forces and protect Eighth Army's eastern flank and rear.

As December opened, the 2d Division, having withdrawn from the Kunu-ri area, continued a planned, phased withdrawal to the vicinity of Yongdung-p'o [south of Seoul]. Enemy elements had exacted a heavy toll during the fighting withdrawal of the division, and the losses were so heavy that a reorganization of all divisional units was mandatory to bring its effectiveness back to a point where it could again assume its role as a major combat element in the combined forces of the United Nations. The strength of the division

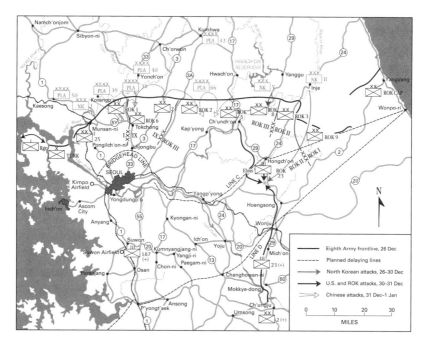

Opening effort of the enemy third phase offensive, 26 December 1950–1 January 1951 (based on U.S. Army Center of Military History map).

had dropped to an aggregate of 10,269 at the end of November. As this represented little more than half of authorized strength, it was necessary to submit emergency as well as scheduled requisitions to fill the replacement requirements. Replacements and returnees totaled 3,371 for the first two weeks of December and, although the flow slowed during the second half of the period, the grand total for the month was 5,070 replacements and returnees. Losses for the period, including both battle and nonbattle, totaled 906 for a net gain of 4,164. Although these gains brought most of the service elements to a strength that permitted comparatively normal operation, the shortage of combat infantrymen remained acute, none of the infantry regiments having within a thousand of their authorized strengths.

The attachment of the French and Netherlands Detachments on 11 December greatly increased the combat potential of the division. The French Battalion, with a strength of 1,020, was attached to the

23d Infantry Regiment while the Dutch Detachment of 630 men was attached to the 38th Infantry Regiment. Although the attached Republic of Korea troops, who numbered a little more than 1,000, showed no indications of improved fighting efficiency or combat effectiveness (which remained at an estimated 40 to 50 percent), the division requested that the ROK personnel be retained until the requisitions for American replacements were filled. Casualties for December were primarily a result of the cold weather. Frostbite and respiratory infections were the most common cause of nonbattle incapacitation.

Major General Laurence B. Keiser, who had been evacuated for medical reasons after the withdrawal from Kunu-ri, was replaced by Major General Robert B. McClure on 7 December. On 10 December, the day that the division initiated a program of training in small unit tactics, physical conditioning, and maintenance of equipment, Eighth Army directed a reconnaissance of the road network to the area extending east to Ch'unch'on and southeast to Ch'ungju. The terrain in the area was to be surveyed to determine its suitability for defense.

During the next few days, the reconnaissance of the road nets and the accelerated training schedule went on concurrently. On 14 December, the 23d Infantry was directed to dispatch a contact patrol to Ch'unch'on to contact the ROK 5th Division and to report on the roads and bridges. The motorized patrol left early the morning of the 15th, arriving at Ch'unch'on at 1245 hours. Contact was made with KMAG representatives with the ROK 5th and 8th Divisions. KMAG reported that these divisions had been under daylong attack by an estimated four North Korean divisions. The left flank of the 5th Division had been penetrated, but the positions had been restored by noon on the 15th. Although the patrol found no evidences of enemy guerrilla activity, they did encounter heavy ROK foot and vehicle traffic on the roads leading into Ch'unch'on.

The Division Operation Plan No. 1 was published on December 16th. This directed that the 2d Division move to the Hoengsong–Wonju-Ch'ungju area and establish blocking positions to deny enemy movement south along the Hoengsong–Ch'ungju axis. All regiments were to begin drawing up their plans; plans were to be based on the

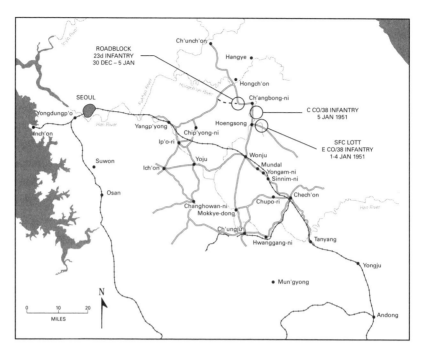

2d Infantry Division area of operations (original map by author).

operation of regimental combat teams, which were to be established upon announcement that the plan was to be executed. Instructions were issued on the same day for the issuance and use of individual panels for frontline identification from the air, which would permit close-in tactical air support while lessening the danger of exposing the frontline units to strafing from friendly air.

The intelligence elements used every available source to determine the enemy intentions during this period. Both the Military Police Company and the Ivanhoe Security Forces were effective intelligence collecting agencies and, in addition, they prevented infiltration by enemy agents.* The division intelligence estimates gave as the enemy capability most likely to be adopted the continuation of

*The Ivanhoe Security Force was a provisional company of South Koreans assigned to the 2d Infantry Division and organized for rear area security operations.

the enemy attack by the reorganized North Korean military units backed by a Chinese force of 150,000, who could be thrown into sectors where the North Koreans were experiencing the greatest difficulty. The size of the organized North Korean force was estimated at 140,000, exclusive of 23,000 guerrillas operating in rear areas. By the middle of the month, the refugee problem had ceased to be acute, and the Ivanhoe Security Force was directed to begin operating in the Wonju sector to learn as much as possible of enemy activity in this zone.

The move of the 2d Division was one of a number made to counter this impending enemy thrust. Operation Order No. 10, published on 23 December, assigned to the 2d Division the primary mission of securing the east flank of the Eighth Army. The 23d Infantry was to prepare and occupy defensive lines while establishing blocking positions along the Ch'ungju-Wonju axis and on the road from Chupo-ri to Ch'ungju. The 38th RCT (-)* was to occupy defensive positions along the Wonju-Chech'on-Tanyang-Yongju-Andong axis. The remaining battalion of the 38th RCT, reinforced, was to ensure the security of the division MSR [main supply road] from Ch'ungju to Mun'gyong. The 9th Infantry was to assemble at Ch'ungju as division reserve and prepare to restore defense positions in the 23d RCT sector or to extend the east flank of the 23d RCT. It was also to occupy defense positions along the Chech'on–Hwanggang-ni axis, not to exceed one battalion, while maintaining the remainder of its force for the protection of Ch'ungju City from infiltrating enemy groups in coordination with the other divisional units stationed in Ch'ungju.

During the next few days, all units were engaged in reconnaissance and the construction and improvement of defensive positions. A major hazard and delaying factor during this period was the condition of the roads, which were icy and hazardous for both tank and truck travel. All of the most dangerous sections of the more traveled roads were sanded by native laborers recruited by the division.

---

* This is standard military terminology to indicate that the unit is not complete because of detachments. Similarly, (+) indicates that a unit has additional forces attached to it.

Eighth Army directed the division to maintain close contact with the ROK II and III Corps at all times. As there was no enemy activity during this period, training was intensified and unit commanders began to survey their areas and prepare detailed demolitions plans, which were submitted to division for immediate use should another general withdrawal be ordered.

After evaluation of all available intelligence had indicated the imminence of an enemy attack in the direction of Wonju, on the 28th of December, Operation Order 14 was published, calling for the primary defense effort on the Wonju-Ch'ungju axis. The 23d Infantry, with artillery attachments but minus the French Infantry Battalion and the 1st Ranger Company, was directed to move to Wonju and occupy defensive blocking positions on the approaches north of town and be prepared to fight a delaying action south along the Wonju-Ch'ungju, and Wonju–Chupo-ri–Ch'ungju axes. The 38th RCT, with 1st Ranger Company attached, was to prepare positions to delay and block enemy penetrations along the Chech'on-Tanyang-Yongju-Andong axis, move one battalion to the vicinity of Chech'on prior to darkness on 28 December, and prepare to block all approaches thereto; the regiment was also to assume responsibility west to Chupo-ri and disperse or destroy all guerrilla units in that area. The 2d Engineer (C) Battalion was directed to maintain the MSR and build fords. The 72d Tank Battalion was told to prepare for employment to the northeast while patrolling road nets and maintaining contact with the Netherlands Detachment. The 9th Infantry with the French and Dutch units formed the division reserve.

Although the 23d Infantry Regiment reported the town of Wonju extremely difficult to defend because of the flat terrain and lack of distinctive features for the defense, Eighth Army notified the division that it was to prepare for a blocking mission at Wonju. On the 29th of December, Eighth Army directed that a site be surveyed in Wonju that would be suitable for an airstrip large enough to accommodate C-47s.

The reports of reconnaissance patrols were so corroborative of the intelligence material already evaluated that at 2325 hours on the 29th, the 2d Division was given the responsibility for defending the Wonju-Hongch'on area—a greatly limited area compared to the one previously held, but much farther north. One RCT was to be assigned to the defense of Hongch'on proper and to be prepared to block enemy movement from the north and east. The other RCTs were to be prepared to counterattack and destroy all enemy units attempting to drive down the MSR.

Operation Order 15, published and disseminated on 30 December, directed the 23d RCT to prepare and occupy delaying positions along the Ch'unch'on-Hongch'on and Hangye-Hongch'on axes; it was also to establish and maintain liaison with the ROK army or police units in Ch'unch'on, Hangye, and Kujand-to. The 38th RCT (with the Netherlands Detachment attached) was to occupy blocking positions south of Hoengsong, patrolling all roads in the vicinity, and prepare to counterattack any enemy penetrations in its zone. An Engineer Detachment was attached to each of the RCTs, and the depleted Engineer Battalion was directed to do everything possible to maintain the MSR. The 9th RCT assembled in Wonju, where it was to form the division reserve. The French Battalion, attached to the 9th RCT, was to secure and patrol the MSR from Wonju to Chupo-ri to Ch'ungju to Wonju.

Reports of enemy probing attacks along the line had been increasing in frequency since the 21st of December. ROK units reported a steady buildup of enemy strength north of Ch'unch'on. Guerrilla activity increased daily. It was believed that the enemy force, consisting entirely of North Korean units, could be expected to attack at any time, and it was anticipated that reinforcement of the attacking North Koreans by Chinese troops was probable should the initial attack fail to penetrate the UN lines.

On the 30th of December, the 2d Division was notified that the commanding general of the X Corps was to visit the division to discuss future plans (the division was to be attached to X Corps early in January). Work on the airstrip was speeded up to permit access to Wonju by air for both cargo planes and air liaison flights.

On the 31st of December, the assistant division commander, forward with the 23d RCT, reported that an enemy column was moving west toward the 23d RCT sector and that a heavy fight was impending. He requested that the maximum available ammunition, gasoline, and rations be sent to the 23d RCT sector and that supporting air be alerted to give support in the impending fight. The 23d Infantry was instructed to suspend the movement of defensive elements to Hongch'on and to devote its major effort to the security of the Hoengsong-Hongch'on road.[1]

Roadblock North of Wonju: 23d Infantry Regiment, 1–5 January 1951

The command reports of the 23d Infantry Regiment for late December and early January describe the ensuing action.

On 28 December the 23d RCT was dispersed as follows: the 1st Battalion held defensive positions on the high terrain just north of Wonju; the 2d Battalion, 3d Battalion, and French Battalion held defensive positions on the roads leading into Wonju from the southeast and southwest. There was no evidence of any enemy buildup in the area. On 29 December, however, B Company, 23d RCT, reported a constant stream of refugees followed by armed police streaming into Wonju. Enemy troops in dark uniforms, and apparently extremely well disciplined, were observed moving in the area in a column of twos.

On 30 December the 3d Battalion moved north of Hoengsong to attack an enemy roadblock on the Hongch'on-Hoengsong road reported by higher headquarters. At the news of this enemy force, and reports by air OP [observation post] that a larger force was building up in this area, the 23d RCT, minus its Tank Company and 1st Battalion, moved through Hoengsong to join the 3d Battalion in eliminating the enemy roadblock and trying to open the MSR so that the ROK II Corps could be withdrawn from the Hongch'on area. The 1st Battalion continued to remain in its defensive positions north of Wonju.

The 3d Battalion led the attack against the enemy roadblock on 31 December, with the 2d Battalion to its right rear facing a possible enemy threat from the east. From well-entrenched positions, the enemy force withstood the assault of the 3d Battalion. Enemy reinforcements were able to come up by means of a trail leading from the mountains on the west down to the Hongch'on-Hoengsong road. On 1 January the 2d Battalion was ordered to attack the enemy by a flanking movement to the left. The 1st and French Battalions were moved forward and ordered to take over the positions vacated by the 2d Battalion.[2]

The 2d Battalion halted its attack at dark on 1 January and assumed defensive positions, with Company E on high ground that dominated the area. Early the next morning, before the battalion could continue the attack, the enemy struck. The actions of Sgt. Junior D. Edwards were instrumental in defeating the enemy counterattack and are described by his commander, Capt. Perry A. Sager, and other members of the company in their recommendations for award of the Medal of Honor to Sergeant Edwards.

CAPT. SAGER: At about 0315 the enemy, using machine guns, small arms, and hand grenades, made a determined attack on the Company E position and succeeded in capturing the highest part of the position. From the ground captured, they began to cover the rest of the position with fire. They emplaced a machine gun on this ground and with it pinned down a portion of the company.

The ground taken by the enemy was in the sector of the 2d Platoon, Company E. In the initial phase of the attack, the squad leader and assistant squad leader of one squad were wounded and the squad disorganized. Sgt. Junior D. Edwards, acting platoon leader of the 2d Platoon, moved to the remaining men of the squad and under intense fire from the enemy reorganized the squad and, with men from other squads not under fire, organized a counterattack. As the fire of the enemy still covered the area, some of the men were reluctant to move forward. Sergeant Edwards then personally led four of the men to foxholes that were within fifty yards of the enemy positions. During these trips he was fully exposed to the fire of the enemy. After he had placed the men in position, he directed their fire on the enemy. At this time Sergeant Edwards realized that the enemy was in a hole that had been dug by our men while they were in the positions and that the flat trajectory weapons in the hands of our men would not be effective against them. He also realized that he could not call for mortar fire on the machine gun position because of the close proximity of friendly troops. Fully aware of the enemy strength and the heavy volume of fire, he took all hand grenades available and left his place of comparative safety and with total disregard for the extremely heavy fire of the enemy, and for his own life, he made a one-man charge on the enemy machine gun position.

SFC JAMES D. DRUMMOND: He ran up the hill, fully exposed to the enemy fire, throwing hand grenades at the position. When his supply of grenades had been used, he returned for more grenades and again single-handedly went forward under heavy machine gun fire in a second attempt to knock it out. He succeeded, [but] his supply of grenades was exhausted [and he] was forced to return to his former position. The enemy moved a second machine gun into position and again directed fire at them. For a third time Sergeant Edwards, with hand grenades, charged the machine gun under intense fire.

FIRST LT. HERBERT P. LIVINGSTON: This time Sergeant Edwards ordered the men to charge the top of the hill as soon as he had knocked out the machine gun. For the third time he started up the hill, throwing grenades as he ran. He again succeeded in knocking the machine gun out of action and killing or wounding all of the crew. Just after the machine gun was knocked out, Sergeant Edwards was fatally wounded by enemy small arms fire. With the machine gun out of action, the other men of the platoon were able to drive the remaining enemy from the hill and restore the company position. This enabled them to use these positions for a line of departure for the successful attack later in the day. The dogged determination and courage of Sergeant Edwards insured the success of the battalion and regiment. His actions were an inspiration to all men and officers who observed him.[3]

First Lt. Jerrell F. Wilson, executive officer, Company G, 23d Infantry Regiment, describes the fighting to eliminate the roadblock after the enemy attack was repulsed early on 2 January.

The mission of the force was to destroy the enemy roadblock in the vicinity of the road junction, about five miles west of Ch'angbong-ni, which was preventing supplies from reaching two ROK divisions somewhere in the vicinity of Hongch'on. ROK trucks attempting to carry supplies through were being machine-gunned and lost off the

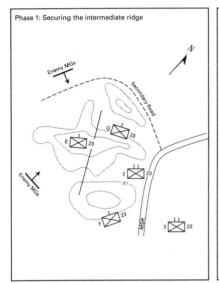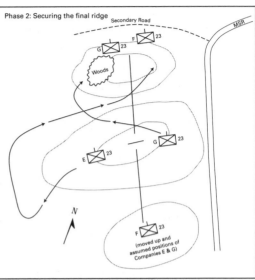

Phases 1 and 2 of the action to eliminate the Hongch'on-Hoengsong roadblock (drawn by Lt. Jerrell F. Wilson; not to scale).

side of the road, which ran along high cliff-like ridges. Information from civilians indicated approximately 1,000 enemy troops were manning the roadblock. However, the enemy was probably only in company strength, for only small-arms and light mortar fire was received during this engagement.

Phase I of the plan for destroying the roadblock was to have the 2d Battalion take the ridge running parallel and to the south of the secondary road making the junction with the MSR; the 3d Battalion preceded the 2d Battalion and made initial contact with enemy forces that occupied part of the ridge.

At 0900, 2 January, Company G moved up behind Company I. Company I had secured part of the ridge during the morning but was pinned down by enemy machine gun fire from the military crest of the hill north of the secondary road. Enemy machine gun fire was also being received from positions in the rear to the southwest. Around noon, Company G relieved Company I, which then moved east of the MSR and joined other elements of the 3d Battalion. With Company E on the left flank and Company F in reserve and as protection of the rear, Company G cleaned out the ridge using small arms and mortar fire. I spent most of the day with the 2d Platoon of Company G on the right flank of the company; the company commander was on the left flank.

At 0100, 3 January, about one company of enemy attacked the Company G position on the ridge. Since the artillery, 81mm, and 4.2-inch mortar forward observers were then at the company CP [command post], I had them lay down fire in front of the company position. This friendly fire was so intense that the enemy attack was diverted to the left, and Company E received the main enemy effort. The platoon on the right flank of Company E broke shortly after the enemy attack, a few men leaving their foxholes and running to the rear, but several sergeants stopped them and sent them back to the line. The fighting was so close in the Company E area that the next morning in one foxhole you would find one of ours, and in the next you would find one of theirs. Company G suffered no casualties. I do not believe that the enemy attack was a determined one.

Phase II of the plan was to have Company E execute a difficult maneuver, that of moving out to the left, then southwest to the rear, to clean out enemy machine guns emplaced behind 2d Battalion's positions on the ridge; Company G was to move left and cover the ground vacated by Company E, then allow Company E to move up on the left flank. Company F was to move up to the ridge and deploy across the front, firing to pin down the enemy as the other two companies moved out. The battalion objective, the high ground west of the MSR, was to be reached by going northwest, then swinging north and cutting the secondary road.

Companies E and G moved out abreast at 0800, 3 January, with Company E's primary mission that of clearing the rear enemy machine guns, and Company G's mission that of clearing and securing the ground for Company E to come through. Company G "pulverized" the area, and upon securing the ground found about fifteen enemy dead and blood trails of the wounded who had escaped.

Company G moved into the draw, meeting no resistance, and mounted the small hill, which was the first objective. Company F, on the ridge vacated by Companies E and G, ceased firing when the lead elements of Company G entered the small patch of woods.

When Company E arrived on the ridge on the right flank of Company G after having silenced the enemy machine guns in the rear, Company G troops were sitting on the ridge and smoking.

The two companies then moved out abreast, crossing the road and attaining the battalion objective without meeting enemy resistance. Shallow graves where the enemy had probably hastily covered their dead in foxholes were found.

One civilian presumed to be a spy and several prisoners taken informed their interrogators they had not dreamed American troops were in the vicinity. In view of the fact that no determined stand or attack had been made by the enemy, I thought the ROKs could have broken through the enemy roadblock without relying on American aid.

In the meantime, the 3d Battalion had reached its objective, the high ground east of the MSR, without meeting great resistance. Company F then moved west on the secondary road until contact with the enemy was made in the vicinity of a village, where a firefight resulted. Company F then withdrew to the small hill south of the secondary road and covered the rear and left flank of Companies E and G. On the following day, Company F returned to bury their dead.

During the next two days, while two ROK divisions withdrew down the MSR from the north, all the companies set out mines, booby traps, and trip flares on the bridges and roads in the vicinity. One engineer detachment arrived and aided in setting the charges. The A&P Platoon of the battalion also assisted.* This was the only intimation the troops had that they would not maintain their positions.

On 5 January, orders to withdraw were received. The 3d Battalion withdrew first, then the 2d, with Companies E, F, and G following in that order. The French Battalion covered the with-

---

* Ammunition and Pioneer Platoon, part of the Headquarters Company in infantry battalions, was responsible for operating the battalion ammunition supply point. The A&P Platoon (technically the P&A Platoon according to doctrine) also performed simple field engineering tasks not requiring technical training or special equipment of engineer troops.

drawal. As Company G was pulling out, enemy troops were seen converging toward the point from the north and the west. The charges were exploded.

The troops started marching back and were met by battalion and regiment trucks and transported to Hoengsong. A shuttle system of alternate motor and foot marches ensued; the troops marched a total of about seventeen miles that day.[4]

The summary of this action in the 23d Infantry Regiment's Command Report provides a perspective quite different from that of Lieutenant Wilson.

With strong air, artillery, and armored support, the enemy roadblock on the Hongch'on-Hoengsong road was eliminated by 1400 hours, 2 January 1951. The enemy roadblock was reduced after a bitter struggle by the 23d Infantry against not only a well-trained, well-entrenched enemy, but also the mountains and extreme cold, temperatures falling as low as 25 degrees below zero. This operation by the 23d RCT destroyed an estimated NK division.

The 23d RCT manned blocking positions on the Hongch'on-Hoengsong highway until 5 January, while the II ROK Corps withdrew through it. Then orders were received for the 23d RCT to withdraw to a defensive line running generally north of the Wonju-Ch'ungju Highway.[5]

Securing the Wonju Road: 38th Infantry Regiment, 1–5 January 1951

Clearing this roadblock allowed the trapped ROK divisions to the north to withdraw. While the 23d Infantry was removing the roadblock south of Hongch'on, the 38th Infantry was patrolling to the rear and flanks to prevent the North Koreans from infiltrating and cutting off the 23d Infantry. One patrol action is described by SFC Raymond Lott Jr., 1st Squad Leader, 3d Platoon, Company E, 38th Infantry Regiment. The enemy troops, estimated to be about 3,000 strong, that were observed by SFC Lott's patrol were most likely part of the North Korean II Corps, which slipped through and around UN forces and moved deep into the UN rear areas.

On 1 January, I was a member of a regimental patrol consisting

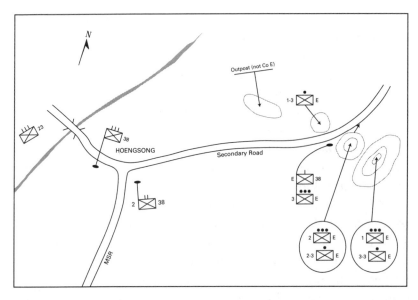

Company E positions, two miles east of Hoengsong (drawn by SFC Raymond
Lott Jr.; not to scale).

of Company E troops: Lieutenant Harver, 3d Platoon leader; the 1st
Squad (myself and seven men); and a fifteen-year-old South Korean
interpreter. The mission of the patrol was to locate the enemy and
study the terrain in front of the regimental positions. The patrol, in
three jeeps, went north about ten miles, then east about ten miles to
ROK lines, where information was secured from the ROK forces.
The patrol, without making physical contact, had seen an estimated
3,000 North Koreans, who had apparently shifted their main forces
toward the right flank of the 38th Infantry Regiment. The patrol
returned and reported its information to regiment.

During the night of 1 January, my squad was on a small hill
about two miles from the center of Hoengsong. Arms included two
BARs, four rifles, and one carbine. At daybreak, 2 January, one of
the men in my squad saw thirty enemy troops dispersed ten yards
apart in a column of twos, coming up the road from the northwest.
I could not send a runner to the platoon CP to inform them of the
enemy approach because the enemy would have seen him. The squad
waited until the enemy had approached to within 200 yards of our

positions, and then fired on them. Friendly troops on the hill across the road commenced firing also. All the enemy soldiers were killed. A runner from the platoon CP came to my hill to make certain my squad was all right.

About one half hour later (0630) the second hill on my right was attacked from the east. A firefight lasted about one hour, and the enemy was repulsed. I estimated fifty-five men were defending the hill.

Nothing occurred until about 2400, 3 January, when both hills on my right were attacked from the east. Artillery support aided in repulsing the attack. Again at 1200, 4 January, the same attack took place, and the same results were effected. My position was not disturbed.

That afternoon, 4 January, ROK forces withdrew from the north, passed through American positions, and continued south on the MSR. Company E, 38th Infantry Regiment followed, and I went to the clearing station at Wonju for medical treatment.[6]

By 5 January all of Eighth Army was withdrawing in the face of heavy Chinese and North Korean pressure. In the west the I and the IX Corps were falling back to Line D, anchored on P'yongt'aek, some thirty-five miles south of Seoul. From P'yongt'aek, Line D ran generally northeast through Wonju and then east to the coast at Samch'ok. In the center above Wonju, the ROK II and III Corps had been rapidly pushed out of position by strong attacks, while a large number of North Koreans had slipped around the eastern flank of the ROK II Corps and were moving into the vulnerable rear areas. The U.S. X Corps under General Almond assumed control of the central sector from the two battered ROK corps and ordered the 2d Infantry Division to withdraw to and hold Wonju, blocking the key mountain roads to the south. Before the order could be acted upon, before dawn on 5 January, a force of 300 to 500 North Koreans attacked and overran Company C, 38th Infantry Regiment, in position six miles north of Hoengsong. The command report of the 38th Infantry Regiment describes the action.

During the afternoon [of 4 January], the 1st Battalion commander requested that he be permitted to withdraw Company C.

They were in his opinion "extended too far forward." This request was forwarded to division but permission was denied.

At 0555 hours small arms and automatic weapons fire were heard from the Company C positions along the east-west road. The 1st Battalion reported that it had communications with the company just before the activity; however, communications were now cut and the battalion was unable to contact the company. Regiment immediately contacted the field artillery requesting they contact their forward observer with the company. The artillery replied shortly thereafter that they could not raise the FO by either wire or radio. While the field artillery was replying to the request, approximately fifteen explosions were heard coming from the rear of the Company C lines. The 1st Battalion reported that this was probably Company C firing a field artillery mission; however, on questioning of the artillery, the men reported none of their batteries were firing a mission. Trained field artillery observers reported that it was mortar fire of a medium caliber. A rapid check of the Netherlands company, which was situated to the right of Company C, disclosed that its men were not in a firefight, nor could they observe any enemy. The company did report, however, that there appeared to be a firefight going on in the Company C area.

At 0820 the executive officer of Company C, along with three wounded men, came into the forward field artillery battery's position. They were immediately forwarded to their battalion. Shortly thereafter, the company first sergeant, with some fifteen stragglers, reported in to the Netherlands' position.

They all reported a harrowing experience. As each tale was compiled and pieced together, the facts became more apparent: At approximately 0550 hours, the roadblock to the west of the company's position observed approximately 200 soldiers marching along the road toward their positions. One member of the roadblock shouted, "Don't shoot, they're ROKs"; this call was carried down the line toward the company. Apparently the members of the roadblock mistook the enemy for ROK troops, whose patrols were active in this area. As the soldiers came abreast of them, members of the roadblock discovered that they were enemy. It was too late; the enemy quickly overran the roadblock and headed straight for the mortar positions. Simultaneous with this action, another group of enemy, also numbering approximately 200, skirted the flank of the company and came up a draw into the rear of the company, going directly toward the CP. In this maneuver, a rifle platoon was entirely cut off from the remainder of the company. The enemy group, heading toward the company CP, went directly up to individual soldiers in foxholes and in the CP area and motioned for them to give up their arms. Three enemy walked into the CP proper and directed the company commander by arm and hand signals to turn over his weapons to them. A soldier standing behind the commander stepped to one side, and with a burst from his automatic carbine, killed all three enemy.

Meanwhile the group of enemy, which had penetrated to the mortar positions, turned the mortars to the south and fired approximately fifteen rounds.

By this time, the company was fighting in separate groups. The isolated platoon began fighting its way back toward the Netherlands company. The heavy weapons, forming the roadblock and mortar crews, fared the worst. Having lost their crew-served weapons, they joined the rifle platoons and fought their way to friendly positions.

Men from Company C continued to arrive in friendly lines. When the ground fog had lifted, regiment requested that a liaison plane reconnoiter the area in which Company C had its action. At noon, the aircraft reported that the enemy was moving north, carrying their wounded with them. The aerial observer reported observing a 150-man carrying party taking casualties to the north. Artillery was placed on this target and an estimated 50 enemy were killed.

During this action, Company C, with its supporting weapons, sustained 4 killed, 4 wounded, and 19 missing in action.[7]

On 5 January, the same day as the attack on Company C, 38th Infantry, the 9th Infantry Regiment, along with the attached 1st Battalion, 23d Infantry, was ordered by X Corps to move south to keep open the Wonju-Chech'on road. By late on 6 January the 23d (minus its 1st Battalion) and the 38th Infantry Regiments were in defensive positions around Wonju.

Chapter 3

ACTION AT WONJU

23d and 38th Infantry Regiments, 6–7 January 1951

Col. Paul Freeman, commander of the 23d Infantry Regiment, describes the situation at Wonju.

Arriving at Wonju on 6 January, the three battalions of the 23d Infantry Regiment and the French Battalion (attached) sent out patrols to contact an ROK division, which was supposed to tie in with the left flank of the 2d Infantry Division; these patrols, some operating as far as eleven miles to the west, failed to reach any ROK forces.

On the afternoon of 6 January, after the 9th Infantry Regiment had left the division, General McClure, the 2d Division commanding general, decided that the ground around Wonju was not defensible, and he determined to establish a new defense line anchored on mountains about five miles south and southwest of Wonju. Moreover, the route to the south over the Wonju-Ch'ungju road was precarious and contained several mountain passes.[1]

Defense of Wonju

The 23d and 38th Infantry Regiments formed the defensive perimeter around Wonju. The 2d Battalion, 23d Infantry, covered the northwestern portion of town; the 3d Battalion, 23d Infantry Regiment, and the French Battalion the southwestern sector; and the 2d and 3d Battalions, 38th Infantry Regiment, covered the northeastern and southeastern parts. The 1st Battalion, 38th Infantry Regiment, south of the airfield, was in reserve. On 6 January, while

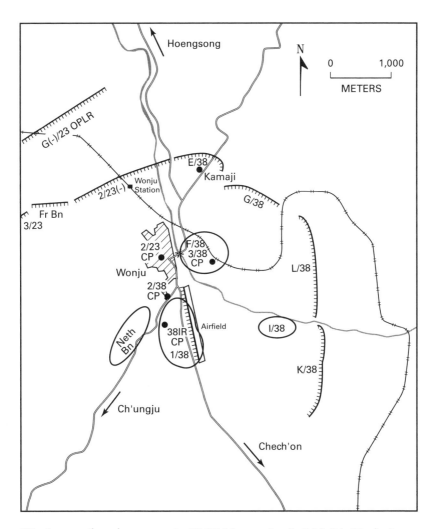

Wonju area (based on maps in CMH Manuscript 8–5.1A BA 31, Action at Wonju).

stockpiled supplies were evacuated from the town by road and rail, the UN forces prepared both for combat and for the expected withdrawal to the south the next day. First Lieutenants John Heath and Jerrell Wilson, both of Company G, 23d Infantry Regiment, describe the defensive positions of their battalion.

LT. HEATH: Company G moved to the battalion assembly area near a school (approximately three miles north of Wonju), arriving in position about 1700. About 2200 Company G moved into the northern outskirts of Wonju and tied in with Company F on the northwest. Company F had a roadblock on the Wonju-Hoengsong road. Company E was to the rear and tied in on the left across the railroad track with the 1st Platoon of Company G. The French were tied in on the rear flank to the southeast. The mission of the 2d Battalion was to defend Wonju against attack from the north. Company G set up its mortars along the railroad, and established an OPLR [outpost line of resistance] with the 2d Platoon, commanded by Lieutenant Finn. The outpost was approximately 1,000 yards north of Company G's positions.

LT. WILSON: Since Company G was under strength (I estimated only ninety to a hundred combat soldiers in the company; about fifteen additional service personnel were cooks and clerks), and since the line to be manned covered a distance of about five miles, the company set up a series of strongpoints, with several men at each point. These troops were not to return enemy fire in case of an attack during the night; their mission was to determine the direction and number of any enemy attacking, make these facts known to the company CP, and withdraw toward Wonju. I stayed in the battalion CP in Wonju with two jeep drivers awaiting word from the company outposts, so that in case of an enemy attack, the drivers could go out and meet those who had made contact with the enemy and would be withdrawing. The MLR [main line of resistance],* manned by Companies E and F, was about one mile south of the OPLR.[2]

Thousands of refugees continued to flow south on the main road through Wonju all day on 6 January. Air observers reported

---

* The main line of resistance (MLR) is an imaginary line that connects the forward edges of the frontline defense areas of the battle position. The outpost line of resistance (OPLR) is established forward of the MLR to provide warning of the enemy approach; orders establishing the OPLR may prescribe that the OPLR must be held against the enemy a certain amount of time to delay and disorganize the enemy and to deceive him as to the location of the battle position.

*up to 15,000 North Koreans in the area south of Hoengsong. De-
spite the American outpost line and defensive perimeter, the enemy
began to infiltrate into Wonju the night of 6–7 January. Sergeant
Raul Villarreal, a mortar squad leader in Company H, 38th Infantry Regiment, was in position between the town and the airfield to
the south and describes the fighting that night.*

From north of Wonju, Company H withdrew to Wonju, arriving about 0800, 6 January. The mortar platoon troops set up their
weapons near the airstrip. Most of that day the platoon cleaned
weapons, registered in, and sat around. That night the platoon was
told that an enemy attack was expected to hit the area around 0300.
Security was set up for the night; at 2400, security around the mortars was doubled.

Hearing small arms and burp gun firing in the vicinity of the
railroad and highway crossing about 0230, 7 January, I went out to
check my mortar. Shortly thereafter the platoon leader, Lieutenant
Gillen, assembled the squad leaders near the road to the west of the
mortar emplacements. The platoon leader informed the squad leaders that the battalion S-2, coming into town from the north with
two jeeps, had just been ambushed at the railroad and highway
crossing. The S2 and his party had escaped without casualty, but
had had to abandon their jeeps. Lieutenant Gillen warned the squad
leaders to "stay on the ball."

Immediately, at about 0300, guards were placed on stations surrounding the mortars. Men of the Number 1 mortar guarded the
road; Number 2 covered the area to the rear of the mortars; Number 4 covered the dike overlooking the river; my men of the Number
3 mortar took care of the area to the front of the mortar emplacements. The mortars were set up on a small street among the houses
and huts of the town; alleys honeycombed the area.

Around 0400, I heard talking on the other side of the river. It
sounded as though someone (friendly) was checking his platoon.
Soon afterward, Lieutenant Gillen came and got the squad leaders
of the 3d and 4th Squads, and together we checked the guards at the
dike. While we were there, an enemy green flare went off in the vicinity of the bridge. I saw about a platoon of enemy troops coming
down the path alongside the dike and about a platoon of enemy

forces coming down along the river. They were about 200 yards away. Fortunately, we happened to be in shadow when the flare went off and were not detected by the enemy. Lieutenant Gillen told the squad leaders to report back to their squads and tell the men that enemy troops were in the area.

About 0500, a second green flare went up, and this must have been the signal for the enemy to attack, for enemy fire from burp guns began to be received by the mortar platoon from two sides, from the area in front of the mortars, and from the river. Although it was still dark, I could see the enemy, dressed in white, infiltrate and scatter into the area between the river and the road, using the houses and huts for cover.

The mortar platoon returned the enemy fire, and although the enemy continued their fire, they did not advance on the mortars. During a lull in the firing, I heard one of the enemy shout over the dike: "The People's Army of Korea does not wish to hurt you. Surrender, and I will see that you get back safely to America." The man spoke pretty good English. No one answered his proposal.

The platoon leader at this time sent the platoon sergeant to tell the squad leaders to withdraw their men to the battalion CP. There was no time to take the mortars out of position or to destroy them. The platoon had two jeeps parked in the alley near the main road, but only one could be started, so the platoon left one jeep and trailer behind. As the withdrawal was being made, an enemy grenade was thrown over the dike into the area, and two men were wounded, one seriously, the other very lightly. The trailer also was spattered by the grenade.[3]

While the North Koreans were infiltrating through the American lines and, according to some reports, moving openly down the Hoengsong road as if they were a South Korean unit, a few isolated American outposts were attacked. On signal at about 0500 hours, the enemy inside Wonju and those massed outside the American lines attacked. The action along the outpost line and the main line of resistance of the 2d Battalion, 23d Infantry Regiment, is described by Lieutenants Wilson and Heath.

LT. HEATH: At 0230, 7 January 1951, the outpost line was attacked by approximately a hundred North Koreans, who flanked the OPLR and hit Company F, preventing a possible withdrawal of the 2d Platoon through Company F's position. At the same time, the 2d Battalion ordered two squads of Company G from the OPLR to reinforce the battalion CP, which was under attack. This left one squad on the OPLR, which was then ordered back to Company G's position. The squad had to fight its way back. An artillery liaison plane, not recognizing the squad (it was just breaking dawn), ordered artillery fire on its approach. Three men were killed and four wounded. At 0600 the remainder of Company G, ordered to the defense of the 2d Battalion CP, drove off approximately thirty North Koreans. The firing ceased about 0630, and the platoons moved back to the MLR. The 2d Platoon patrolled the area to recover the wounded and dead.

LT. WILSON: In spite of the OPLR and the MLR, enemy forces estimated about company size infiltrated into Wonju. The Company G outpost on the right flank under SFC Chambles made contact about 0500. Chambles pulled back according to instructions, but meeting enemy elements between him and town, Chambles took his group in a southwest direction, laterally behind the OPLR, and then probably lost his sense of direction. The group received fire from the outposts and from artillery; three men were killed, and five were wounded.

In the meantime, the other company outposts withdrawing in Wonju toward the battalion CP received some friendly fire from the French Battalion, which was in the area to the west.

In Wonju, the first knowledge of enemy infiltration into town came when small arms fire struck the stone building, which housed the battalion CP. The enemy must have followed telephone wires to the house. Lt. Col. James Edwards, the commanding officer of the 2d Battalion, 23d Infantry, walked out on the porch about 0530, and, seeing several enemy soldiers fifteen yards away moving past one of the gates of the stone wall around two sides of the house, he shot and killed one with his .45 pistol. The enemy force around the CP numbered about a company. They fired small arms and machine guns against the stone sides of the CP and occasionally tossed grenades over the wall into the court. At 0600, about twenty ROK men slipped over the board fence behind the CP building (a detail was guarding this area), and aided the CP defenders. No concerted attack was made by the enemy, and I think the reason for this was the fact that the man killed by Lieutenant Colonel Edwards must have been the enemy leader. Company G, less Chambles's group, arrived at the CP around forty or fifty minutes after the ROK troops.[4]

On the eastern side of the Wonju perimeter, the 2d Battalion, 38th Infantry, also came under attack. Sgt. Richard W. Carey, a squad leader in the 3d Platoon, Company E, describes the attack on one part of this battalion.

When it was just breaking dawn, 7 January 1951, heavy fighting could be heard in Wonju. Various houses in the town could be seen burning. Company E, 38th Infantry Regiment, was dug in north and east of Wonju. The company CP was in the small village of Kamaji [about one kilometer north of Wonju]. The 1st Platoon was dug in to the north of the village; the 2d Platoon was on a high ridge slightly to the north and east of the 1st platoon; and the 3d Platoon was defending the village from the east. Two squads were dug in on a high knoll, and one squad was on a finger extending southward. The 3d Platoon CP was located about 500 yards to the north. The CP was in a house beside a Buddhist temple.

Company G was dug in to the east and the 23d Infantry Regiment was dug in across the valley to the west of Company E's position.

During the night before, small arms could be heard firing in Wonju. As dawn was breaking, the rate of firing in Wonju increased and seemed to be coming toward the rear of Company E's positions. At first, I thought Company G was under attack. Red and green flares could be seen in the direction of Wonju (approximately one mile away), and my men were trying to figure what they meant.

From my position a long column of men could be seen, going north up the valley below. I counted eighty and then stopped counting. Not having been told who they were, and assuming they were friendly troops, I held up fire. In the meantime I noticed that communications were cut off from the 3d Platoon CP (my squad had an

SCR 300 and an SCR 536* with them). The channels seemed to be jammed and full of static. As I was trying to get communications through, I glanced out of my foxhole and saw a North Korean standing about six feet away. This was the first time that I knew that the column was enemy troops.

My squad left our foxholes and chased approximately forty or fifty enemy down the hill, by small arms fire, into a small valley below. I heard later that this group of North Koreans had overrun the 3d Platoon CP, forcing the platoon sergeant and one squad to flee. The platoon leader was at the company CP at this time.

At the time the enemy was approaching my position, the other squad on the hill fled. The squad sergeant had taken an SCR 300 to the company CP, and the men wouldn't stop for me. This left me and three or four men on the hill.

The enemy, after being forced off the hill where I was, went up the hill where the 2d Platoon was situated. One squad fled with the squad from the 3d Platoon. In the meantime, the platoon sergeant, platoon guide, and the reserve squad of the 2d Platoon withdrew to the company CP, having thought the rest of the platoon had been overrun.

We remained in position on the hill. I directed the men to get the light machine gun abandoned by the squad that fled. At this time, several other stragglers joined the group, making a total of nine men with one machine gun and three boxes of ammunition. The first thing the men did was to go to the northern slope of the hill and fire on the enemy that had overrun the 2d Platoon's positions. They hit some and received small arms fire in return. I then ordered my men back to the original positions on the ridgeline.

Around 0700, I saw a group of Koreans about 1,000 yards be-low the position in the valley below. Not being sure who they were,

---

* The Signal Corps Radio (SCR) 300, or walkie-talkie, was a short-range frontline company-to-battalion FM radio weighing about forty pounds, with a range of one to three miles. The SCR 536, or "handie talkie," was a short-range frontline platoon-to-company radio weighing about ten pounds, with a range of about one mile.

I stood up and hollered "Ittywa—come here." The group scattered, and I ordered my men to open fire. I then got the group together and withdrew to another hill to make better use of the machine gun. From this point, American units could he seen withdrawing down the Hoengsong-Wonju road toward Wonju. While moving to this hill, my group was under enemy small arms fire. Several small enemy groups of five to ten men were repulsed coming over the skyline from the south. I thought they were stragglers trying to rejoin the main enemy force.

From this hill, I could see some American troops on the hills to the left of the road. I knew they were Americans by their dress. They had air panels out, and they were firing south. Around 0800 we joined forces with them. It was the 1st Platoon of Company E, 38th Infantry Regiment. The company commander, Capt. Robert Allen, and the 1st Platoon leader, a lieutenant, were with the men. Another officer was there directing mortar fire on enemy positions. Captain Allen told me that he was certainly glad to see me and the men, and further stated that the machine gun, which I had brought with me, was the only one in the platoon. The men scattered out and dug in a tight 360-degree defensive perimeter, with the machine gun on the top of the hill. During this time the hill was under small arms and machine gun fire from the village of Kamaji, from the ridge to the northwest and from the flats where the 23d Infantry Regiment had been. I could see houses burning up and down the valley. Friendly mortar fire and machine gun fire kept the enemy pinned down, and the platoon remained in this position for about one hour.

Around 1015, the platoon was relieved by Company E, re-grouped and led by Lieutenant Harvey. The enemy was put to flight and fifteen or twenty were taken prisoner, including one Chinese. I couldn't begin to estimate [how many enemy were opposing the platoon], but in one foxhole where I thought there were only two North Koreans, they took out eleven bodies.

Around 1100–1200, the company withdrew to Kamaji, which had been cleared of enemy opposition. We were issued more am-munition and were told to go back to our original positions and prepare for an enemy counterattack. The company remained in these positions until dark without further enemy contact.[5]

Private 1st Class Herbert D. Wiggins, a mortar man in Company E, 38th Infantry Regiment, was in a defensive position east of Wonju at the time of the attack. He describes what happened.

Early in the morning on 7 January, the company position was suddenly attacked by enemy armed with mortars and automatic weapons. The surprise element of the attack caused the company, with the exception of the company commander, Captain Allen, me, and fourteen others, to break and withdraw. I was later told that those who withdrew were reorganized by Lieutenant Harvey and given the mission by Colonel Skeldon, the commander of the 2d Battalion, of supporting the strongpoint being held by Captain Allen. Counterattacking, they succeeded in making their way back to Captain Allen, killing, capturing, and dispersing the North Koreans. This ended the firefight in the Company E area on 7 January.[6]

Master Sergeant Olen L. McGregor, first sergeant of Company F, 38th Infantry Regiment, describes other portions of the fighting in the 2d Battalion's area. Company F manned the outpost line with one platoon and retained the other platoons in reserve ready to react to emergencies.

On 7 January 1951, Company F was bivouacked in buildings on the east side of the river, near the bridge, in Wonju. At approximately 0400, the 2d Battalion S-3 notified Company F's commanding officer, Captain Shelton, that the enemy had set up a roadblock in a railroad underpass [where the Hoengsong road crossed the railroad north of Wonju]. At this time, Company F had 36 men on an OPLR under the command of Lieutenant Opolas. The men on the OPLR were attacked and surrounded by an estimated 200 to 300 North Koreans. Lieutenant Opolas gave radios to the different outpost positions and kept an SCR 536 radio with his section to maintain contact. A prearranged signal to withdraw (three shots and the setting off of smoke grenades) was decided upon by the lieutenant in case of radio failure. When the enemy attacked near

Lieutenant Opolas's outpost, the SCR 536 radio would not work, and after firing the three rounds and setting off the smoke grenades, the lieutenant's outpost started to withdraw. The other outpost squads were depending on the platoon leader (Lieutenant Opolas) to notify them when to withdraw, but evidently failed to see or hear the signals. Twelve men out of 36 returned. Three were captured by the North Koreans and were immediately released. The twelve men returned to Company F's position by withdrawing back to the railroad and following the tracks to the main line of friendly troops.

During this time, Company F was given the mission to reduce the enemy roadblock at the underpass. The advance was made in a staggered diamond formation. The two rifle platoons were followed by the weapons platoon.

As the Company neared the bridge, I could hear American voices yelling. Approximately fifty North Koreans were crossing the bridge from the center of Wonju, pushing two GI medics in front of them, and the medics were shouting for Company F to hold their fire. Some of the men opened fire on the enemy. I saw the North Koreans shoot one of the American prisoners in the back of the head, while the other fell to the ground. Company F immediately engaged the enemy. During the firefight Captain Sheldon was wounded. Six North Koreans were killed on the bridge, and the rest fled back toward the center of Wonju. At the time the enemy tried to rush the bridge, approximately an enemy squad tried to ford the river by wading slightly to the north of the bridge, and this attempt was driven back, with about five North Koreans killed. At this time, one platoon from Company E reinforced Company F. The enemy used small arms and automatic weapons in the attack.

At the same time that the enemy was trying to cross the bridge and ford the river, approximately a platoon of North Koreans launched a whistle-blowing banzai attack down through the underpass around the roadblock. The quad-fifties from a section of the 82d AAA [antiaircraft artillery] Battalion attached to Company F opened fire and repulsed the attack, causing the enemy to flee to the north, leaving about nine dead behind. All of this action occurred between 0400 and daylight. The weather was very cold and the sky was overcast.

After the attack was repulsed, the platoon from Company E took a position on the high ground [about one kilometer north of Wonju]. Company G was on the high ground east of Wonju.[7]

With the repulse of the attack on the defensive perimeter, the Americans went about the process of eliminating the remaining North Koreans who had infiltrated into Wonju. A large group of enemy was found near the airfield, south of the area where the mortar platoon of Company H, 38th Infantry Regiment, had come under attack before dawn. Sergeant Villarreal continues the account of his mortar platoon.

By about 0600, the platoon had successfully withdrawn to the [battalion] CP, and while Lieutenant Gillen went inside to report the action, the platoon formed a perimeter defense around the CP. A friendly rifle platoon came down the road from the hills to the north, attacked the enemy in the area around the bridge, while the mortar platoon went back up the road and advanced on the enemy from the south. The rifle platoon cleared out the area, and when the mortar platoon reached our mortars, we found my mortar with a hole in it; the other three had not been touched. The jeep and the trailer were also recovered; the only damage the trailer had suffered was a blown-out tire.

The platoon moved its mortars back close to the battalion CP about 0800 and set them up there. The platoon leader and an officer from battalion went back and surveyed the area where the mortars had been, and Lieutenant Gillen reported to the platoon that thirty enemy dead had been found in the area. He did not know how many were dead along the river.[8]

Across the river from Sgt. Villarreal's mortar platoon, the North Korean infiltrators appeared at the 3d Battalion, 38th Infantry Regiment's command post. Maj. John Lapotka, Headquarters Commandant, 3d Battalion, 38th Infantry Regiment, describes the action.

The battalion arrived in Wonju at approximately 1700 [6 January], and the 3d Battalion CP was set up in the vicinity of the airport with the various companies of the battalion scattered out in a pe-

rimeter north and east of Wonju. The 38th Infantry Regiment CP
was in Wonju.

At 0530, 7 January 1951, firing could be heard from the vicinity of the [highway] bridge in Wonju. I was informed that several
companies of North Koreans infiltrated through the 23d Infantry
Regiment's positions from the east and were trying to cross the
riverbed. A wire crew from the 38th Infantry Regiment, going to
fix wires that had gone dead, surprised the enemy, who in turn
fired upon them with small arms. The attempt to cross the riverbed
was repulsed.

After the two enemy companies failed in their attempt to cross
the riverbed, they swung around and went across a field between
the airstrip and the 3d Battalion CP. At approximately 0615, the
battalion commander, Lieutenant Colonel Maixner, spotted the
enemy (approximately 200) and called the commanding officer of
Company I, Capt. John Totten, and instructed him to bring up the
company and establish a perimeter around the battalion CP. Company I was in reserve at the time. The enemy troops were wearing
white parkas and were not immediately recognized, so Major De-
vos, 3d Battalion executive officer, called out, "GI." The enemy
hollered back "GIs" and opened fire with small arms. At the same
time they jumped into a ditch bordering the airstrip and placed machine gun and mortar fire on the 3d Battalion's positions. The firefight lasted from approximately 0615 to 0815, at which time the
enemy fled into the hills to the north. Thirty-five were killed, 25
wounded, and 25 were taken prisoner, including some North Korean officers and noncommissioned officers. No Chinese (CCF)
were involved in this action.[9]

*Capt. Michael H. Swatko from the 38th Field Artillery Battal-
ion was liaison officer with the 3d Battalion, 38th Infantry Regiment. He provides this account of the action around the 3d
Battalion's CP.*

In accordance with 2d Division commander's order, at 0330 in
the morning everyone in the 3d Battalion command post was awake,
up, and dressed. At 0415 Captain DeBrock, 3d Battalion S-2, got a
phone call from the S-2, 38th Infantry Regiment, to the effect that

a wire crew had been ambushed at the road bridge across the Wonju River, and Company E had been ordered to investigate the bridge and the railroad trestle. The regimental S-3 estimated two companies of enemy to be in that area. At 0445 I heard rifle fire and mortars in the direction of the road bridge, and at the same time, Lieutenant Colonel Maixner, 3d Battalion commander, ordered Company I to report to the battalion command post. At 0500 the Company I commander came into the battalion command post bringing Lieutenant Wymer, the artillery forward observer, with him. At 0600 command post guards reported that there were men moving in some rice paddies fifty to a hundred yards east of the command post. These enemy being armed with burp guns and estimated at about 100, were opened up on by the perimeter guard, with Company I taking up the firefight in the vicinity of the 3d Battalion command post, the Company I 60mm mortar shelling the enemy, with Lieutenant Wymer observing. The 38th Infantry regimental headquarters was notified concerning the firefight and an improvised group started out for the 3d Battalion command post coming from the north end of the airstrip. Daylight occurred at 0700. At 0715 I poked a hole through a rice paper window in the command post and using field glasses was able to see heads bobbing around on a bank of the edge of a rice paddy about seventy-five yards distant. I knew they were enemy because they did not wear helmets. I fired thirty rounds of ammunition at them from my carbine. At around 0730 Colonel Maixner had some South Koreans yell to the enemy to surrender. Since daylight the perimeter guard on the high ground had had the same advantage of shooting the North Koreans in the rice paddies that one has "shooting ducks in a barrel." According to Captain DeBrock, 77 of the enemy surrendered, 42 killed were counted in the vicinity of the highway bridge and the 3d Battalion command post; 9 wounded Northern Koreans were brought in and placed in a building. I covered one about seventeen years old with my blanket. The 3d Battalion lost one man killed and 6 wounded.[10]

The 1st Battalion, 38th Infantry, was in reserve south of town near the airstrip. They counterattacked to restore the defensive pe-

rimeter where it had been penetrated and then cleared the area of infiltrators. Second Lt. David Brisbane, a platoon leader in Company B, 38th Infantry Regiment, describes the actions of his platoon.

At 0300, 7 January, I heard machine gun fire coming from the high ground northeast of the railroad in the approximate vicinity of Hill 233. I assembled my platoon on the road, and on order from the company commander advanced to the road junction [of the Ch'ungju and Chech'on roads just north of the airfield]. As it was getting light, I led my platoon east and northeast across the rice fields. On the other side of the river, an estimated 200 enemy troops firing from a gully or canal southeast of the Company I CP had pinned down Company I. My platoon engaged the enemy, killed an estimated 100, and took 45 prisoners, as elements of Company C came north across the airstrip and met us at the gully. My platoon then cleared the village [the buildings just east of the river]; no enemy troops were found. Company I at this time moved out of the village and deployed along the railroad and the barracks [part of the buildings east of the river].

My platoon, on company order delivered by runner, moved up to and crossed the bridge. Spreading out in a skirmish line, the platoon turned to the right, and cleared the center of town from the bridge to the railroad, between the left bank of the river and the first street. At the center of this area, the platoon met and passed through elements of Company G.[11]

An Eighth Army Military History Detachment reconstructed the events at Wonju and summarized the reasons for the enemy surprise of the UN forces and why the surprise attack failed.

From the interviews, which form the basis of the action described above, it would appear that enemy troops estimated in battalion strength infiltrated into the town of Wonju between 2400, 6 January, and 0300, 7 January, with the intention of harassing United Nations forces in town. An estimated battalion of enemy forces marching in column, two or three abreast, and moving south on the Hoengsong-Wonju road was observed by 38th Infantry Regiment elements, which assumed the column to be ROK forces and thus did not fire. Another enemy column, assumed to be friendly, was observed moving north in the small valley east of Wonju. The main body of enemy most probably infiltrated into Wonju through the valley along the Wonju River, entering the town along the dikes to the road bridge in the center of the town. It was suggested that the enemy element, which attacked the CP of the 2d Battalion, 23d Infantry Regiment, might have followed telephone wires to the building.

Having achieved the element of surprise by his successful infiltration into Wonju, the enemy did not exploit his position with any marked degree of effectiveness. Enemy forces in attack, although coordinated, failed to strike with vigor sufficient to cause considerable damage. His attacking elements appear to have been dispersed over too great an area. Although some confusion among United Nations troops resulted, friendly troops repulsed each individual segment of the attack as it occurred and made possible the orderly withdrawal from Wonju on 7 January, according to plan.[12]

Withdrawal from Wonju: 2d Infantry Division, 7 January 1951

After the North Korean infiltrators were cleared from Wonju, the UN forces prepared to withdraw from the city. The 2d Battalion, 38th Infantry Regiment, and an engineer platoon were designated to remain behind as rear guard to cover the withdrawal of the other 2d Division units and to burn all military supplies and those buildings and facilities in the town that might be used by the enemy. First Lt. Walter Hurtt was platoon leader of the Ammunition and Pioneer Platoon of the 2d Battalion, 38th Infantry Regiment. He describes his attempt to keep his unit supplied with ammunition and his actions in the destruction of supplies and facilities before the withdrawal from Wonju.

I left the 3d Battalion on 4 January and proceeded to Wonju with the two battalion ammunition two-and-a-half trucks with one trailer. The ammunition train contained a basic load for the battalion. A basic load consists of 57mm and 75mm recoilless rifle ammunition, 60mm and 81mm mortar shells, 2.36-inch and 3.5-inch rockets, 400 lbs. of C-3, 5,000 dynamite blasting caps, and small arms ammunition. There were about thirty railroad cars containing ammunition sitting at Wonju Station with no one about the station except a few refugees. About 300 yards west of Wonju Station, a field artillery battery was set up and firing north. I helped myself to the ammunition, finding in the cars everything from carbine to 105 rounds. The carbine ammunition was in poor condition, and the M-1 ammunition had only five to eight rounds to a clip.

The 2d Battalion, 38th Infantry Regiment, arrived at Kamaji [about one kilometer north of Wonju] at 0400 6 January. The battalion headquarters set up at Kamaji and the rifle companies took up positions across the Wonju River from Wonju. I was ordered to take the two ammunition trucks to the 38th Infantry regimental headquarters, which was located on the west side of the Wonju-Chech'on road about one mile south of Wonju. Across the road from the regimental headquarters were about eight Quonset huts, and on the other side of the Quonset huts, the southern end of the Wonju airstrip, which ran north to the southern edge of Wonju.

On the night of 6 January I went to sleep at headquarters, 38 Infantry Regiment. According to regimental SOP by order of Colonel Peploe, commanding officer, the 38th Infantry Regiment has a general alert each morning at 0330. At 0345 I heard firing in the vicinity of the road bridge across the Wonju River. Small arms fire broke out along the banks of the Wonju River in the general vicinity of Wonju, and I saw the flashes of concussion grenades and heard explosions, which I believed to be mortar shells since later on in the morning I saw mortar duds of a light caliber lying on the streets of Wonju. At 0415 the 38th Infantry regimental S-3 told me, "Get the trucks the hell out of the compound." The S-3 felt that if a mortar round hit one of the two ammunition trucks, the explosion would silhouette the entire 38th Infantry regimental position to the benefit of the enemy. Knowing that the 2d Battalion would need additional ammunition to replace that expended in the firefight, I started toward Wonju, riding in the lead truck. Five hundred yards up the road I was met by fifty to a hundred American soldier stragglers coming south. Some of these men hollered, "Roadblock! Enemy 200 yards ahead." I stopped my truck in order to drop the trailer to enable us to maneuver across country around the roadblock. At the time I stopped I found that the ammunition sergeant had deserted his second truck. The sergeant later on turned up in Chech'on. The shotgun guard on the back of my truck had also deserted his post; therefore, I had difficulty with just two men to help me drop the trailer. I next attempted to turn the stragglers around and start them back to their units. I supplied twenty-five to thirty men, who had either lost or thrown away their weapons, with excess arms from the ammunition trucks, the weapons being carbines and one "grease gun." Some of the men got up on the running board of the truck, and they started north. The men soon got off the truck, and I do not know whether they returned to their units.

Reaching the road junction, I was unaware of the fact that the 2d Battalion, 38th Infantry Regiment, command post was located in a building about 50 yards west of the road junction and proceeded south on the Wonju-Ch'ungju road about 200 yards when I ran into some soldiers who knew the location of the 2d Battalion. This 2d Battalion, which was located just off the road, turned out to be the 2d Battalion, 23d Infantry Regiment. I continued south down the Wonju-Ch'ungju road, passing some Dutch soldiers just south of the 23d Infantry Regiment, and reached the 2d Division forward command post at Mich'on [about ten kilometers south of Wonju] at 0545. At division I found no one who knew where the 2d Battalion, 38th Infantry Regiment, command post was. I talked with the G-4 and with a major at G-3. The G-4 suggested that I move back with division headquarters when they withdrew. At 0600 a stray jeep from Company H, 38th Infantry Regiment, arrived at division headquarters, and I placed the jeep with the ammunition truck. At 0630, by using the phone at G-3, I was able to contact the 38th Infantry Regiment S-3, who told me that the 2d Battalion, 38th Infantry, command post was up near the roadblock [near the airfield], and I was to go on up to the 2d Battalion command post with my ammunition trucks; however, a major at G-3 told me not to go up to Wonju. At 0730, after I had waited around an hour, I said the hell with it. I got in the jeep, told the truck driver to crank up, and started back to Wonju. In the vicinity of the Dutch trucks I found my second ammunition truck. The driver reported he had lost the first truck in the dark and had pulled in with the Dutch troops for the night. A 2d Battalion, 38th Infantry Regiment, S-2 man met the ammunition train at the road junction and directed me to the battalion command post, which I reached at 0800. Jeeps came in from the companies and replenished their ammunition. At 0900 I took a three-quarter-ton weapons carrier to Wonju Station to replenish the battalion ammunition supply. On the way I noticed about 200 dead North Koreans and a few enemy mortar duds scattered through town. I found when I reached the station that a train had removed some of the boxcars the night before, but there were still sixteen boxcars standing there. Wonju Station was protected by two .50-caliber machine guns situated about fifty yards west of the station and one .30-caliber machine gun located about thirty yards south of the station. The two .50s were firing short bursts of harassing fire. I replenished the 2d Battalion ammunition supply from the ammunition in the boxcars and returned to the 2d Battalion command post. At 1300 I observed the French Battalion starting to pull out of Wonju and estimated that their last unit cleared the town by 1330. At 1400 we loaded eleven bodies of the 2d Battalion, 38th Infantry Regiment, killed in the firefight of that morning on one ammunition truck and sent the two ammunition trucks to the rear.

On 7 January an engineer team placed explosive charges at Wonju Station with a forty-five-minute fuse, the railroad bridge across the Wonju River with a two-minute fuse, and the road bridge across the river with a two-minute fuse. Standing at the Wonju Station were eleven out of the sixteen boxcars containing about eighty tons of explosives. The original order was for me to set off the charge at the three points after the 2d Battalion, 38th Infantry Regiment, had cleared Wonju; however, this was changed, and about 1400 I was given the mission of burning Wonju. It was decided that Company G would burn the southeast portion, Company E the eastern part, Company F the region in the vicinity of Wonju Station, and the Ammunition and Pioneer Platoon would set the fires in Wonju west of the river and south of the railroad station. At 1500 Lieutenant Colonel Skeldon, 3d Battalion commander, decided not to burn Wonju, because he thought the burning town would silhouette the withdrawal of the 2d Battalion, which was to occur at dusk that night; instead, he ordered me to destroy military objectives. The only materials that I had to destroy military objectives were the five-gallon gas cans, and the military objectives that he deemed most important were rice sacks. All rice sacks found in Wonju were saturated with gasoline and burned. Some explosives inside rice sacks located in the center of the town were ignited, and a large rice mill with about 100,000 lbs. of rice stored was set on fire.

Dusk occurred at about 1700, at which time the 2d Battalion, 38th Infantry Regiment, started to withdraw from Wonju, being the last United Nations unit of battalion size to leave. Company E pulled out of its position, crossed the river, and started on foot down the Ch'ungju road, leading the battalion, followed by Companies G, Headquarters, H, and F, also moving by foot, in that order. By 1800 Company F had cleared the road junction, the last squad just clearing before the 38th Infantry Regimental Special Engineer Team moved north from regimental headquarters past the road junction and on to the road bridge, which drew fire. I did not hear the railroad bridge explosive charge go off, but I did see flames come from the bridge. I heard at no time an explosion from the delayed fuse charge at Wonju Station and do not believe it exploded. The 2d Battalion, 38th Infantry Regiment, left thirty-six wounded Northern Korean prisoners in Wonju when it withdrew.[13]

When the withdrawing column reached a mountain pass about twelve miles south of Wonju on the road to Ch'ungju, orders were received to reverse direction and return. The town, which had been successfully defended at some cost early on the morning of 7 January and had then been delivered up to the enemy at no cost, now had to be regained. The return to Wonju would be long and expensive.

Chapter 4

RETURN TO WONJU

2d Infantry Division, 8–20 January 1951

General Almond, X Corps commander, directed the 2d Division immediately to reoccupy Wonju. General McClure, the 2d Division commander, argued that the terrain around Wonju made defense of that area difficult and that a much better defense line could be established on the high ground several miles south of town. Almond recognized that a defense of Wonju would be difficult, as the North Korean attack on 7 January demonstrated, but believed that the high ground immediately south of and overlooking the town had to be retained. From this terrain, UN forces could build a strong defense, and their artillery could dominate the town and make it unusable for the enemy. Moreover, Almond was reacting to the concerns of General Ridgway. On 5 January Ridgway had reluctantly ordered the withdrawal of UN forces to rear defensive positions, designated as Line D, and was clearly upset about the apparent willingness of UN forces, and especially American units of the I and IX Corps, to withdraw unnecessarily and their failure to inflict punishment on the enemy when retreat was necessary. Earlier Ridgway had specifically ordered that Wonju, on Line D, be held. In addition, Almond's orders to McClure to hold Wonju had been clear and unequivocal, and he was furious when McClure fell back and gave up not only the town, but also the high ground about one to two miles to the south on the Ch'ungju road. After Almond ordered the 2d Division to retake Wonju, the 2d Division in turn directed the 23d Infantry Regiment to send one battalion along the road toward the town, considerably less of an effort than envisioned by General

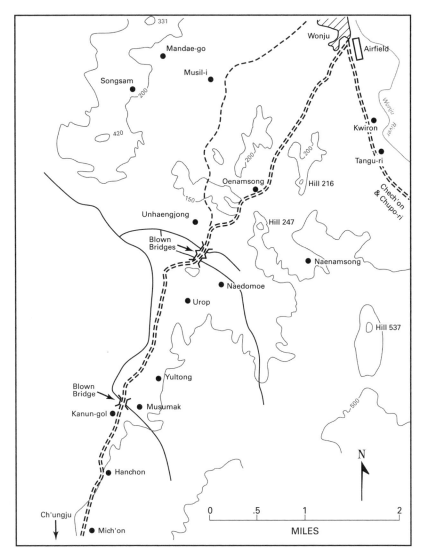

High ground south of Wonju (original map by author).

*Almond, while the remaining battalions of the 23d and the 38th In-
fantry Regiments guarded the Ch'ungju road and the 9th Infantry
Regiment with the attached battalion from the 23d Infantry continued to patrol the Chech'on road. The command reports and daily
journals of the 2d Division and the 23d Infantry make note of the
orders received and those issued for the return to Wonju.*

At 0330 hours on the morning of 8 January, the chief of staff of X Corps relayed a warning order to the 2d Division. The division was to occupy the high ground directly south of Wonju with not less than four battalions and make a reconnaissance in force, with not less than a battalion, beginning at daybreak, to clear the town and airfield. Armored patrols were to keep the road from Wonju to Ch'ungju and from Wonju to Chupo-ri open. Withdrawal from the Wonju area was not to be contemplated unless ordered by the X Corps Commander.[1]

The 23d Infantry Regiment received orders at 0400 hours to send one battalion to Wonju to clear the enemy from the town and the airfield and to take [up a] position to keep the enemy from [re-taking] Wonju. The 23d Infantry [remainder of the unit, including two battalions attached from the 38th Infantry Regiment, was] to defend in present position against an attack from the north.[2]

General McClure obviously was more concerned about the vulnerability of his division in the mountainous terrain south of Wonju than he was about recapturing the town. The enemy had repeatedly demonstrated its capability of moving large forces over rugged terrain around the flanks of road-bound UN troops, cutting their lines of supply and forcing costly, and sometimes disastrous, withdrawals. Consequently, only one battalion of the 23d Infantry was ordered north toward Wonju, and the remainder of the regi-ment remained in defensive positions astride the Ch'ungju road about four miles south of town. The other regiment located on the Ch'ungju road, the 38th Infantry, was about four miles further south guarding a key pass through the mountains. The battalions of the 38th Infantry, which had been attached to the 23d Infantry, moved into defensive positions halfway between the two regiments as additional security for the road.

Taking the High Ground: 23d and 38th Infantry Regiments, 8–13 January 1951

As the 2d Battalion, 23d Infantry, moved out toward Wonju, it was alone and proceeded cautiously. The weather was overcast with a heavy fog. First Lt. Jerrell Wilson of Company G describes the action.

On 8 January, orders were received to move up toward Wonju in order to find out where and in what numbers the enemy was concentrated. After breakfast about 0900, the 2d Battalion moved out in a column of twos with Companies E, F, and G in that order. Troops were on foot, carrying all gear and ammunition. The weather was miserably cold. At the bridge destroyed by 2d Battalion the previous night about four miles south of Wonju, Company G crossed the streambed, entered the woods to the right of the MSR and walked about one and one half miles until the crest of the second hill two or three miles south of Wonju was reached. Company E sighted a concentration of enemy troops in the village below, called up artillery, and directed small arms and mortar fire, which killed an estimated 200 men and caused considerable confusion. In the afternoon, around 1500, although there was no enemy pressure on the battalion, the troops were withdrawn to their previous positions. The reason for the withdrawal was the observation of enemy forces attempting to envelop the 2d Battalion's position.[3]

Cpl. Julius L. Stephens, a member of the 3d Platoon of Company E, provides this account of the action of his unit.

The next morning [8 January], Company E started to walk back toward Wonju (about two or three miles); it was snowing very hard, and visibility was poor. Company E's mission was to contact the enemy, kill as many as possible, and then withdraw back to the 2d Battalion assembly area. In the advance toward Wonju, Company E came across an estimated battalion of enemy troops asleep, with the exception of one outpost. The enemy was dug in on the forward slope of a hill and in a small village. The company commander called for and received artillery concentrations and 81mm mortar fire on the enemy's positions. Company E received small arms and automatic weapons fire in return. The company then withdrew back to the 2d Battalion assembly area. Company E had no casualties from this encounter with the enemy.[4]

Although the 2d Battalion had surprised an enemy battalion and apparently inflicted a large number of casualties, they had also stirred up a hornet's nest. A regiment-size enemy force organized a vigorous counterattack and quickly moved around both flanks of the 2d Battalion, threatening to cut them off. Upon receiving reports of the situation, the regimental commander ordered the battalion immediately to withdraw. That night X Corps ordered that the advance on Wonju be resumed the next day stating that "the moderate enemy resistance and heavy enemy losses indicated that an attack on Wonju would prove successful." The 2d Division was to keep four battalions in position just south of Wonju, which would be permitted to retire only on X Corps order. Two battalions were to be utilized in an air and artillery supported attack to retake Wonju and the Wonju airfield. The 2d Battalion, 38th Infantry, was attached to the 23d Infantry and was given the mission of joining the 2d Battalion, 23d Infantry, in a renewed attack toward Wonju. The two battalions were to be under the control of the commander of the 2d Battalion, 38th Infantry, Lt. Col. James H. Skeldon. The 2d Battalion, 38th Infantry, would attack on the left, and the 2d Battalion, 23d Infantry, would attack on the right.

The situation in the 2d Battalion, 38th Infantry, is described by two members of Company F, M. Sgt. Olen McGregor, the company first sergeant, and 1st Lt. Frank J. Barnes, a platoon leader.

MASTER SERGEANT MCGREGOR: At 0400, 9 January 1951, orders were received for the 2d Battalion to retake Wonju. All bedding, packs, and personal equipment were left behind at Kanun-gol. Only ammunition and weapons would be carried. The order of advance was to be Company G, followed by E. Company F was to be in support. The battalion assembly time was set at 0800, and the companies jumped off together at 0830. The French came up later. The rifle companies advanced in a skirmish line in cold and overcast weather—typical Korean weather. The attacking force followed a rough trail to the right of the Wonju-Ch'ungju road just below the ridgeline. Artillery fire could be heard to the front, probably friendly artillery just harassing the enemy. The morale of the men in Company F was low. Several men had shot themselves through the hand. The company was hampered by a shortage of key noncommissioned officers.[5]

FIRST LIEUTENANT BARNES: At 0330, 9 January 1951, Captain Forney, commanding officer of Company F, 38th Infantry Regiment, received orders to go back into Wonju. The order of march was to be Company G spearheading the attack, followed by Company E, and Company F being the reserve, bringing up the rear. The 2d Battalion was to take several intermediate objectives before reaching Wonju. Captain Forney told me that the 2d Battalion was to recover the airstrip at Wonju. Wonju, according to Captain Forney, was the key to all of the roads in the immediate vicinity, and the recapture of the town was necessary. The battalion left the jump-off point (approximately one-half mile north of Musumak) around 1000. French troops were dug in around Musumak. Company G spearheaded the advance, followed by Company E. The advance of these companies was in the form of a skirmish line.

The morale of the men was lowered when they were told of being ordered back into Wonju. They believed that the battalion was going into the 2d Infantry Division reserve around Ch'ungju. Company F had only 47 men out of 170. Company E had only 50-some men at this time of the advance on Wonju.[6]

The approach and attack of the 2d Battalion, 38th Infantry, is described by Sgt. Rena F. Lattorre-Lopez, a machine gun squad leader from Company H, attached to support Companies E and G.

At 0600, 9 January 1951, Lieutenant Rhotenberry told me that we were going back into Wonju—and I mean back. One section of the Heavy Machine Gun (HMG) Platoon, of Company H, commanded by the lieutenant was to support Company E. Sergeant 1st Class Hudson took charge of the section supporting Company G; I was a squad leader of this section. According to information received by Lieutenant Rhotenberry, the 2d Battalion, 38th Infantry Regiment, was to hold in front of Wonju and support the 9th Infantry Regiment, which was to hit the enemy from the right flank. Company G was to spearhead the attack of the 38th Infantry Regiment. Company G, with attached sections, left the bivouac area at 0700, 9 January 1951. All heavy equipment and ammunition were hauled by two jeeps and trailers following the HMG section. Upon arrival at an assembly area (approximately one mile south of a bombed-out bridge), the men carried the weapons and as much ammunition as possible. About 1100 they left the jeeps in the assembly

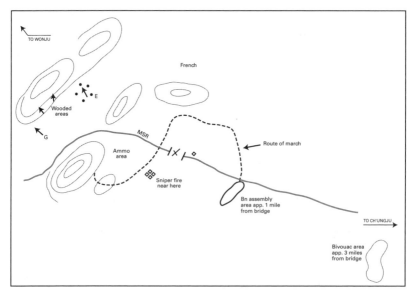

Attack of 2d Battalion, 38th Infantry, 9 January 1951 (drawn by Sgt. Rena F. Lattorre-Lopez).

area, crossed to the right of the road just south of the bridge, skirted a hill, recrossed the road again to the left side, went through a rice paddy, and then passed through a small village. The HMG section went up a rough trail a short distance and then went into position on a small hill. A smaller hill was to the immediate rear and was separated from the large hill by a shallow saddle. The only time the "Chinks" (I am not sure if they were Chinese or North Korean troops) could have seen the approach of the company to its jump-off position was when we recrossed the road. It was about 1200 hours when the HMG section went into position.

The approach to and the establishment of the firing line met no enemy opposition or sniper fire. It was quiet, and visibility was good up to 600 yards, except when the action started. It then started to snow enough to get you wet. Artillery was firing as the HMGs went into position, but their target could not be seen.

Sergeant Villarreal, the other squad leader, set up one light machine gun approximately ten feet to the left of me, and we established a field of fire crossing the light machine guns. Although called the heavy machine gun section, we had been issued brand new HMGs and spindles, but no tripods, steam-condensing devices, or water cans had been issued. The guns were just hauled around in a jeep and never used.

After the firing line was established, Companies E and G started their advance. Company E's advance was slightly to the right front of my gun. I could not see the advance of Company G from my position. Although my mission had been to support Company G, the situation demanded that my gun be used to support Company E. Up until this time, no enemy activity had been observed. Suddenly I heard Lieutenant Jack Knight, commanding officer of Company G, yell, "There's beaucoup enemy up there. What are you waiting for, Rhotenberry? They're trying to flank Easy Company from the left."[7]

Sgt. Frank J. Monte, ammunition sergeant and squad leader of Company G, 38th Infantry, describes the action in Company G's area.

At about 1330, while Company G was advancing on some hills, someone hollered, "Enemy!" then several soldiers hollered, "Enemy!" Company G commander, Lieutenant Knight, quieted the men down by stating firmly that there was no enemy around. Just as he had finished making that statement a machine gun began to chatter off to the left, and small arms fire broke out in the same sector. The enemy fire came from small arms, machine guns, and mortars. We fought back with small arms, BARs, machine guns, and mortars. I was pulled from my duties as ammunition sergeant and placed in charge of a squad in the 2d Platoon during the firefight. Sergeant 1st Class Elmer Wood commanded the 2d Platoon. Company G did not receive any artillery support during the action, although there was an artillery forward observer (FO) section with the company. During the firefight Company G suffered the loss of two machine guns, which were not recovered. Twelve Company G men were injured in the firefight.[8]

The fighting in the Company E sector is described by Sergeant Lattorre-Lopez and by two soldiers of Company E, Sergeant 1st

Class Peter H. Palamidy and Sergeant Richard W. Carey, along with the mortar FO, Sgt. Raul Villarreal.

SERGEANT LATTORRE-LOPEZ: By the time fire was placed on the enemy, some of the men from Company E had reached the trenches. I saw two or three climb up the hill to the trenches and then topple backward as the enemy opened fire. The volume of enemy fire was about company strength. Rifles and burp guns were mostly used; I don't remember any mortar fire falling on friendly positions.

I laid fire from Company E's left flank to the wooded area in order to keep the enemy pinned down. Sergeant Villarreal was crossing fire with my gun. The gunners had to keep changing gun positions because of the steam rising from the guns. It had been eighteen below zero the night before. During this time my ammunition bearers drew fire and returned it with their carbines. Although the hill started to draw only sporadic fire, Lt. Rhotenberry ordered the men to dig in. Ammunition was running low, and the orders came from Lt. Rhotenberry to fire on only sure targets. It seemed that artillery fire was falling over the target and to the right. I don't understand this, because an artillery FO was on the same hill as I was, and I could hear the FO calling for fire. Lieutenant Bundy was also calling for mortar fire on the target at the same time. The Company G commander, Lieutenant Jack Knight; the 2d Battalion commanding officer; the 2d Battalion Adjutant; the commanding officer, Company H; as well as the artillery FO were on the same hill.

SERGEANT 1ST CLASS PALAMIDY: At 1030, the company advanced in a skirmish line. The 1st Platoon was on the right, and the 2d and 3d Platoons were on the left. The 4th Platoon was in reserve. No enemy was contacted on the first hill. The attack continued on to a hill to the north across the Wonju road. As the advance continued, the platoons moved in a diamond formation, providing for more maneuverability. As Company E approached the second hill, heavy enemy resistance was met (approximately one company). At first the approach was quiet, and no enemy could be seen, but as soon as some of the men started to climb up on the trenches, the enemy opened fire. The enemy trenches were just below the crest of the hill, with machine guns firing on both flanks of the company and forcing the company to withdraw.[9]

SERGEANT CAREY: Around 0900–1000, 9 January 1951, the whole 2d Battalion jumped off in an attack on Wonju. The weather was rather warm and clear in the morning, and the snow was melting, but later that afternoon it started to snow very hard. The 3d Platoon spearheaded the attack in Company E's sector. The battalion advanced overland over very rough terrain with numerous hills and ridges. The advance moved roughly 4,000 yards to the north when the enemy was contacted. We were two hills away from our objective; my squad was advancing to the right of the peak of the ridge, and the other squads were advancing to the left, when all hell broke loose. The enemy opened fire with small arms and burp guns along the entire front (a high hill with a trench just below the ridgeline) and from the left flank.

My squad was pinned down by the enemy fire, but we returned fire in the general direction of the enemy, although we couldn't see them. When I saw the other squads withdrawing, I ordered my squad to withdraw—and rapidly. The withdrawal of the entire company was very disorganized and was witnessed by the 2d Battalion commander, Lieutenant Colonel Skeldon, from a hill to the rear. He told the officers and men that he never wanted to see such a disorganized withdrawal again.

The company went to the reverse slope of the hill to the rear and regrouped. Company G was there also, regrouped first, and moved right out. Company E stayed there for about two hours, during which time I took some men and carried fifteen or twenty wounded back to the road and brought back ammunition (mostly mortar rounds). During the time of the attack it was snowing very hard and all the men were wet.[10]

SGT. RAUL VILLARREAL: I was forward observer with Company E. Heavy weapons support for the 2d Battalion, 38th Infantry Regiment, was arranged in this manner: Companies E and G had with them forward observers for the 4.2-inch and 81mm mortars; Company F had with them the artillery forward observers.

No enemy resistance was encountered until Company E attacked a hill about one and one half miles south of Wonju. It started to snow slightly, and Company E, meeting resistance, withdrew back to the hill to the rear. During this withdrawal, my radio operator slipped and broke his ankle; he was evacuated for medical treatment. I had to carry the radio. The Company G forward observer and I were able to see the enemy indistinctly on two hills to the north, and we called for the mortars to register in eight rounds. I also asked my platoon to send me another radio operator, and he arrived shortly. At this time, the mortars of my platoon were about 900 yards to the rear, behind a small hill.[11]

Sergeant Lattorre-Lopez tells what happened to him next and provides some insight into the problems of the company.

My gun jammed at this time, and I was ordered to withdraw to the small hill to the immediate rear to fix it. During this time, Company G also withdrew to the hill behind the firing line to reorganize, and I got three boxes of ammunition from them. I was really glad to get it because I had only one-half can left.

After I rejoined the firing line, the enemy started to concentrate their fire on our position. I think the steam rising from the gun gave my location away. I pulled my gun from the top and was reaching for an ammunition box when I was wounded in the arm. After being hit, I went to the bombed-out bridge, where there was a jeep waiting. On the way back, we were under sniper fire, and we could hear fighting on the right flank. I was evacuated to a clearing station of the 2d Medical Battalion near Ch'ungju.

The attack of Company E was too exposed to enemy fire. The reconnaissance was poor, because the enemy was not sighted until Lieutenant Knight saw them. The main problem was that the men were too tired and cold. Each man had only one blanket. We would rather walk or dig all night than sleep. If we stopped, the perspiration would freeze inside our boots.

During this initial contact with the enemy, Company F remained to the rear in support. The company's perspective on the action is provided by Master Sergeant McGregor.

Company F then moved to a small hill, which dropped off sharply to the Wonju road to our front, where two small blown bridges were plainly visible. Companies G and E had crossed to the left of the road, and Company F was to support their attack. The objective of the 2d Battalion was a high ridge overlooking Wonju about a mile to the northeast of our position. The 38th Infantry Regiment was to advance on the left of the road, and the 23d Infantry Regiment on the right. Captain Forney received orders by radio from the 2d Battalion to bring up all ammunition, but the men had only what they could carry. Captain Forney took the entire company and crossed over under the second blown bridge to the left of the road. Just before crossing, one man from Company F was hit by a stray bullet. The company moved up around 1300. General Almond, X Corps commanding general, was observing the attack on Wonju; the general's aide called Captain Forney to the CG's jeep and asked him who ordered him off the hill. The aide told the captain that Company F was not supposed to be off the hill and that Captain Forney would be notified when to report to General Almond. The captain never heard anymore about this. Company F moved back to the hill and established defensive positions.

Orders were then received from the battalion to cover the possible withdrawal of Companies E and G down the road. Our hill position was excellent for this purpose, because the hill dropped off sharply and permitted fire high enough over the road. The hill had a few small pine trees on it but not much brush. Company F remained on the hill approximately one hour, and then was ordered by the battalion to come behind Companies E and G, which were 500 yards to the front on high ground to the left of the Wonju road.

Meanwhile, the 2d Battalion, 23d Infantry, advancing on the right of the 2d Battalion, 38th Infantry, was also experiencing problems as 1st Lt. Jerrell Wilson, executive officer of Company G, 23d Infantry, relates.

On 9 January, the 2d Battalion, 23d Infantry Regiment, received the same mission, that of getting as far into Wonju as possible. The move was to be made abreast with the 2d Battalion, 38th Infantry Regiment, on the left of the road. The same route was taken except that the troops marched farther to the east of the road. Contact with the enemy was made at the same place, but this time the enemy was reinforced. Visibility was poor due to snow, which fell from time to time, and the enemy used white phosphorus shells to locate

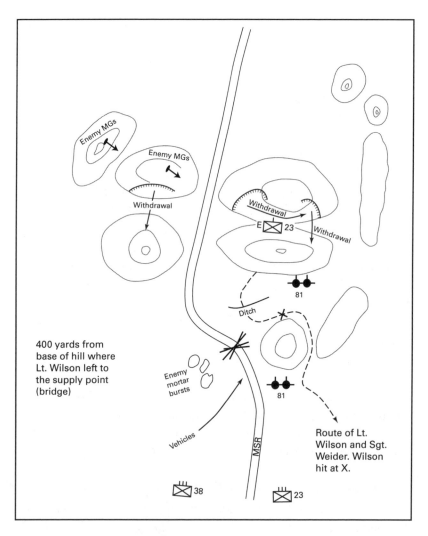

Attack of 9 January 1951 (drawn by Lt. Jerrell F. Wilson).

where their rounds were hitting. For some unknown reason, units of the 38th Infantry Regiment that were abreast of Company G, 23d Infantry Regiment, and west of the MSR, pulled back about noon. This caused enemy fire to fall on the Company G position from the left flank, and the company pulled back 300 or 400 yards behind the hill to get out of the fire.

At about 1300, because mortar and machine gun ammunition was running low, I went to the rear toward the destroyed bridge in order to meet the vehicles carrying ammunition supplies. On the way back I met Sergeant Weider, who was wounded and going toward the battalion aid station. We circled around a hill to avoid enemy fire from the northwest. Behind another hill the battalion communications officer, Lieutenant Wagner, and several men who were taking cover in a ditch warned me of enemy fire, but I disregarded the advice. About three rounds of enemy mortar shells fell about 60 yards from the parked vehicles at the bridge. Sergeant Weider and I swung around to circle another hill, when I was hit by machine gun fire in the hand. I made my way back to the MSR below the supply point, reached the battalion area, and was evacuated for medical treatment.[12]

The confusion in Lieutenant Colonel Skeldon's task force is evident from entries in the 23d Infantry Regiment's S-3 Journal for 9 January.

1210 HOURS: Commander of TF Skeldon estimates enemy on Hill 247 as one company; receiving fire from the front. Firefight.

1215 HOURS: Task Force now in contact. Small arms fire increasing in intensity.

1245 HOURS: Task Force ran into strong enemy force on a wide front. 38th lead elements on left had to withdraw, leaving right flank exposed holding up right flank; danger of being outflanked.

1247 HOURS: Commander of 23d Infantry Regiment out of communication with TF Skeldon. Commander, 23d Infantry Regiment, is with commander, 2d Battalion, 23d Infantry. Lt. Col. Skeldon is with 2d Battalion, 38th Infantry. Commander, 23d Infantry, wants to know if the task force is getting reorganized and into position.

1257 HOURS: Commander, 2d Battalion, 38th Infantry, states he is in position, but the unit on the right is withdrawing.

1258 HOURS: Commander, 2d Battalion, 23d Infantry, states he is not withdrawing.

General Almond was displeased with almost all that he saw during his visit to the front lines of the 2d Division, but especially the

attack of Task Force Skeldon. As indicated by various division re-
cords, Almond's visit produced prompt changes in everything from
seemingly routine tasks to artillery support to the plan of attack.

SECOND INFANTRY DIVISION COMMAND REPORT, JANUARY 1951:
The commanding general of X Corps and the commanding general
of the 2d Infantry Division made tours of the front lines and reported deficiencies they had personally noted. These included improper selection of fields of fire, lack of range cards for crew served
weapons, and excessive casualty rates caused by improper foot care.
These and other deficiencies were brought to the attention of commanders for immediate corrective action.

TWENTY-THIRD INFANTRY REGIMENT PERIODIC OPERATIONS RE-
PORT 118, 9 JANUARY 1951: The regimental commander assumed command of the attacking force and ordered the French Battalion forward.

TWENTY-THIRD INFANTRY S-3 JOURNAL, 9 JANUARY 1951, 1400
HOURS: Summary: French Battalion ordered to attack on the left of
the 2d Battalion, 38th Infantry, to secure the objective ridgeline. . . .
Commanding general called 2d Division chief of staff and ordered
the division artillery staff to move forward to operate with the 37th
Field Artillery Battalion. The 38th Infantry Regiment command
group was ordered to the location of the 23d Infantry Regiment's
CP. The 23d Infantry Regiment's command group ordered forward
by the Commander, 23d Infantry Regiment. Commanding general
ordered 38th Infantry commanding officer to assume responsibility
for the defense sector presently occupied by the 23d Infantry Regiment (reinforced). Commanding general, X Corps, arrived approximately 1100 hours and departed 1345 hours.

As several members of the 2d Battalion, 38th Infantry, relate,
the renewed attack against light resistance was successful and the
attacking units took up defensive positions for the night.

LIEUTENANT BARNES, COMPANY F, 38TH INFANTRY: The next immediate objective of the 2d Battalion was a fairly high ridge to the
northeast of Company G's objective. Companies E and F were to
seize this ground. An old enemy trench could be seen on the forward
slope of the ridge just below the crest, and little enemy fire was being experienced at this time.

Company F attacked to the right with Company E on the left. French troops were on the left of Company E. Company G was in reserve at this time. Very little enemy opposition was met—approximately a squad. I was glad the opposition was slight because the rifles were icy, and some could not fire. The attack started around 1500.

After seizing the objective, Company E moved to a ridge about 200 or 300 yards to the north and dug in. Company F remained on the objective and established its defense.

MASTER SERGEANT McGREGOR, COMPANY F, 38TH INFANTRY: Company F was further ordered to attack abreast with Company E. Company F waited in a small village [Unhaengjong] while Captain Forney received attack orders from the acting battalion commander, Major Wilkins.

The attack on the hill met no enemy resistance, but three men were wounded as Company F moved into position for the attack. The men were wounded by mortar fire, which I thought was friendly forces firing short rounds. I was unable to prove this, and the men were listed as wounded in action. The attack jumped off around 1630 in overcast weather. Company E attacked on the left and Company F on the right. Company G was in support at the village. The 23d Infantry Regiment was on the right of the Wonju road. The battalion CP later moved up to the village with Company G.

Later that night, Company F furnished Company E with two squads to outpost a hill to the front. No enemy resistance was met that night, and no firing could be heard. During the night it snowed very heavily. Captain Forney and I slipped all over the place as we went to contact Company F, 23d Infantry Regiment, which was on the immediate right flank of Company F, 38th Infantry Regiment. Captain Forney wanted to see if the lines were properly tied in. Company F, 38th Infantry Regiment, set up its CP in a single house to the left of the Wonju road, and Company F, 23d Infantry Regiment, had its CP in a house to the right side of the road.

The morale of the men in Company F was low. In the holding position below Wonju, Company F had three men go AWOL. There was no enemy action, nor was Company F in attack, so the only logical conclusion was that they were cold and went AWOL. The men had no bedding.

SGT. RAUL VILLARREAL, MORTAR FO WITH COMPANY E, 38TH INFANTRY: Company E jumped off about 1700, attacked the hill to the front, and took it without meeting enemy resistance. It was snowing very hard now. An outpost was sent to the next hill to the front, and it remained there all night. A counterattack was expected that night, but none came. It snowed all night; none of the troops had their bedrolls, for all bedrolls had been collected before the battalion had moved.

SERGEANT 1ST CLASS PALAMIDY, COMPANY E, 38TH INFANTRY: Company E reorganized and attacked again. The enemy fired a few rounds and withdrew. On the objective, the 2d Battalion regrouped. At 1600, the battalion jumped off again, but evidently the other outfits on either flank were not notified of the jump-off and remained where they were. The 2d Battalion was forced to withdraw to its original position. Outposts were established on a ridge to the front.

SGT. RICHARD W. CAREY, COMPANY E, 38TH INFANTRY: Prior to jumping off in attack of the company objective again around 1500, artillery and mortars blasted the enemy positions. Company E attacked the hill in a skirmish line and walked right back up. No enemy resistance was met. When Company E reached the top of the hill, the men dug in. My squad from the 3d Platoon and one squad from the 1st Platoon were given the mission of outposting another ridge to the front (about 2,000 yards), which was to be the company's objective the next day. My squad dug in to a close 360-degree defensive perimeter on top of the highest knoll on the ridge. That night was very cold, and all the men's clothing and weapons were frozen. It was a good thing the enemy did not attack that night, because none of the weapons would fire. One man surrendered to the outpost that night, and said he was a South Korean captured by the North Koreans and then released. I sent him on back to the company CP.

SERGEANT LATTORRE-LOPEZ IN THE 38TH INFANTRY MEDICAL CLEARING STATION: Around midnight, 9 January 1951, Sergeant Hudson, Corporal Mattox, and a medical NCO (Corporal Haggin) were brought into the same clearing station. Hudson and Mattox told me that they were hit by sniper fire when returning to the rear for more ammunition.

Sergeant Hudson told me that the French and Company F had later flanked the hills, went to the top, and rolled grenades down into the "Chink" trenches; and that they were going to sleep that night on top of the conquered hills.

The attack east of the Wonju road in the 2d Battalion, 23d Infantry's sector was partially successful, but the attacking units had to withdraw for the night because the captured position was too large to defend:

FIRST LT. JOHN H. HEATH, PLATOON LEADER IN COMPANY G, 23D INFANTRY: The French were to take Hill 216 at the same time as Company F, 23d Infantry Regiment, took Hill 247. Company G was to support Company F's attack, and Company E was to support the French attack. During the attack, Company F received small arms fire from Hill 247 (approximately two companies of North Koreans were dug in on the hill) and flanking fire from Hill 216 (approximately one company of North Koreans). Both Company F and the French reached their objective and withdrew. The mission of the 2d Battalion at the time was to contact the enemy, determine his strength, and withdraw. The 2d Battalion withdrew to the high ground north and west of Naenamsong and established defensive positions. The battalion CP was located in Naenamsong. No enemy contact was made that night, although firing could be heard to the rear.

CORPORAL BRESLIN, COMPANY G, 23D INFANTRY: Lieutenant Colonel Edwards, battalion commander, was on the hill with the company. Ordered to advance about 1500, the company moved out abreast. My 57mm recoilless rifle (the only one in the company, since the other weapon was reported destroyed) was behind some riflemen about in the middle of the company. Proceeding for a half-mile over two small hills, Company G arrived on the second hill about 1500. My squad had fired about six rounds at enemy personnel. My five-man squad, consisting of gunner, assistant gunner, and three ammunition bearers, carried eighteen rounds of ammunition.

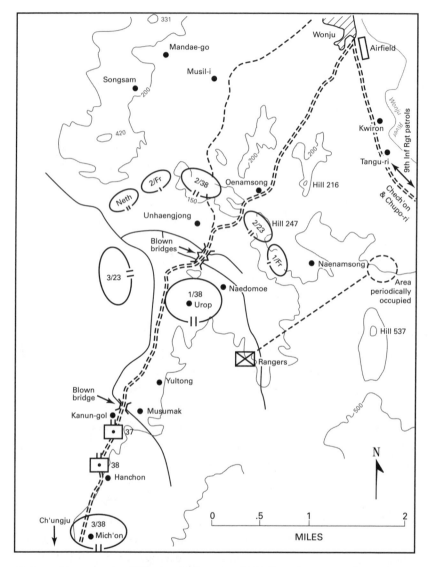

Unit positions south of Wonju, 12 January 1951 (based on maps from CMH Manuscript 8–5.1A BA 31, Action at Wonju).

The company stayed on this hill until about 1700, when it advanced again. As the company was moving down the hill, I was hit by enemy fire in the left hand.[13]

Overnight plans were made for a renewed push to secure the high ground overlooking Wonju.

The temperature was extremely low that night, and the troops, most of whom had been ordered to leave their nontactical equipment in the rear prior to moving out, suffered from the cold. In the morning, many men had difficulty operating their weapons.

The failure of the attempts on 8 and 9 January to retake Wonju made necessary the commitment of additional elements to the attack, and when General Almond, X Corps commander, ordered the attachment of forces sufficient to accomplish the mission, the French Battalion and the 3d Battalion, 23d Infantry Regiment, were brought up on 10 January, and the 38th FA Battalion was moved up to supplement the fires of the 37th FA Battalion already in support. (Note: The 2d Infantry Division lacked a 155mm howitzer medium artillery battalion, because the 503d FA Battalion had lost its entire equipment in a previous action and had not been reequipped.) The four battalions to make the advance were placed under the command of Colonel Freeman. The commander of the 38th Infantry Regiment took charge of the defensive positions.

The troops were deployed in the following manner, from left to right: the 3d Battalion, 23d Infantry; the Netherlands Battalion; the 2d Company, French Battalion; the 2d Battalion, 38th Infantry Regiment; the 2d Battalion, 23d Infantry Regiment; and the 1st Company, French Battalion. The 1st Battalion, 38th Infantry Regiment, was in reserve.[14]

While the other units were moving into position on the morning of 10 January, the 2d Battalion, 23d Infantry, renewed its attack on the right against Hill 247.

First Lieutenant Heath, Company G, 23d Infantry: On 10 January 1951, a coordinated attack was made up the MSR (Wonju-Ch'ungju road) with the 2d Battalion, 38th Infantry Regiment, on the left of the road, and the 2d Battalion, 23d Infantry Regiment, on the right of the road. Company G, 38th Infantry Regiment, tied in on the right with Company G, 23d Infantry Regiment. The attack jumped off at 1000 in a very heavy snowfall. Company G moved into place for the attack, taking supporting positions covering the approach of Company F to Hill 247. Company E was again to support the French attack on Hill 216. While Company G was going into position, it received flanking fire from the 38th Infantry Regiment sector and was forced to withdraw temporarily.

Company F launched its attack on Hill 247 at 1600, and at the same time the French attacked Hill 216. Both hills were secured against moderate resistance (one company). Prior to the attacks, a terrific artillery bombardment of the hills took place. After the objectives were secured, Captain Terrell, commanding officer, Company F, radioed back that he personally counted forty enemy dead. Later that night, the 2d Battalion withdrew back to its positions around Naenamsong.[15]

SERGEANT WHITE, COMPANY E, 23D INFANTRY: About 0830, 10 January, the 2d Platoon, Company E, returned to the hill it had occupied the previous day. One half hour later, the 3d Platoon arrived and deployed on the left of the 2d Platoon. Enemy estimated in company strength again fired from the same position, and the platoons of Company E returned the fire. Difficulty was experienced in getting the rifles to fire because of the cold weather. It was necessary to work the automatic operating rod by hand after each round.

About 1500, a French company reinforced with several 57mm recoilless rifles came forward. Part of the company deployed with the American units on the ridge to form a base of fire, while the other portion of the company skirted the hill for an advance on the enemy position. At 1600, as the men on the ridge commenced firing, the French moved up the hill with bayonets fixed. When the French crossed the top of the hill and disappeared from sight in pursuit of the enemy, the French platoons forming the base of fire followed. The French troops returned after clearing the enemy-held hill and moved to the rear. The platoons of Company E withdrew to the company area near the road and again formed a perimeter defense for the night.[16]

The situation in the 2d Battalion, 23d Infantry, sector around Hill 247 is summarized in the 23d Infantry's Periodic Operations Report:

The 23d Infantry continued the attack at 1000 hours on 10 January, advancing approximately 800 yards and capturing Hill 247. However, both flanks had to be extended to prevent being outflanked by an estimated enemy battalion on each flank. This extension of the zone of attack required all reserves except for one platoon from the French Battalion, which was placed in regimental reserve with priority of employment in the French sector. Before flanks could be tied in with the 38th Infantry defensive positions, a group of approximately 150 enemy succeeded in flanking the left flank and in engaging the French Battalion from the rear. Meanwhile on the right of the line, the 3d Company, French Battalion, attacked to secure the southeast nose of Hill 247. The objective was taken by a platoon assault with fixed bayonets. The defensive horseshoe was shortened to strengthen the line. A company of the Netherlands Detachment extended the 38th Infantry defensive perimeter to close the gap between the 38th and 23d Infantry. The infiltrated enemy was cut off and eventually eliminated from the defensive perimeter.[17]

To the west of the Wonju road, the 10th of January was relatively uneventful for the 2d Battalion, 38th Infantry, as the battalion moved forward and dug in on the next ridge.

SERGEANT CAREY, COMPANY E, 38TH INFANTRY: The next day [10 Jan], around 0800, Company E moved out to the OPLR, and a company defense was set up with the 2d Platoon tied in on the right with Company F, which also moved up. The 1st Platoon was on the left and tied in with the French. Company G later replaced Company F on line. The 3d Platoon, Company E, was left back at the hill to the rear of the OPLR as a support platoon in case of a withdrawal. The 23d Infantry Regiment was to the right of the Wonju-Ch'ungju road.

During the day, Company E sent patrols to the north. One patrol led by Sergeant Palamidy in the morning went into Oenamsong and found several wounded North Koreans, who were captured, and several antitank guns were destroyed. No enemy action was had on the 2d Battalion's front. From the OPLR, an estimated two companies of North Koreans could be seen moving into positions north of the 23d Infantry Regiment's lines; I don't know whether the 23d Infantry Regiment was informed of this. During the night, a firefight could be heard several hills away on the extreme left (French), but there was no action that night on the 2d Battalion's front.[18]

FIRST LIEUTENANT BARNES, COMPANY F, 38TH INFANTRY: Around daybreak, 10 January 1951, rations and ammunition were brought up to the troops. At noon, Captain Forney ordered Company F to reinforce the ridge occupied by Company E. The order was to defend the ground at all costs. Company E was too thin to defend the ground by itself; they couldn't make a full company out of the whole battalion.

During the day a firefight could be heard to the rear. On the left front enemy troops, around regimental strength, could be seen on the slopes of a high hill, and artillery concentrations were hitting the positions. The French were shouting on the left flank, and the enemy was trying to infiltrate to the left of the French. Company E fired small arms and 60mm mortars at the enemy positions, but I stopped my men from firing after a few rounds were expended, because the range was too great and I wanted to conserve the ammunition for closer fighting. During the night, the enemy infiltrated to the rear, and firing could be heard on all sides.[19]

MASTER SERGEANT MCGREGOR, COMPANY F, 38TH INFANTRY: At approximately 1200, 10 January 1951, Captain Forney was ordered by the 2d Battalion to move the company up to the OPLR. Companies E and F moved up while Company G remained back in the vicinity of the battalion CP. Both Company E and Company F left one platoon back at their position of the night before to provide for cover. From the OPLR an enemy OP could be seen, but Companies E and F were unable to knock it out. It was on a high hill to the northwest. Approximately ten to twelve mortar rounds fell behind the OPLR. Around dark, Captain Forney decided to move the support platoon up on line, and in the process the support platoon ran into an enemy patrol trying to infiltrate to the rear of the OPLR. The enemy threw two grenades and opened fire with an automatic weapon before it withdrew, wounding three men from Company F. No enemy dead or wounded were found. The platoon tied in with the company on the right, covering the draw to the rear. The company commander and I moved the company CP into the front line, using an abandoned enemy trench, which was dug just below the crest line of the hill. After the brief encounter with the enemy patrol, the rest of the night was quiet. Sergeant 1st Class Smith, acting platoon leader of the support platoon, was wounded and Sergeant Sanchez hurt his leg. A medical NCO, Sgt. Buster Hall, took over the platoon for the night. It was extremely cold that night, and it snowed. It was so cold that the snow would freeze to the skin before you could brush it off.[20]

The problems with retaining Hill 247 continued as explained by the 23d Infantry Regiment's Command Report for January and soldiers of the unit:

TWENTY-THIRD INFANTRY COMMAND REPORT: Hill 247 was lost and recaptured at least four times, with the 2d Battalion, 23d Infantry, taking the hill in the daytime and withdrawing at night, setting up dummy positions, with booby traps, barb wire entanglements, and calling for artillery to place interdiction fire on the vacated positions. Also, when the enemy was observed moving into these vacated positions, air strikes and the combined fires of the Heavy Mortar Company and two artillery battalions were placed on him. From 13 to 14 January 1951, Hill 247 was held, despite renewed enemy attacks and the extremely cold weather. During the reorganization on top of Hill 247, many enemy dead were found in the foxholes, a result of the combined efforts of air strikes, mortar fire, artillery fire, booby traps, and the attacking riflemen.[21]

SERGEANT WHITE, COMPANY E, 23D INFANTRY: On 11 January, the hill previously occupied by Company E troops was held by North Koreans. Artillery and mortar fire were placed on the hill during the morning, and in the afternoon the 3d Platoon occupied the hill, withdrawing again in the evening. On 12 January, the 2d Platoon again moved back on the hill without meeting enemy resistance.[22]

First Lieutenant Heath, Company G, 23d Infantry: At 0900, 12 January 1951, Company F was to retake Hill 247, but the attack was delayed. An artillery liaison plane spotted two companies of North Koreans in well-prepared positions atop the hill. Air strikes were called for but not received due to foggy conditions; consequently the attack by Company F was delayed. At 1500, four air strikes were made on Hill 247 and Hill 216. F80s and P51s strafed enemy positions and dropped napalm bombs. At 1600, Company F and the French took their objectives with no enemy resistance, and mined and booby-trapped the rear slopes before they withdrew under the cover of darkness.

About 0300, 13 January 1951, the enemy attacked Hill 247 and Hill 216. As the mines and booby traps exploded, the enemy opened fire on the top of the hills. About daylight they reached the top of Hill 247 and were immediately brought under fire by Company G, forcing them to withdraw back to the rear. Mortar and artillery fire were also brought to bear on the enemy.

The 2d Battalion remained in position between 13 and 15 January 1951, sending patrols to the north. No enemy contact was made.[23]

To the west of the Wonju road a minor war of outposts and patrols continued until early morning of 13 January, when the enemy attacked in this sector at the same time they launched their assault on Hill 247 east of the road. Sergeant 1st Class Palamidy, Company E, 38th Infantry, describes the fighting.

Outposts were established on a ridge to the front, and the next day, 10 January 1951, Company E moved up and dug in. Company F reinforced Company E on the 10th and 11th of January 1951. On the morning of 12 January 1951, Company G relieved Company F.

During the night of 12 January 1951, Lieutenant MacNanamy and I set up trip flares in front of our positions. Enemy trenches in the vicinity were booby-trapped with antipersonnel mines. Later in the night, the lieutenant and I burned an enemy village just below the hill. The village, Musil-i, was just below a long finger of the hill we occupied. Several wounded North Koreans were captured along

with some antitank guns. One prisoner was extremely healthy looking and was dressed in a Chinese (CCF) uniform. Chinese money
was found in his pockets.

Around 0450, 13 January 1951, an estimated two companies of
enemy troops hit Company E's position. The first attack was repulsed by the 1st Platoon.

It was extremely cold, and the weapons would not work. During the first attack I called on a field phone to Lieutenant Mac-
Nanamy for instructions as to what to do. The lieutenant instructed
me to tell the men to urinate on their weapons. This enabled the
men to get fourteen out of nineteen guns into operation.

The second attack was repulsed by the bravery of Private 1st
Class Lewellyn. Private Lewellyn left his foxhole and walked down
the slope, in the midst of the enemy. Lewellyn just cut them down.
When Lewellyn was returning to his foxhole, he was killed by artillery fire. I think it was friendly artillery fire; the ground was black-
ened near our foxholes by the artillery blasts.[24]

*Other eyewitnesses to Private 1st Class Lewellyn's heroism
describe his actions in their recommendations for his Distinguished
Service Cross.*

CAPTAIN ALLEN, COMPANY E, 38TH INFANTRY: During the initial
attack around daybreak, Private Lewellyn was stunned by an enemy
concussion grenade, but quickly regained his composure and managed to crawl back to his position and materially aided in repulsing
the banzai attack by placing his dependable fire on the enemy. Once
again the enemy rallied for another fanatical banzai charge, and once
again Private Lewellyn aided materially by moving about the defense
line, with complete indifference to his personal safety, through the
heavy enemy small arms and automatic fire, by distributing his fire
on the enemy. During this time he was wounded, but refused to
leave for medical attention. The enemy rallied for a final attempt,
which was against Lewellyn's position. As they drew near, Lewellyn
leaped from his foxhole to a more advantageous position, exposing
himself to the enemy in so doing, and by his fire personally killed
several of the enemy who had crawled to within grenade range of his

position. It was while he was engaged in this gallant action that he received a fatal wound.

First Lieutenant Knight, Company G, 38th Infantry: Private Lewellyn was a rifleman in a foxhole on the limiting point between my company and his. In the early morning hours, we were attacked by a large force of fanatical screaming enemy in a banzai-type attack. The men in my company on the immediate right of Lewellyn reported to me that from the initial assault of the enemy up to the time he was killed, Lewellyn fought savagely and successfully to hold off the fanatical enemy force. Private Lewellyn's position was right at the point where the enemy attempted to get through. Early in the battle an enemy-thrown hand grenade blew him clear out of his position, but he crawled his way back up, and though wounded and dazed, continued his valiant performance, making maximum use of his weapons. As the enemy continued to swarm toward his position, he jumped out of his hole and yelled at the enemy, "Come on up and fight, you sons of bitches." At this time he killed several enemy within a few yards of his position, but was killed himself by the enemy fire.

This individual's action was particularly outstanding because he was a new replacement who had only joined the company the night before. It is most unusual to find a man so freshly initiated into combat under the additional hardship of the bitter cold and snow we had to contend with, who will show such extraordinary heroic conduct. Such great courage and supreme sacrifice as that displayed by Private Lewellyn is what made possible the holding of the vital Wonju salient against overwhelming odds.[25]

Sergeant Carey, Company E, 38th Infantry, describes the end of the fight:

Around 0500 [13 Jan] I could hear enemy small arms fire increasing in tempo on the company's position. I was back with the 3d platoon. Mortar rounds started to come in on the company's positions. I don't know whether it was friendly or enemy mortar fire; I know friendly mortars were zeroed in on the valley in front of the OPLR, and mortar fire was dropping in between the OPLR and the 3d Platoon's positions. Artillery rounds were falling short on the 1st and 2d Platoon's positions, and one man was killed by concussion. I was ordered by my company commander to take my squad and reinforce the 1st and 2d Platoons. I sent two men to the 1st Platoon and three (including myself) to the 2d Platoon. When I was in position, the enemy banzai'd three times and was repulsed each time. I estimate the enemy strength as two battalions; they were attacking along the entire front. Friendly artillery fire aided in dispersing the enemy. It was just getting light when the enemy attacks stopped, and the rest of the day was cold and fairly clear. Company E remained in position and prepared for another counterattack, which did not come.[26]

The lack of air support due to bad weather was one of the major problems in the fighting for the high ground overlooking Wonju. Artillery by itself was unable to prevent the enemy from moving in the open during daylight hours due to a shortage of ammunition. Once the weather cleared, the situation changed drastically as revealed by entries in the 23d Infantry Regiment's daily journal.

10 JANUARY, 1100 HOURS: Message to commanding general, 2d Division: am continuing attack as ordered. Very strong enemy forces threaten both flanks, particularly the left. Continuation of attack is considered unsound. Request instructions. Signed Col. Freeman. Ordered to continue the attack.

10 JANUARY, 1100 HOURS: Summary: estimate 1,500 enemy opposing the advance with another 2,000 to the front. Air support believed to be imperative, but no air for two days.

10 JANUARY, 1240 HOURS: Commanding officer [Col. Freeman] briefs commanding general by phone: I have advanced 800 yards. Have had to extend both flanks to keep from being outflanked. Now have Hill 247. Impossible to bring air strike in. Have had no air for two days.

10 JANUARY, 1500 HOURS: Situation Report to division: estimate 5 battalions of enemy: one opposing our advance, three battalions on our left with two extending over Hill 420 moving down the valley running southeast to northwest of Hill 420 and one battalion on south side of valley opposing 3d Battalion, 23d Infantry. One battalion along northwest base of Hill 537 in Naenamsong.

11 JANUARY, 1430 HOURS: Air support arrives. Priority targets: Hill 216, Hill 231 [east of Chech'on road], Hill 420, and all villages in vicinity.

11 JANUARY, 1520 HOURS: Air strike on Kwiron, town in flames. Air strike on Hill 420.

11 JANUARY, 1530 HOURS: Situation Report to Division: Hill 247 taken. Have had two air strikes.

12 JANUARY, 0300 HOURS: Division informed us of B-29 strike as follows: Time for strike 1045 to 1115. Variable time and delayed action bombs will be dropped.

12 JANUARY, 0920 HOURS: Situation Report to division: 2d Battalion and French Company will attack Hill 247 at 1000 hours to reestablish the line. Attempting to deliver air strike on east slope of Hill 247 with a pass on the east slope from south to north.

12 JANUARY, 0955 HOURS: Started air strike on Hill 247. Strike delivered on northwest, top, and east slopes by 4 F-4Us and 4 ADs with excellent results against an estimated enemy battalion dug in on top of Hill 247 in slit trenches and on the east slope in communication trenches. 1010 HOURS: Mosquito [airborne FAC] found sleepers on south slope of Hill 247. Will bring fighters in on them. 1018 HOURS: Mosquito says there are 450–800 enemy on Hill 247. 1053 HOURS: One company of enemy on top of Hill 247 firing on the French. Will adjust mortar fire on them.

12 JANUARY, 1055 HOURS: Fighters coming in, cease fire on mortars. 1115 HOURS: 8 Corsairs dropped napalm on Hill 247; hit wide. 1118 HOURS: Asked division for more air support. 1120 HOURS: Dropped another napalm, right on target; will work over top of hill. 1122 HOURS: F-80s coming in on Hill 247 now. 1123 HOURS: B-29s are coming in; targets are east and west of Wonju. 1126 HOURS: 11 B-29s are overhead now. 1128 HOURS: Got clearance from 38th Infantry S-3 to work over ridge from Hill 247 to Hill 537. 1150 HOURS: B-29s dropping bombs now. 1155 HOURS: Air strike over, start using artillery and mortars. 1159 HOURS: More fighters coming; artillery and mortar cease-fire. 1220 HOURS: F-80s finishing air strike now. 1221 HOURS: Estimate enemy battalion on Hill 331; 4 F-80s will work it over. 1230 HOURS: F-80s made last pass; another flight coming in now. 1233 HOURS: Asked air for permission to fire 4.2 mortar

observed fire on west slope of Hill 247; may fire when air is clear; 1252 HOURS: Another flight of planes on Hill 537; start firing artillery on Hill 247. 1420 HOURS: 2d Battalion and French Company launch attack on Hill 247 at 1405; 11 F-4Us attacked Hill 331.

12 JANUARY, 1625 HOURS: Message from division G-3: use all air possible to destroy buildings in Wonju that could be used by the enemy.

12 JANUARY, 1926 HOURS: Bombers in air now. Contact them on Charlie Channel; mark targets with white phosphorous.

12 JANUARY, 2025 HOURS: Situation report to division: All quiet; received air support. Worked over north of Tangu-ri to north of Wonju. No Firefly [flare-dropping C-47 aircraft] arrived. Planes working on roads north of Wonju. Some fires in Wonju still. Firefly will be here 2300–0300.

13 JANUARY, 0745 HOURS: French Battalion request air strike on Mandae-go, Musil-i, Songsam. Estimate three battalions in villages. 0820 HOURS: French Battalion reports enemy to front are withdrawing north. Request air strike.

13 JANUARY, 0820 HOURS: Division states air should arrive 0910 hours. Flights curtailed for lack of aviation gas. CG will be informed of situation.

13 JANUARY, 1032 HOURS: X Corps commander arrived at command post and briefed by commanding officer; 1106 HOURS: X Corps commander departs command post to visit all battalions.

13 JANUARY, 1130 HOURS: Message by phone to Capt. Wood, 2d Division G-3 Section to be transmitted to X Corps (Col. Guthrie) to be sent by L-17 to Gen. Ridgway personally. Message as follows: To Ridgway, signed Almond. I am at the CP of 23d Infantry most forward coordinating element of the 2d Division. The combat team commander estimates from 8 to 10,000 enemy in the force attacking him. These are excellent targets for all the air that can be employed in this area. The first Mosquito arrived in the area at 0800. It should have been here at daylight. Size of strike at 0830 was 8 fighters and 1 bomber. I believe 50 planes over this area all day long is a minimum requirement. Jets with MG ammo are considered ineffective. Required is napalm and bombs. It is my understanding that the only pressure on the Army front is here. I am informed

there is a curtailment of gas for planes resulting in decrease in sorties. If true, I hope that this can be corrected at once and that adequate air support can be furnished this area.

The enemy attack on 13 January was the last major action in front of Wonju. The fighting by the 2d Division had been fierce at times, but overall, many of the problems, other than the cold weather, were of their own making. Comments by 2d Division soldiers are informative:

SERGEANT CAREY, COMPANY E, 38TH INFANTRY: NCOs need maps and compasses. The men were not briefed as to why they were in a certain position or how long they would be there. In my opinion it was because the company officers did not know. The replacements we received were not physically fit for combat. Many would drop out on forced marches.

FIRST LIEUTENANT BARNES, COMPANY F, 38TH INFANTRY: There was an acute shortage of maps on company and platoon level. Shoepacs made the feet sweat too much. There was a shortage of clips for the BAR. No one seemed to know exactly what was going on. My company commander, Captain Forney, called back to find the location of certain troops in the area. The only answer he could get was, "they're on the firing line." The outposts are put out too far; in some instances they are three miles out. The men do not get warm meals. The kitchen trucks were forty miles to the rear of the action at Ch'ungju. The French would get hot meals while my men had to eat cold rations. The men could not understand why this happened. Only half of the men had entrenching tools. You can't dig a foxhole with just a pick or an axe.[27]

FIRST LIEUTENANT HURTT, A&P PLATOON, 2D BATTALION, 38TH INFANTRY: Supply was a difficult problem since American engineers had blown the bridge [on the Wonju-Ch'ungju road just north of Kanun-gol]. Two-and-a-half-ton trucks had to stop and be unloaded on the south side of the blown bridge. On the north side, jeeps and weapons carriers would be loaded and carry the supplies to the companies. The kitchens, having been sent to Andong before the firefight in Wonju on 7 January, did not return while the 2d Battalion was in this defensive position; however, the last two days before pulling out, auxiliary kitchens were set up. C rations were used from the time the kitchens left for Andong until the auxiliary kitchens were set up. It was a lack of aggressiveness on the part of the S-4 that the kitchens had been sent so far to the rear at Andong and did not rejoin the battalion in the defensive position.

The shoe-pacs cause many problems. On the march quite a few men arrive with blisters on their feet caused by the shoe-pacs. In the defensive positions south of Wonju some men were bothered by frozen feet also caused by the shoe-pacs, since perspiration on the felt soles inside the shoe-pacs turned to ice, and it was like placing your feet in an insulated icebox. What was needed was a breather above the water line of the shoe-pac.

The morale of the 2d Battalion, 38th Infantry, was fair. This can be attributed to, first, C rations and cold meals instead of hot meals; second, the men were not adequately briefed on the situation; third, the battalion was under strength; fourth, the extremely cold weather.[28]

Protecting the Flank: 9th Infantry Regiment, 6–17 January 1951

Meanwhile, to the east on the road from Wonju to Chupo-ri and Chech'on, the 9th Infantry Regiment, with the attached 1st Battalion, 23d Infantry, had the mission of keeping the road open and protecting the eastern flank of the 2d Division.

During the early morning hours of 6 January 1951, the regimental commander received a letter of instructions with verbal orders to move the regiment to the vicinity of Sinnim-ni, to establish defensive positions and protect the east flank of the division against enemy attacks, to patrol the Wonju-Chech'on road against infiltration and the establishment of roadblocks by the enemy.... At 2045 hours [on 7 January] the 1st Battalion, 23d Infantry, was attached to the regiment....

With the main enemy strength reported to the east of the Sinnim-ni–Wonju road and at Wonju, roadblocks were established at strategic points along the road with motorized and foot patrols covering all natural avenues of approach from the east.... Contacts with the enemy were many and varied, from groups of platoon size to two- and three-man patrols. Small-scale attacks were launched against the regimental roadblocks, but patrols of the regiment continued to inflict numerous casualties against the enemy.[29]

The 2d Battalion, 9th Infantry, operating from its patrol base at Sinnim-ni was to patrol north toward Wonju. The result was several combat actions with the enemy. Members of Company E describe one on 8 January.

SERGEANT HADLEY, COMPANY E, 9TH INFANTRY REGIMENT: I was 2d Squad leader in the 1st Platoon of Company E, 9th Infantry Regiment. On the morning of 8 January I overheard the 2d Battalion commander give the Company E commander the mission of patrolling the road from Chech'on to Wonju, the company being at that time near Chech'on. The men were issued three C rations; the company was loaded on trucks and moved out on the Chech'on-Wonju road, detrucking at a road junction near the center of the town of Sinnim-ni.

The company moved out on foot on the MSR, which ran in a northwestern direction, the men in a deployed formation. The 1st Squad of the 1st Platoon acted as the point; my squad (2d) was the connecting file. The terrain was mountainous, the road running through a narrow valley between high mountains. Paralleling the highway but farther up the slope, the railroad entered several tunnels between Sinnim-ni and Wonju. One of these tunnels was reached at about 1500, and while a squad from the 1st Platoon checked the tunnel, the Korean interpreter with the company interrogated refugees who reported North Korean soldiers up the road to the northwest. After the squad that checked the tunnel returned, the company continued up the road, the point passing Mundal, a small village that lay to the right of the road surrounded by rice paddies. The connecting file was about twenty yards back of the point and the main body about 100 yards behind the connecting file.

At about 1630 the connecting file and the main body were hit by automatic fire and some mortars, which came from houses in Mundal, 75 yards right of the road, and from a hill 300 yards to the right of the road. Most of the enemy had automatic weapons, especially in the dug-in positions. The company, upon being hit, deployed to the left in obedience to previous instruction, hitting a ditch, which ran by the side of the road. The fire of the enemy moving down the railroad track indicated an attempt to gain the rear of Company E's position. Lieutenant Hope, 1st Platoon leader, said later that they could have been cut off by the North Koreans advancing down the railroad track and establishing a roadblock in the rear of Company E. To extricate the company from the ditch, two half-tracks, with quad fifties, were brought up. One went into position on the road ahead of the point, the other at the rear of the column. The one 60mm mortar that the company had was set up in a draw to the west of the road just south of the town. The draw afforded little cover for the mortar. The company withdrew, by crawling down the ditch, which had snow and water in it. Company losses were three men killed: a jeep driver, the 4th Platoon sergeant, and a new replacement. There was no friendly artillery fire. The company pulled back to Yongam-ni and spent the night of the eighth and all day the ninth there.[30]

SERGEANT SHOCKEY, COMPANY E, 9TH INFANTRY REGIMENT: I was chief of the radio section of Company E and served as radio operator for Captain Walker, the company commander. On 8 January Company E was given the mission of patrolling the road from Chech'on to Wonju. In the vicinity of the entrance of a railroad tunnel, the enemy was contacted, and Captain Walker notified by radio, the 2d Battalion commander, Lieutenant Colonel Barberis, that the company was in a firefight. Colonel Barberis's orders were to stay where we were and to get a count of the enemy numbers, weapons, and location. Colonel Barberis did not say that help was coming. There were two half-tracks with quad fifties mounted on them accompanying Company E. They went into operation and kept the enemy down. One 60mm mortar belonging to Company E fired six rounds. The other mortar remained on a jeep, because guerrilla fire prevented the mortar men from placing it in position. Company E being unable to proceed to Wonju, Captain Walker asked the battalion commander for permission to withdraw, and he gave it. Company E lost in the encounter one jeep, two 57mm recoilless rifles, and one 50-cal. machine gun.[31]

PRIVATE 1ST CLASS JOHNSON, MEDICAL COMPANY, 9TH INFANTRY

REGIMENT: I was an aid man with Company E, Captain Walker, commanding. Some squads of Company E went down the railroad track paralleling the road. At 1330 Company E got around three miles from Wonju, where they could see the North Koreans on high ground overlooking the road trying to surround them. At 1445 the enemy started shooting, attempting with their fire to pin Company E down and to cut off the column from its avenue of withdrawal. Steadying his company, Captain Walker stood in the middle of the street saying, "Take it easy men; I'll get you out of here." Company E had to leave behind two jeeps with one or two recoilless rifles when they withdrew. There was a little, young artillery second lieutenant serving as forward observer with Company E, trying to raise another station with his radio in order to shoot, but he couldn't even get Company G. He kept giving his call and trying.[32]

On the 10th of January, the 2d Battalion advanced north once again on the Wonju-Chech'on road. The next day near Mundal, the location of the 8 January action, they encountered a strong enemy force as described by members of the battalion.

SERGEANT HADLEY, COMPANY E, 9TH INFANTRY REGIMENT: On the morning of the tenth, the 2d Battalion moved out toward Wonju. Company F spent the night of the tenth in the railroad tunnel, Company G on a hill just south of the tunnel, and Company E behind Company F. There were some buildings on fire toward the road from Company E, and the men took turns going to the buildings and heating their rations. On the morning of the eleventh, Company E advanced; the formation was staggered, men being from five to ten paces apart. In about the same sector, in which Company E was ambushed on the eighth, it was hit again. This time, besides enemy being in houses on the right of the road and on the hill to the east, there were snipers on Hill 535 located 300 yards southwest of the battalion. The friendly artillery support was good. I was wounded by a sniper in the opening stages of the firefight.[33]

SERGEANT SHOCKEY, COMPANY E, 9TH INFANTRY REGIMENT: On 11 January the 2d Battalion received the mission of proceeding north on the MSR to Wonju. If there was no enemy there, the battalion was to return. Captain Walker called the platoon leaders and platoon sergeants together and briefed them. Company E proceeded down the road; Company F took to the high ground to the right entering a railroad tunnel; Company G proceeded on the high ground to the left of the road. Company E contacted the enemy in the vicinity of Mundal.

The point of Company E, which was about 600 feet in front of the company immediately, went into some shacks beside the road. The shacks contained a few North Korean soldiers. The point remained separated from the company from 1000 until they rejoined the company during the night of January 11, taking with them the North Korean soldiers as prisoners.

Company F was pinned down in the tunnel since guerrillas were on high ground overlooking the tunnel and Company E's position. Around noon, an air strike was called for and delivered on the enemy located about 300 yards to the left flank of Company E's position. Ammunition running low, Colonel Barberis ordered the battalion to withdraw, at which time Company F came running out of the tunnel in a disorderly fashion. Their company commander regrouped them in the gully beside the Wonju-Chech'on road just below the tunnel entrance. They then withdrew to the rear in single file, each man about five yards from the other, and went back about four miles.

In Company E Captain Walker continued to walk up and down, cautioning his men to keep low. He was unarmed, since he had given his weapon to a man who lost his M-1 rifle. The wounded from Company E were evacuated next; there being but two litters, it took two men to carry each wounded man. The three dead were the platoon leader of the 4th Platoon, a jeep driver, and one rifleman. After the wounded were evacuated, Company E started to the rear in single file. Company G, which was on high ground to the left and which did not make contact with the enemy, was pulled back when the other two companies withdrew. Company E withdrew with the rest of the battalion taking up positions further southeast on the MSR.

The field artillery support, under the direction of Lieutenant Kessler, forward observer from the 15th FA Battalion, was very good, and Lieutenant Kessler had excellent communication by radio. Unfortunately, during the firefight the proximity of the enemy necessitating close fire missions, one round of friendly artillery fell short, injuring one man in Company E. The 4.2-inch mortars attached to the battalion shot well, and the morale of the battalion was raised by the air strike. The enemy possessed no artillery or mortars, their only weapons being rifles and burp guns. The weather was cold.[34]

FIRST LIEUTENANT BALAFAS, COMPANY G, 9TH INFANTRY REGIMENT: At 0300 hours [11 January] Lieutenant Colonel Barberis, 2d Battalion commander, had a company commanders' call, which Captain Munoz attended. From information gathered at the call Captain Munoz informed me that the 2d Battalion would attack that morning north up the MSR toward Wonju. Company F was to go up the MSR; Company E would cover the hills to the right of the road, and Company G the hills to the left of the road. The three companies were supposed to advance abreast on a line.

The advance started at 0600, with Company G soon falling behind because of the height of the mountains, difficulty of climbing ridges, and the hardness of breaking tracks. At Mundal and on the high ground on both sides of the road, a number of North Koreans opened fire on Companies E and F, who were advancing northwest along the MSR. At 1500 Colonel Barberis radioed Captain Munoz (Company G was on high ground 2,000 yards south of Mundal at that time) that we were immediately to envelop the enemy, coming in from the south and catching the North Koreans in a pincer movement. Companies E and F coming up the MSR were to form the other claw of the pincer. Captain Munoz complied with the 2d Battalion commander's order, and Company G advanced due north only to be halted at 1545 by Colonel Barberis, who informed Captain Munoz that there would be an air strike in the vicinity of the hills at Mundal, and he felt that if Company G continued its advance it would move into the area of the friendly air strike. After the air strike, during which the planes used rockets and machine guns for strafing, Company G continued north, around 1630 arriving at Tosogol. While the rest of the battalion started to disengage the enemy at 1700, Company G searched the town of Tosogol, finding only enemy dead there. From then to 17 January the 9th Infantry Regiment engaged in patrolling the Wonju-Chech'on road.[35]

General Withdrawal and Return to Wonju:
2d Division, 14–20 January 1951

Although the 9th Infantry Regiment was unable to advance its patrols north toward Wonju on the Chech'on road, the 23d and 38th Infantry Regiments had taken the high ground astride the Ch'ungju road overlooking Wonju. This partial success, however, did not save General McClure, and on 14 January he was relieved of command by General Almond. The new commander was Maj. Gen. Clark L. Ruffner, former chief of staff of X Corps. Along with the new commander came orders to withdraw to the south to consolidate the defensive line, allowing ROK units to be pulled out of the front line and freeing up additional forces to deal with the North Koreans who had infiltrated through ROK lines in the east into the X Corps rear. Colonel Freeman of the 23d Infantry was disappointed with the withdrawal order.

The advancing force [23d Infantry Regiment with attached units] reached a position about one and a half miles south of Wonju, and while it was unable to advance further, it dominated Wonju with artillery and infantry fire. Concurrently, patrols from the 9th Infantry Regiment were attempting to reach Wonju, coming up from the southeast on the Wonju-Chech'on road. The 23d Infantry Regimental Task Force held and defended its advanced position for six days, in a blinding wet snow during the first three days, in below zero weather during the last three. The enemy force defending Wonju, estimated at 25,000 North Koreans with CCF on the east flank, had as weapons small arms with a very few light mortars on the west side of the position. The enemy attacked the 23d Infantry Regiment in daylight and darkness, on the last morning engaging in a series of banzai attacks, which were repelled with considerable loss to the enemy. The North Korean force was finally defeated and dispersed, and when further advance became possible, the entire 2d Division was ordered to withdraw to defend a line approximately ten miles north of Ch'ungju.[36]

The new division line was 40,000 yards long, and was anchored

on the Han River in the west, where contact was established with
the 24th Division, and Chech'on in the east, where the 7th Division
was operating. While the 23d and 38th Infantry Regiments manned
the defensive positions, the 9th Infantry Regiment continued ag-
gressively to push patrols up the Wonju-Chech'on road. Soon after
the 2d Division had withdrawn to the new line, the patrols discov-
ered that the North Korean V Corps, which had fought at Wonju,
was also withdrawing, having suffered heavy casualties and ex-
hausted its supplies. First Lieutenant Mallory of the 2d Battalion,
9th Infantry Regiment, describes the return to Wonju.

From 14 January on, motorized jeep patrols got closer to Wonju
on the Wonju-Chech'on road. The mission of these patrols was to
burn buildings, search hills for enemy, and push up toward Wonju.
On 15 January a patrol reached Kwiron [less than a mile south of
town]. Later I heard Captain Walker say that he took his Company
E into Wonju on 17 January and spent the night, returning with
several prisoners. The town had been leveled by the fighting; the
men did not have sleeping bags, and it was too cold to sleep. The 2d
Battalion S-3 told me that the 23d Infantry Regiment was also sending patrols into Wonju. On the night of 18 January Company G, 9th
Infantry Regiment, went into Wonju and stayed. On these patrols
there was good air liaison, red panels being used for communication
with the planes. Artillery observers accompanied the patrols. The
evening of 18 January Lieutenant Colonel Barberis, commanding
the 2d Battalion, held a company commanders and staff call, at
which time he said that the 2d Battalion was going back into Wonju
on 19 January, which came as no surprise to me. Since the patrols
had not hit anything new, it was a sure bet we were going back. It
was estimated that there was one regiment of enemy in Wonju.

On the morning of 19 January at 0730 the 2d Battalion left
Sinnim-ni, accompanied by two tanks and two artillery (105mm)
pieces towed by their prime movers. When the 2d Battalion moved
out, the 1st Battalion moved into Sinnim-ni. The south end of the
airstrip was reached at 1000, and the 2d Battalion continued north,
running into some small arms fire on the edge of Wonju at 1500 and
retiring to the south end of the airstrip for the night. The next morn-

ing, 20 January, the S-4, Captain Pierce, bringing up PX supplies and moving in a convoy of three jeeps manned by automatic weapons and one two-and-a-half-ton truck with fifteen men, ran into a roadblock in the vicinity of the Mundal railroad tunnel. The men dismounted from the truck and jeeps and succeeded in driving the enemy off.

At 1000 the 2d Battalion, reinforced by Company E, 38th Infantry Regiment, jumped off and secured the airstrip without running into any enemy activity. About 1500 in the afternoon, Generals Ridgway and Ruffner landed at the [Wonju] airstrip to pay a visit to the sector.[37]

Chapter 5

HILL 312

1st Battalion, 5th Cavalry Regiment, 28–30 January 1951

While X Corps battled the North Koreans in the central sector in mid-January, the I and IX Corps on the west probed forward of their defensive positions on Line D in search of the Chinese, who had not closely followed the UN forces in their withdrawal south of Seoul. Reconnaissance forces failed to find large enemy concentrations near Line D, and on 25 January, I and IX Corps began a strong and carefully coordinated reconnaissance in force, Operation Thunderbolt, across the entire front of both corps. X Corps was ordered to maintain contact with the IX Corps advance on the west.

Although initial opposition was light in front of I Corps, strong resistance was met by IX Corps as the 8th Cavalry Regiment, 1st Cavalry Division, advanced from Paegam-ni to Yangji-i. By 26 January, the advance had stalled on the heights above Yangji-i. The next day the 5th Cavalry Regiment passed through the 8th and moved west toward Kumnyangjang-ni. This approach surprised the Chinese, and the 5th Cavalry was able to turn north and continue the advance astride the road to Kyongan-ni. On 28 January near Hill 312 about four miles north of Kumnyangjang-ni, the 1st Battalion, 5th Cavalry Regiment, made contact with the enemy. Major Gibson, the battalion executive officer, describes the battalion's advance.

After passing through the 1st Battalion, 8th Cavalry Regiment, the 1st Battalion, 5th Cavalry Regiment, started searching check-

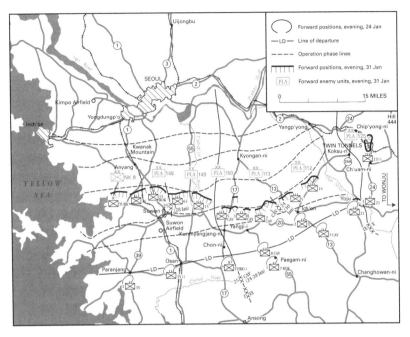

Operation Thunderbolt, 25–31 January 1951 (based on U.S. Army Center of Military History map).

points 9 and 13 (terrain features numbered for convenience). Kumnyangjang-ni was in friendly hands, and the 2d Battalion, 5th Cavalry Regiment, moved up the left, or west, side of the road while the 1st Battalion advanced on the right, or east, of the road leading north. No enemy resistance was met until Checkpoint 44, Hill 312, was approached. On 28 January, late in the afternoon, Company A, in the valley just south of Hill 312, received enemy fire. Because of approaching darkness, the 1st Battalion formed a perimeter defense for the night, planning to search out the enemy on the following day.[1]

An Army combat historian in Korea, 1st Lt. Martin Blumenson, who collected accounts of the ensuing action, describes the situation.

Hill 312 was a key point in the enemy defenses. It dominated the surrounding terrain. It permitted enemy observation of the MSR

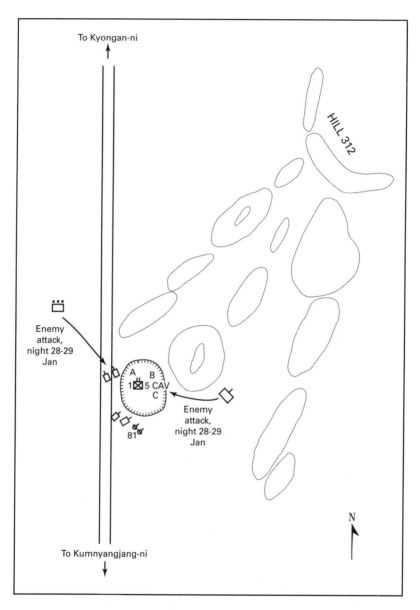

To Kyongan-ni

HILL 312

Enemy
attack,
night 28-29
Jan

A   B
1⊠5 CAV
C

Enemy
attack,
night 28-29
Jan

81

N

To Kumnyangjang-ni

Attack on 1st Battalion, 5th Cavalry, night of 28–29 January 1951 (based on
a sketch by Maj. James M. Gibson; not to scale).

and friendly movements north from Kumnyangjang-ni and vicinity. The hill was strongly defended by entrenchments and emplacements, and the two most accessible avenues of approach were covered by machine guns and automatic weapons, well dug in, and excellently camouflaged.

After making initial contact with the enemy on 28 January, the 1st Battalion, 5th Cavalry Regiment, supported by one platoon; Company A, 70th Tank Battalion; and one platoon, Heavy Mortar Company, 5th Cavalry Regiment, formed a perimeter defense for the night. Elements of the 61st Field Artillery Battalion were in support. During the hours of darkness, the battalion repelled an enemy attack, which ceased just before daybreak.[2]

The battalion perimeter was just east of the main road, about 2,000 yards southwest of Hill 312. Several members of the battalion describe the enemy night attack in the early morning hours of 29 January.

SERGEANT MASON AND MASTER SERGEANT CHIKAHISA, COMPANY B, 5TH CAVALRY: When Company B moved into the battalion perimeter on the night of 28 January 1951, it tied in between Company A on the left and Company C on the right. The 3d Platoon, Company B, outposted a group on the finger ridge extending up Hill 312. At 0230, 29 January, the outpost came charging through the company area and alerted the battalion for an enemy attack, which occurred first in the area defended by the tanks of the 70th Tank Battalion, and later, about 0300, against the 1st Platoon, Company C, which at first gave way, but was later reassembled in place. The enemy troops could be seen descending the ridge from Hill 312, outlined against the skyline and snow. The enemy using machine gun, automatic weapons, and small arms fire, as well as grenades, came within ten yards of Company B, but was repulsed. After a thirty-minute pause, the enemy attacked again at 0400. Fire ceased just before daylight.[3]

SERGEANT 1ST CLASS ATWOOD AND SERGEANT 1ST CLASS HUDSON, COMPANY B, 5TH CAVALRY: During the night of 28 January 1951, the 2d Platoon, Company B, was tied in on the battalion perimeter with Company C on its right flank. That night three attacks made between 0300 and daylight, 29 January, against the battalion perimeter by enemy estimated at company strength were repulsed. Sergeant Mason's squad took the brunt of the attacks because they were on the point, the easiest approach to the platoon position. The moon was shining and reflecting off the snow, and the enemy could be clearly seen. Tracer bullets and one friendly mortar round of white phosphorous illuminated the area.[4]

MASTER SERGEANT CLARK, COMPANY C, 5TH CAVALRY: I was platoon sergeant of the 2d Platoon of Company C. Company C, on 28 January, set up its defense in the battalion perimeter south of Hill 312. At 0200, 29 January, an enemy attack ran the 4th Squad of my platoon out of position. I reorganized the men and got them back. The fight continued until daybreak, about 0630. The company suffered three WIA and one KIA.[5]

SERGEANT 1ST CLASS MANFREDI, COMPANY C, 5TH CAVALRY: I was platoon sergeant of the Weapons Platoon of Company C. During the night of 28–29 January, Company C moved into the battalion perimeter, registered its mortars, and posted its guards. At 0300 I heard firing from the direction of the battalion CP, and I saw tracers across the battalion area. Immediately afterward, an enemy attack struck the 2d Platoon of Company C, which called for mortar fire. Approximately 500 rounds of 60mm mortar fire were thrown against the enemy, who retired about 0530.[6]

The battalion's operations log provides a count of enemy casualties and the information gained from prisoner interrogations.

ENTRY FOR 29 JANUARY, 0900 HOURS: Actual count of enemy dead in encounter this morning: immediate CP area—2; Baker area—22; Charlie area—6. Counting incomplete. Two wounded POW. One stated he is from 3d Regiment; 23 years old; approximately 500 enemy on Objective 44 [Hill 312], well dug in; came here 10 days ago; had 20 WIA from artillery; had 7 heavy machine guns and 1 has been destroyed; more enemy on hill across valley in Swing White area [code name for 2d Battalion, 5th Cavalry]; states has no mortars or artillery, but this is dubious.[7]

Company C was ordered to attack Hill 312 on 29 January. Captain Rezac, the company commander, describes the action.

After an artillery preparation from 1000 to 1015 on Hill 312, Company C, reinforced by the 1st Platoon, Company B, for right flank security, moved out at 1015. The 3d Platoon, with a section of machine guns attached, and the 2d Platoon, with one 57mm recoilless rifle attached, moved toward the objective while the 1st Platoon, with attached .50- and .30-caliber machine guns, laid down a base of fire. Forward observers of the 81mm mortars, the 4.2-inch mortars, and the artillery, all in support, were with me.

The 3d Platoon took the first of a series of knolls along the ridgeline toward the crest of Hill 312 without opposition. Then with the 2d Platoon as a base of fire at that position, the 3d Platoon moved to the next knoll until enemy small arms fire from outposts drove the 3d Platoon back.

About 1200 I reorganized the company. I caused the supporting weapons to move forward, and I placed the 60mm mortars just behind the company. As artillery and mortar fire were directed against the hill, I requested an air strike, which arrived about 1400. The hill was marked with white phosphorus by the artillery, and a spotter plane directed four F80 planes with rockets, napalm, and machine gun fire on the target.

I then had the 3d and Weapons Platoons act as a base of fire while the 2d Platoon moved forward in frontal assault and the 1st Platoon crossed to the left in an enveloping movement. But before the platoons assaulted, the battalion S-3 phoned and instructed the company to wait for a second air strike, which arrived at 1500. Three or four Australian Mustang planes struck the hill. The artillery forward observer adjusted his fire for the final barrage as the two platoons moved out.

During this attack, the 1st Platoon, Company B, assaulted also, advancing between the 1st and 2d Platoons, Company C. With the three platoons abreast, the assault proceeded to the top of the hill, where the leading six or eight men were met and repulsed by an enemy grenade attack. This assault had moved over 150 yards of ground exposed to enemy small arms and machine gun fire. The platoon leader, 1st Platoon, Company B, was killed in this attack.[8]

Soldiers of the 1st Platoon, Company B, describe the actions of their platoon leader, 2d Lt. Green B. Mayo, in their recommendation for his award of the Distinguished Service Cross.

MASTER SERGEANT PENDERGRAFT: While Lieutenant Mayo's platoon was moving into the attack, the platoon and Company C came under heavy enemy fire. All of the platoon was under heavy fire and was pinned down except one machine gun section that was covering Lieutenant Mayo. He spotted two enemy machine guns that were delivering the fire, and after ordering his platoon to stay in their positions, he attacked one machine gun position. While he was assaulting the position and diverting fire from the rest of the company, an enemy grenade landed under him and killed him. The act was outstanding, because Lieutenant Mayo could have waited and gotten assistance from the artillery and supporting units; however, this would mean more casualties and a delay in the attack. So rather than sacrifice his men, he went after the position alone. As a result, Company C and Lieutenant Mayo's platoon were able to withdraw to better positions.

PRIVATE 1ST CLASS VANDERBURG: When Company C jumped off in the attack, we were ordered to attack with them. Three enemy machine guns on Hill 312 were holding up the advance of our troops. Our platoon sergeant, seeing them, said he was going after one, and after he had left, Lieutenant Mayo, I, and one machine gun section from our platoon went after the other machine gun. Lieutenant Mayo ordered me to throw a smoke grenade to cover his advance, and he then advanced alone toward the machine gun nest. He threw several grenades at the machine gun and called back to me for more grenades. When he looked back, an enemy grenade landed between his legs and went off, killing him. We were forced to withdraw due to heavy grenading.[9]

Captain Rezac continues his description of the fighting.

A second assault over the same ground was made without success. I then directed the 1st Platoon to move to the extreme western approach to Hill 312, but this force was driven back by grenades thrown by the enemy from the top of the hill.[10]

The platoon leader of the 1st Platoon, Company C, 1st Lieu-

tenant Eismann, had recently been assigned to the company after his recall to active duty. This was his first combat action with Company C, and little time had been available to build cohesion within his platoon. Lieutenant Eismann describes the attack on Hill 312 after the air strikes.

Two air strikes were made on Hill 312. After additional artillery preparation, the 2d and 1st Platoons moved up in skirmish line. The 1st Platoon advancing in frontal attack was pinned down by enemy automatic weapon and machine gun fire. Captain Rezac called the 1st Platoon over to the left flank finger ridge where the 2d Platoon was located. While I was moving over, I noticed that my platoon was remaining where it was. I was unable to get my men to move.

Captain Rezac asked me whether I thought I could proceed to the extreme left flank and envelop the enemy. I said I would attempt to do so. But when I tried again to move my platoon over, the men remained where they were. Because my carbine had failed to operate, I exchanged it with a soldier for an M1 rifle, then set off alone. I moved to the extreme left of Hill 312 and reached a point twenty-five yards from the top of the hill. From my position I was able to see the enemy trenches dug along the crest of the hill.

I had four hand grenades, my M1 rifle, and one bandolier of ammunition. I threw one grenade into the enemy position. It failed to explode. I threw a second, which failed to explode. My third grenade was thrown back by enemy troops. My fourth grenade operated effectively. When I attempted to fire on two enemy soldiers operating a machine gun, my M1 rifle failed to fire.

I then decided I would endeavor to get some men up with me. I motioned without result. I started descending the hill, and after proceeding about ten yards, I received a piece of shrapnel in my leg. I informed Captain Rezac that I thought Hill 312 could be taken from the left flank point, then walked down the hill to the aid station. I met the battalion executive officer at the CP and informed him that the hill could have been taken if the men had done their jobs. In my opinion only twenty-five or thirty men in the company were working that day.[11]

Captain Rezac continues.

Enemy machine guns were targets of the 76mm guns of the tanks attached to the battalion [in position in the valley and firing generally northeast] and also for the 57mm recoilless rifle attached to Company B's platoon.

At close to 1800, the battalion commander ordered one more attempt to take the hill. I brought up my 3d Platoon, and the final assault was made by the 1st, 2d, and 3d Platoons, Company C, and the remnants of the 1st Platoon, Company B, all moving up the finger ridge on the southwestern side of the hill until pinned down by enemy machine gun fire. The order for withdrawal was given, and the company descended the hill.

I estimate that an enemy force of 200 defended the crest of Hill 312. Enemy defensive positions and emplacements had been prepared to cover the two main approaches to the crest, one long ridgeline and one finger pointing southwest. With the exception of these approach routes, the sides of Hill 312 were steep and bare. Trenches were entirely connected around the crest of the hill. Machine guns had excellent fields of fire. Positions were logged in and covered with dirt. Individual holes were dug back under the surface of the ground for protection against air attack and napalm. Positions and emplacements were well camouflaged. Enemy 60mm mortar positions were later found in the vicinity of unnumbered Hill 300 [400 yards to the northeast]; 82mm mortar positions were found behind Hill 193 [2,000 yards to the north].[12]

Company C pulled back into the battalion perimeter for the night while air strikes worked over the enemy position atop Hill 312. Major Gibson, 1st Battalion executive officer, and Captain Stewart, assistant operations officer, 5th Cavalry Regiment, explain the air operations.

MAJOR GIBSON: That evening the regimental S-3 informed the battalion that division was making a plane available for close tactical support at night, an experimental operation that had been used with success in the 24th Division sector. An Air Force tactical air control officer arrived at regimental headquarters to direct the air strike, which was controlled by a company forward observer in communication with the regimental S-3.

The air strike on Hill 312 started about 2400 and lasted to 0330. Most of the time was spent in coordinating the operation. The artillery marked the target with a round of white phosphorous. Then a flare ship, watching for the shell, illuminated the target area with flares. The B26 plane then made a dry run, and the forward observer checked to make certain that the pass was on target and made in the correct direction. Then the air strike was made. Bombs were dropped 600 yards in front of the 1st Battalion troops.[13]

CAPTAIN STEWART: Between 2100, 29 January, and 0005, 30 January 1951, four planes dropped twelve rockets, two napalm bombs, five 500-pound fragmentation bombs, and six 500-pound firebombs on Hill 312, and strafed enemy positions with 3,300 rounds of .50-caliber ammunition, in a tactical close support air strike during the hours of darkness.

This was accomplished in the following manner. A forward observer with one of the companies of the 1st Battalion was located about 700 yards from the target and was in telephone communication with the regimental S-3. The regimental S-3 was in communication with the supporting artillery and also with the Tactical Air Control Party (TACP) officer who was located 200 yards from the regimental headquarters. The TAC officer, Captain Haythorne, was in radio communication with the planes.

The azimuth and time of flight from the regimental CP to the target were given to the guide plane, which then dropped flares on the enemy positions to be struck. An artillery round of white phosphorus further pinpointed the target. The B-26 planes then made a dry run, which was checked by the forward observer; when all was correctly coordinated, the air strike was made, 1,000 to 1,500 yards from the friendly troops.[14]

MAJOR GIBSON: In my opinion, the air strike did not knock out any enemy weapons or emplacements. But the air attack had a psychological advantage. It must have stunned the enemy forces on Hill 312, and it certainly kept them awake. It also probably prevented the enemy from organizing for a counterattack, which the battalion was definitely expecting.[15]

Major Gibson describes the action the next day, 30 January.

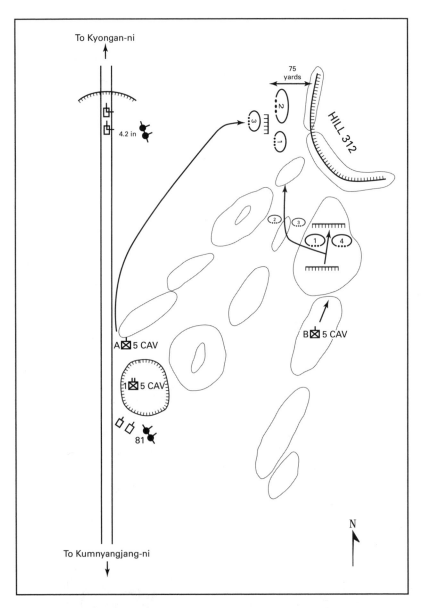

To Kyongan-ni

75 yards

HILL 312

4.2 in

3

2

1

2

3

1

4

A 5 CAV

B 5 CAV

1 5 CAV

81

N

To Kumnyangjang-ni

Attack on Hill 312, 30 January 1951 (based on a sketch by Maj. James M. Gibson; not to scale).

On 30 January 1951 at 0900 hours, a coordinated attack with two companies was launched by the 1st Battalion, 5th Cavalry, at Hill 312. After an artillery barrage, B Company was instructed to make a holding attack over the same ground that C Company used the day before. A Company was to be the maneuvering element and make the main effort. They advanced north up the road and turned to approach Hill 312 from the west. A section of tanks from the 1st Platoon, Company A, 70th Tank Battalion, and the 2d Platoon of Company D were given the mission of protecting the left flank of Company A on its approach to Hill 312 and to cover the battalion positions from the north.

At 0920 hours B Company had moved to within 500 yards of the objective. The 1st and 4th Platoons formed a base of fire on the ridge, and the company commander took the 2d and 3d Platoons across a small draw to the base of Hill 312. As they began working up the hill, they came under small arms and automatic weapons fire. The enemy was still holding the top of the hill.[16]

Soldiers of Company B provide more details of the fighting.

FIRST LIEUTENANT BAILEY, EXECUTIVE OFFICER OF COMPANY B: In the assault on Hill 312, I set the 1st Platoon, the 4th Platoon, and part of the company headquarters of Company B on a ridge 500 yards to the right of the battalion objective to lay a base of fire for the attacking elements of Company B and give them close-in support with the 60mm mortars and the 57mm recoilless rifles, in order to keep the enemy pinned down while the company moved to positions from where the final assault could be made. The Weapons Platoon was behind the ridgeline in defile while the riflemen and the 57mm recoilless rifle fired from the geographical crest.

Approximately five enemy soldiers who were observed infiltrating the right flank of Company B, with the apparent mission of neutralizing the machine gun and rifle fire, were killed or wounded.

Volume of fire was directed at supposed enemy positions. Several enemy pillboxes could be seen, and one was neutralized by a direct hit of the 57mm rifle. In general, however, firing was laid on enemy smoke and fire flashes.

The base of fire enabled Company B to move within grenade

range of the objective, and during the final fifty yards of the assault, mortar and machine gun fire was lifted so that the mortar rounds landed on the reverse slope of the hill against enemy troops attempting to withdraw or against ammunition bearers, while the machine guns fired over the heads of the assaulting elements in an endeavor to keep the enemy pinned down in his holes.

The company commander ordered the base of fire to cease firing when the company was in the final assault stage of cleaning out the enemy positions.[17]

CAPTAIN DOBSON, COMMANDING OFFICER OF COMPANY B: On 30 January Company B moved up the hill. I placed the 1st Platoon on the first high ground south of Hill 312, and the Weapons Platoon just behind it. Small arms, mortar, and automatic weapons fire from here was effective against enemy positions.

The 2d and 3d Platoons moved to the west across a small draw and joined Company A's right flank. At this time, the company began to receive heavy small arms fire and suffered some casualties. The platoons drawing intense small arms and mortar fire worked up the ridge to the right of Company A to the last cover on the hill, fifty to seventy-five yards from the top.

At a coordinated time (I was in radio contact with the commanding officer of Company A), Company A and the two platoons of Company B with bayonets fixed assaulted the crest of Hill 312. Twenty yards from the enemy trenches at the top, a rain of grenades fell on the assault part, but the attackers overran the enemy positions with grenades and bayonets. Enemy troops were shot, bayoneted, or grenaded in their holes.[18]

PRIVATE 1ST CLASS BROWN, 3D PLATOON, COMPANY B: It was not particularly cold on 30 January 1951, but there was snow on the ground. After Company B moved out to take Hill 312, Captain Dobson instructed Lieutenant Bundy, my platoon leader, to leave one machine gun on the first knoll on the ridge leading to the crest of Hill 312. Lieutenant Bundy ordered me, my assistant gunner, and one ammunition bearer, all under Sergeant Baines, to take position. I picked out a place, and as I set up my gun, the platoon moved around the edge of the knoll to the left.

When Captain Dobson, who was 30 yards distant, ordered the

machine gun to commence firing, I opened up against a small saddle 150 yards to the right front, where I suspected an enemy position. I fired about 400 rounds in short bursts of three and four when a sniper's bullet from the left struck the ground near me. A second round hit me and threw me back from my gun. Sergeant Baines took over when a third bullet hit Corporal Tobias, the assistant gunner. At this time the assault platoons were 300 yards up the hill, and as I was carried off the hill, friendly mortars opened fire.[19]

SECOND LIEUTENANT BUNDY, 3D PLATOON LEADER, COMPANY B: On the morning of 30 January, Company A was ordered to move around the left flank of Company B and make the main effort, while Company B approached Hill 312 over the route taken by Company C. Company B planned to form a base of fire with its 4th and 1st Platoons, while the 2d and 3d Platoons moved to the left of the base of fire and to the right of Company A assaulting the hill.

With the 2d Platoon leading, Company B left the battalion positions shortly after 0800. My 3d Platoon, following the 2d Platoon, crossed the ridgeline that led to Hill 312 and remained on the left of the ridge to avoid enemy flanking fire that was being received from the right shoulder of the hill. I placed one machine gun on a knoll to search and traverse this enemy shoulder, and I moved up to contact Captain Dobson, commanding officer of Company B. I was able to see the men of Company A moving up the approaches of Hill 312. Captain Dobson stated that something was holding up the 2d Platoon, so I moved forward to Lieutenant Withers, platoon leader, and learned that enemy fire from the right was keeping Company B from getting over the ridgeline.

I called for my other machine gun to come forward to fire to the company left, and the machine gunner and I covered each other as we moved up the slope. At this time I was hit in the face by enemy small arms fire, and after my face was bandaged, I stood up and waved my platoon up. The 2d and 3d Platoons arose, with bayonets fixed, and shouting, ran forward up the hill. At the same time, Company A assaulted the hill. Grenades thrown by the enemy from the reverse slope of the hill were kicked out of the way as the men of Companies A and B continued assaulting the crest.[20]

SERGEANT 1ST CLASS ATWOOD AND SERGEANT 1ST CLASS HUDSON,

2D PLATOON, COMPANY B: On 30 January Hill 312 was assaulted as follows. Company A attacked on the left flank. The 2d and 3d Platoons, Company B, assaulted the center. The 1st and 4th Platoons, Company B, on the right fired in support. Company C remained in reserve.

When Company A reached effective firing range against the enemy, the 2d and 3d Platoons, Company B, were pinned down. Lieutenant Bundy, who had been wounded in the face and was bandaged, stood up and yelled, "All we need is force." One man said he couldn't move because he was wounded. "Wounded!" shouted Bundy. "I'm wounded too." Everyone moved out, made a great deal of noise, and assaulted the top of the hill.

The riflemen of Companies A and B moved in on the top of Hill 312 and grenaded the main trench from a distance of ten to twelve yards, then swept over the top of the hill.[21]

SERGEANT MASON AND MASTER SERGEANT CHIKAHISA, 2D PLATOON, COMPANY B: On 30 January the 2d and 3d Platoons, Company B, attacked Hill 312 with Company A on the left. The 2d Platoon, Company B, moved on the right flank of Company A. As we approached the crest, the assaulting elements were pinned down, about 1030, by automatic weapons fire.

On order of Lieutenant Withers, platoon leader, 2d Platoon, after Lieutenant Bundy was wounded, the 2d and 3d Platoons formed a skirmish line and walked up the hill, well over 100 yards, firing against likely enemy positions. Enemy troops could be plainly seen when they raised their heads to fire or to throw grenades. It took about one hour to cross this open ground, and when in range, the platoons threw grenades on the crest of the hill, and assaulted the top.[22]

Major Gibson, who was with Company A, describes the company's approach to Hill 312 and subsequent attack.

In the meantime Company A approached from the left and reached a point about seventy-five yards from the crest of the hill before they were detected by the enemy, who was concentrating on Company B. At 0940 hours Company A deployed on a small ridge under heavy small arms fire and prepared to assault the objective.

The 3d Platoon laid down a base of fire. The 4th Platoon moved up behind the 3d and placed the mortars in a small draw. Machine gun sections from Company D and 4th Platoon machine guns were placed in position with the 3d Platoon. The 1st and 2d Platoons were designated the assault element, 1st on the left and 2d on the right.

At 1100 hours the 1st and 2d Platoons jumped off in the assault after a mortar concentration by the 1st Platoon of Heavy Mortar Company. To reach the objective the 1st Platoon of Company A had to scramble hand over hand up a steep cliff side. The enemy, from dug in positions on the crest fired into the advancing platoons and tossed hand grenades down the slope on the Americans as they labored up the cliff. As a grenade landed near a man he attempted to throw it back or in many cases kick at it with his foot or bat it away from him with his hands. It would roll further down the slope to the misfortune of the men below. The 2d Platoon was advancing across rugged ground and was receiving a large volume of automatic weapons fire. From behind the crest, the enemy threw his potato masher–type hand grenades. From eight to twelve grenades at a time were seen in the air, arcing toward the 2d Platoon.

The 3d and 4th Platoons continued to lay down a heavy concentration of fire at the enemy positions on the crest. As the men of the 1st and 2d Platoons reached the crest, the covering fire was lifted. The men in the assault platoons tossed their grenades up on and over the crest, and pushed their way up the last few feet. By this time most of the men in the assault platoon had expended their hand grenades (three apiece when they started). Some of the rifles had become clogged with mud as the men scrambled up the cliff. The Chinamen stayed in their holes as the Americans moved up the crest. Up and down the 150 yards of dugouts and trenches on the crest, the Americans could be seen struggling hand to hand with the Chinese. The battle swayed back and forth on the hilltop. Chinamen fell under the blows of the rifle butts and bare bayonets; grenades exploded; wounded Americans, covered with blood, turned and staggered from the line. Screams of the wounded rang above the calls of the officers and NCOs urging their men on. At this point the battle hung in the balance.

The 3d Platoon, Company A, was committed and came charging up the slope to help their comrades. The assault platoons of Company B, who had been covering Company A, now charged forward. The reinforcements completely overwhelmed the enemy, and the line swept over the hill. Many well-camouflaged holes were overlooked in the confusion. The enemy stood up and threw grenades and fired into the backs of the Americans as the line swept past them. Small and desperate hand-to-hand engagements took place all over the hill. By 1215 the hill was secured.[23]

Soldiers of Company A provide more details of the attack on Hill 312 on the left of Company B and particularly the heroism of the 2d Platoon leader, 1st Lt. Robert M. McGovern, who was posthumously awarded the Medal of Honor.

FIRST LIEUTENANT KADER, WEAPONS PLATOON LEADER, COMPANY A: On 30 January, with Company B advancing over Company C's route of approach on the right, Company A proceeded out of the village and up the valley to the north to approach Hill 312 from the left. The companies were aided that morning by a very dense fog that enabled Company A to move up under artillery fire to within 100 yards of the objective before the company was discovered and pinned down by enemy fire. With the Weapons and 3d Platoons as a base of fire, and the 1st and 2d Platoons as the initial assault platoons, Company A moved up against the crest of the hill. The 2d Platoon, led by Lieutenant McGovern, who was killed while cleaning out a machine gun nest, reached the crest of the hill, and as the men of the platoon engaged the enemy in a grenade battle, the other two rifle platoons assaulted and overran the hill, using bayonets. I saw three men using bayonets on Chinese who were in dug-in positions. Lieutenant McGovern's leadership of the 2d Platoon, in my opinion, was the factor that kept Company A moving.[24]

Lieutenant McGovern, after being seriously wounded seventy-five yards from the crest of the hill, reassured his men that he was all right, that all they did was shoot away his compass, and then proceeded to lead his men forward, exposing himself to intense automatic weapons fire. Casualties in his platoon were increasing, and the morale of his men was very low, when he stood up and assaulted a machine gun emplacement. He had his carbine shot away, and using his pistol and hand grenades when only ten yards away from the gun, killed seven enemy before he fell mortally wounded almost on top of this machine gun. His men, enraged by what happened, charged the hill with bayonets and grenades and took their objective. The act of valor of Lieutenant McGovern saved many lives of men in his platoon, and it alone made it possible for the platoon to complete its objective.[25]

CPL. GEORGE R. HICKSON, 2D PLATOON, COMPANY A: I saw Lieutenant McGovern, when about seventy-five yards from the crest of the hill, stop for just a moment as one does when one gets hit. I asked him if he was all right, and he said, "Sure. All it did was hit my compass." I knew that he was hit because later on I saw him put his hand in his jacket and there was blood on it. But he kept us moving forward into this heavy fire that was coming from machine guns to the right and left of us and especially the one to our front, which had good fortifications. The enemy kept throwing and rolling grenades down at us. Lieutenant McGovern threw back a lot of the grenades, and when his carbine was shot away, he was using his pistol and grenades. When Lieutenant McGovern was only ten yards away from the machine gun, he was hit by a burst of fire from the gun and fell mortally wounded on top of the machine gun. He killed those seven men who were manning the machine gun. Lieutenant McGovern's act of heroism gave all of us enough courage and rage to take the position with bayonets and hand grenades.[26]

PFC LOUIS AMOS, 2D PLATOON, COMPANY A: I was a member of Lieutenant McGovern's platoon during the assault on Hill 312 and saw him, when we were about seventy-five yards from the top of the hill, pause a bit as if he was hit. But he assured us that nothing had happened except for his compass, which was damaged by gunfire. I found out later that he was seriously wounded, but to keep up the morale of the platoon, he never showed it. He continued to lead the men forward, exposing himself to intense automatic weapons fire from three machine guns, one especially to our front. After his carbine was shot away from him, he was using his pistol and grenades, and rushed up to the machine gun, killing seven enemy soldiers before he fell mortally wounded about a foot away from the knocked-out weapon. If it had not been for Lieutenant McGovern's guts and go-get-them spirit, I am sure that most of the men in the platoon would have been killed, but seeing what he had done and seeing him lying there by that machine gun, the rest of us charged the hill with bayonets and took our objective.[27]

SERGEANT 1ST CLASS FORD, 3D PLATOON, COMPANY A: Company A moved out at 1000, 30 January, with the mission of taking Hill 312, and by 1120, the company had reached the first knoll situated about halfway and about 250 yards from the top. With the 3d Platoon behind the knoll acting as a base of fire, the 1st Platoon covered half the remaining distance to the hillcrest, when it laid down fire to enable the 3d Platoon to move up.

Crawling under enemy machine gun fire, Corporal Klein and Private 1st Class Sanchez, 3d Platoon, were able to get within grenade range of this machine gun nest, and they knocked it out. Lieutenant McGovern, following these men, was killed there.

After the machine gun was neutralized, all the platoons of Company A walked up the hill and over the top. Enemy grenades rolled among the men making the assault. I saw one man jump into the enemy trench and bayonet an enemy soldier who had been throwing grenades.[28]

MASTER SERGEANT POE, 1ST PLATOON, COMPANY A: About 0800 30 January, Company A moved out in a heavy fog. After advancing north about 1,000 yards, the company turned east up Hill 312. Because of the heavy overcast, I was able to see only a few yards ahead. Company A reached a ridge that ran off the western side of Hill 312; Company B was moving up Hill 312 from another direction. I understood that both companies were to assault simultaneously. The 2d Platoon, Company A, leading the company, got to 150 to 200 yards from the top of the hill when it was fired on by the enemy and was temporarily halted by several casualties.

A preparatory barrage had been laid on the hill before Company A had moved out, and when the company moved up the mountain, artillery continued to fire a harassing fire. The tanks also fired from the valley.

When the 2d Platoon was pinned down, Captain Wolf, Commanding Officer, Company A, took his automatic weapons and his section of machine guns attached from Company D and set them up as covering fire. The 1st Platoon moved up behind the 2d Platoon, and then to the left into a parallel draw, and both platoons assaulted together at 1125. The 2d Platoon seemed to assault the steepest part of the hill, and when the leading squad reached a point thirty to forty yards from the top, the enemy threw concussion grenades over the top of the hill. Unless these grenades exploded very near a man, they were not effective. The men jumped out of the way or fell flat, then continued after the explosion. Grenade casualties were light in comparison to the number of grenades thrown by the enemy.[29]

FIRST LIEUTENANT KADER, WEAPONS PLATOON, COMPANY A: The Weapons Platoon was placed in a draw 250 yards from the objective, about minimum range for the 60mm mortar. One 57mm recoilless rifle was operating with the 3d Platoon base of fire. When the enemy began leaving his positions and running down the reverse slope of the hill, the mortars lifted and hit the draw between Hill 312 and the adjacent peak.[30]

Major Gibson describes the consolidation on the objective and the enemy counterattacks.

Company A reorganized to defend the hill, and Company B pushed on through toward Hill 300, which was about 1,000 yards north. Company B had moved about 150 yards when the enemy, 200 strong, counterattacked from Hill 300. They crossed to within fifty yards of Company B, and a desperate battle took place. The battle raged until about 1700 hours, when the enemy was beaten off by accurate rifle fire and 60mm mortar fire. The enemy made another small probing attack shortly after dark (about 2100 hours) that resulted in an exchange of hand grenades. The hill remained secure in the hands of the 1st Battalion, 5th Cavalry.

Seventy-five enemy dead were counted on Hill 312 and its approaches. Twenty-one enemy dead were found in Company C's area (result of night attack, early hours of 29 January). Two enemy dead were found in the battalion CP area killed by the 1st Platoon, Company A, 70th Tank Battalion. Two prisoners taken on different days both state that Hill 312 was defended by 300 Chinamen supported by another 200 on Hill 300 and more (number unknown) in the valley north of Hill 312. From this it can be determined that the area was defended by at least one battalion probably reinforced.

The enemy had constructed dug-in emplacements with excellent fields of fire. The positions were constructed so that during air strikes and artillery barrages the enemy moved their weapons into the hillside. Afterwards they again occupied the firing positions. The positions were connected by communication trenches approximately four feet deep. Mortar positions were found on the reverse side of the hill about 100 yards from the crest.[31]

Other soldiers of the battalion discuss this phase of the operation and provide their observations and comments on the attack.

FIRST LIEUTENANT BAILEY, EXECUTIVE OFFICER OF COMPANY B: On the top of Hill 312, the enemy had well-dug-in trenches. The individual holes went down and back under. The tight enemy perimeter was able to defend itself against an attack from any direction. I estimate 500 men or a reinforced battalion had occupied these positions. Had the enemy had mortars and artillery in great numbers, he could have held his positions, and the lack of this material by the enemy was an important element in the success of the attack.

Thirty minutes after the hill was secured, the enemy counterattacked Company B. I think this attack was made to delay additional forward movement of friendly elements rather than an attempt to regain the hill. If no counterattack had taken place, Company B would have pushed forward, and the enemy would have had to withdraw across open ground in daylight. The enemy counterattack was repulsed, but it did succeed in stopping the battalion forward movement.[32]

SERGEANT 1ST CLASS ATWOOD AND SERGEANT 1ST CLASS HUDSON, 2D PLATOON, COMPANY B: An enemy trench dug all around the top of the hill to a depth of five feet provided excellent cover and enabled wounded to be evacuated down the reverse slope of Hill 312 without being seen; replacements also could reinforce the defenders of the hill without exposure. Automatic weapons and machine guns were effectively dug in. Bunkers and pillboxes were lined with logs, and dirt walls were three to six feet thick.

Although the top of Hill 312 was burned bare by napalm, it was felt that most enemy casualties were caused by small arms fire, rather than by mortar, artillery, or air strikes.

Enemy material—including 60mm mortars, one .30-caliber American water-cooled machine gun, carbines, M1 rifles, Bren guns (both English and Japanese), American tommy guns and "grease guns," and a large amount of ammunition and grenades—was found at a supply point on the reverse slope of Hill 312.

On the following day, the battalion moved toward its next checkpoints. No enemy contact was made.[33]

CAPTAIN DOBSON, COMMANDING OFFICER OF COMPANY B: Major Gibson, battalion executive officer, who had followed Company A up the hill, ordered Company A to remain and consolidate Hill 312, while Company B moved to the next high ground north of the hill. I moved two platoons forward to the next high point. Shortly thereafter, the enemy counterattacked in a force estimated between fifty and seventy-five, from the draw to the north, in an effort to regain the high ground north of and slightly lower than Hill 312. This enemy counterattack was pointed out by an observation plane that made two very low passes to indicate the approaching enemy to Company B. Company A troops on Hill 312 also observed enemy forces regrouping for a counterattack.

Enemy troops crawled up the ridge to within forty yards of Company B, and a small arms firefight lasted about one hour. Forty-five minutes after the attack was repulsed, an observation plane led four jet planes in on an air strike 100 yards north of Company B.

Major Wilson, battalion S-3, at this time called and ordered the company to consolidate on its position. But I asked and received permission to withdraw to Hill 312. As the company was digging in, Major Wilson ordered Company B to withdraw to the battalion perimeter. Company C relieved Company A on top of Hill 312.

On the following morning, Company B advanced and found that the enemy had withdrawn, apparently in haste, leaving weapons, ammunition, and food.

In my estimation, air strikes and artillery had had comparatively little effect on the enemy due to his covered bunkers. Napalm was the most effective weapon. Artillery with delayed fuse might have had more effect in penetrating the bunkers.

It was SOP in Company B to fix bayonets before an assault. The effect of this was for the most part psychological, a good morale factor for friendly troops. Furthermore, the enemy seemed to fear a knife of any type. I estimate that of the sixty-five men in my two platoons making the assault, fifty-four reached the crest of Hill 312. Of these an estimated ten engaged the enemy with the bayonet, either in combat or in disposing of wounded but dangerous enemy soldiers.

For additional support, I had one section of three tanks of Company A, 70th Tank Battalion, with which I had radio contact. The tanks in the vicinity of the village southwest of Hill 312, 1,500 yards from the target, could not fire effectively, because they could not observe the target due to a heavy morning mist hanging over the top of the hill.

The enemy troops defending Hill 312 were in my opinion well disciplined and willing to fight. Very few fled.[34]

The enemy force that the 1st Battalion, 5th Cavalry, drove off of Hill 312 was a regiment of the Chinese 112th Division of the 38th Army. To the east, the 7th Cavalry also encountered a regiment of this same division. All along the front of the I and IX Corps, enemy resistance was stiffening, with six divisions now opposing the Eighth Army advance. However, the success at Hill 312 and elsewhere led General Ridgway on 30 January to turn the reconnaissance in force into a full-scale advance by authorizing each corps to bring forward all available troops to hold the ground gained.

Meanwhile to the east, X Corps units moved forward to protect the right flank of the IX Corps advance. This soon led to another engagement between UN forces and the enemy near the Twin Tunnels area south of Chip'yong-ni.

Chapter 6

TWIN TUNNELS

3d Battalion, 23d Infantry Regiment, and
French Battalion, 30 January–2 February 1951

The 23d Infantry Regiment, with its attached French Battalion, occupied the western end of the X Corps defensive line, tying in with the right flank unit of IX Corps at Yoju. In response to orders from Eighth Army to maintain contact with the reconnaissance in force of IX Corps to the west, the 23d Infantry moved its 2d Battalion forward about ten miles to Munmang-ni, a village about ten miles east of Yoju, to establish a patrol base. On 27 January a reconnaissance patrol advanced to the dominating terrain south of Chip'yong-ni, where two railroad tunnels cut through the mountains. It returned to base without any enemy contact. Two days later another patrol to the same twin tunnels area encountered strong enemy forces and suffered heavy casualties. An Army combat historian in Korea, 1st Lt. John Mewha, who documented the ensuing operations, describes the consequences of this patrol.[1]

On 29 January 1951 a reconnaissance patrol was ambushed by a strong enemy force in the tunnels area. Lt. Gen. Edward Almond, X Corps Commander, directed the commanding general, 2d Infantry Division, to send a combat patrol in force to develop the enemy's positions and destroy him. On 30 January the 23d Infantry Regiment was given the mission of occupying the commanding terrain in the tunnels area. A secondary mission of finding and destroying the enemy in the area was also given the regiment.

The tunnels area consists of two high ridgelines running north and south with a small valley in between. It is through these high ridges that railroad tunnels have been constructed. The small valley

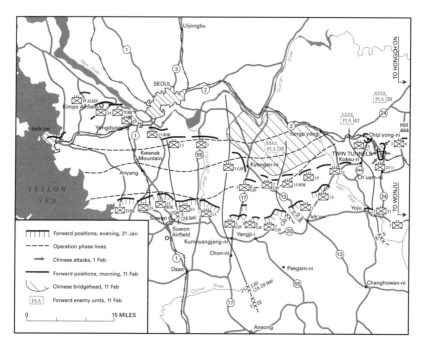

Operation Thunderbolt, 1–11 February 1951 (based on U.S. Army Center of Military History map).

is closed at the north by a small east-west ridge, and is completely encircled at the south by Hill 453.

The 3d Battalion, 23d Infantry Regiment, and the attached French Battalion were given the mission of clearing the tunnels area.

Colonel Freeman, the commander of the 23d Infantry Regiment, directed the two designated battalions to move the night of 30 January into an assembly area near Changsan, about four miles northeast of Yoju. The 1st Battalion, 23d Infantry, was to move forward to the Munmang-ni area and patrol to the north and northwest to maintain contact with the two attacking battalions; the 2d Battalion, 23d Infantry, was pulled back to the X Corps defensive line. The units began moving at 1630, and all had closed into their new positions by 2230 hours. The next morning the attacking battalions left their assembly area at 0600 and moved north about 6,000 yards to the line of departure near Chisan-ni, which they crossed on time at 0900

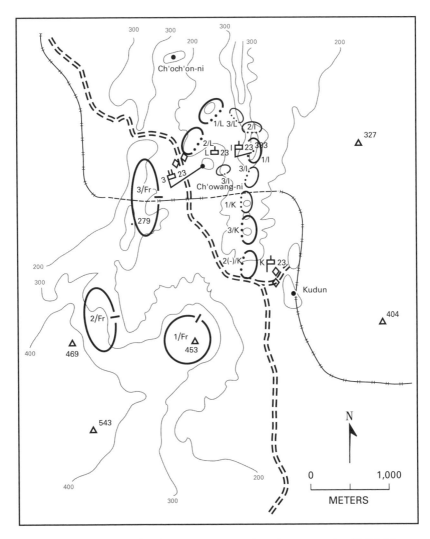

Twin Tunnels area and defensive positions (based on maps in CMH Manuscript 8–5.1A BA 84, Twin Tunnels).

hours. Lieutenant Mewha describes the advance north to the twin tunnels area and the occupation of defensive positions.

The French had a 1,000-yard front to the left of the Chip'yong-ni road, and the 3d Battalion was on the right side with a 2,000-yard front. The weather was clear and cold, and several inches of snow were on the ground.

The 3d Battalion moved out on foot in a column of companies in the order of Companies K, I, and L with the mission of "finding, fixing, and destroying the enemy." Company K screened the highest ground to the right of the road; Company I screened the lower ground from the base of the high ground to the road; and Company L was in battalion reserve following behind Company I. Tanks from the regimental Tank Company and several flak wagons [antiaircraft self-propelled weapons] from the 82d AAA Battalion preceded the vehicular column (vehicles of the battalion forward CP, the heavy weapons company, and organic vehicles of the French Battalion), paralleling the advance of the troops on the high ground on each side of the road. The battalion rear CP, consisting of battalion headquarters (-), medics, kitchen trains, ammunition point, battalion S-4, and battalion motor pool, remained at the assembly area but later moved to the vicinity of Chisan-ni. The 37th Field Artillery was in position at Chisan-ni and was supporting the advance of the attacking battalions. Company B, 23d Infantry, provided the security defense of the rear area.

Company K screened the high ground on the right without enemy contact but was forced to hold on Hill 404 until the French Battalion came on line to the left. The French Battalion had extremely high ground—Hill 453—in its sector. The tanks and flak wagons proceeded on to the road junction west of Kudun, and Company I followed behind them. As Company I was passing Company K, 1st Lt. Charles Roberts, Company I executive officer, spotted two men, with field glasses, observing the 3d Battalion's advance from a high ridge 2,000 yards to the rear. This was reported to the 3d Battalion CP, and an L-5 liaison plane was sent over; no further contact with the men was made. Company I continued on to Kudun, passing some abandoned GI equipment and empty ration cans south of the village.

About 1300, Company I crossed the road junction and advanced up the high ground leading to the north-south ridgeline. The slope was so steep (45-degree angle) that in some places the men had to pull themselves up. The high ground in the twin tunnels area was the only terrain adjacent to the road junction that could be defended effectively. When Company I reached the top, four hills were seen to the north along the ridgeline, and each one was higher than the other—like a ladder. The hills were approximately 300 to 500 yards high and were covered with small pines about the height of a man's head. Thick underbrush covered the slopes, and snow was on the ground, drifted in some places to two to four feet. The company advanced northward up the ridgeline with the 2d Platoon taking the first hill and holding while the 3d Platoon took the next. On the second hill, five American bodies were found. Some were badly mangled as if beaten around the head with rifle butts; others were bandaged and looked as if they had put up a struggle before being shot; one had been shot through the head at close range. The men were mostly Hawaiian or Puerto Rican, but one had red hair. Some of the men in Company I were new men and had never seen a dead GI before and wanted to turn the bodies over. Lieutenant Roberts kept them moving and told them that they were dead Koreans. One man remarked: "It's the first time I saw a red-headed Korean."

The next two hills were taken without incident. Hill 333, the last hill and dominating terrain, was used as the Company I CP. The ridgeline then angled slightly to the left (northwest) and continued to a small saddle then up a small knob about thirty feet high. The knob sloped off to the north into a draw. The 2d Platoon, Company I, was given the mission of defending the knob; the 1st Platoon dug in around the company CP; and the 3d Platoon was on the right flank. One squad from the 3d Platoon outposted a small finger to the rear of the company CP. Company I arrived in position about 1630, and the men still were digging in after dark.

In the meantime, Company L continued northward up the valley and about 1430 reached the road junction where two squads were ordered to mount three tanks and go on an advance reconnaissance up the northwest road. The remainder of Company L proceeded up the northwest road on foot. When the tank-infantry force, together with two flak wagons, reached a point where a ridge finger extended near the right side of the road, the infantry squads dismounted and went to the high ground.

As Company L (-) approached the village of Ch'owang-ni, it observed the wreckage of five jeeps, one three-quarter-ton truck, and five or six bodies. The bodies had been stripped of their cloth-

ing and burned, and the vehicles had been machine-gunned and
napalmed. Someone had shoveled snow on the bodies in an attempt
to hide them. One Korean apprehended in the area said that he
watched a North Korean force ambush the patrol.

At 1700 Company L arrived at the tanks that remained on the
road near the ridge finger. The platoons were each assigned a section of the high ground, and the 2d and 3d Platoons immediately
moved out. The 1st Platoon screened Ch'owang-ni and found five
Korean men, dressed in dirty white clothes, in a bunker-type dugout
to the rear of one of the huts. In the house later occupied at the
company CP, several Korean packs (quilted blankets used to carry
clothes and rations) containing various items of Korean and GI
clothing were found. As the 1st Platoon continued on to the high
ground, 1st Lt. William Sanford spotted a German shepherd dog
running northward on the ridge. When the men finally reached the
top, the dog was seen running northward up the valley to the northwest, never stopping or slackening at the houses. The men thought
the animal might have been carrying a message.

The ridge finger defended by Company L went up sharply from
the road and gradually sloped upward to the east for approximately
500 yards and then went into a saddle (50 yards) that led to a high
rocky peak (75 feet) near the north-south ridgeline. A saddle then
extended to the south of the rocky peak along the north-south
ridgeline. The 2d Platoon, Company L, defended the ground nearest
the road; the 1st Platoon defended the rocky peak; and the 3d Platoon defended the saddle on the north-south ridgeline. The 2d Platoon, Company L, tied in by fire with the French Battalion on the
left side of the road (Hill 279). Company L dug in after dark.

The entire ridge finger occupied by Company L was covered
with heavy underbrush and small pines about waist high; several
inches of snow covered the ground. The 3d Platoon had a front of
600 to 700 yards to cover with thirty-five men; gaps of 50 to 100
yards existed between the squads; and one squad had a 200-yard
front to cover with six men. The 1st and 3d Platoons, Company L,
were unable to dig foxholes in the rocky shale, and it was also impossible to dig rocks from the frozen ground to make barricades.
The 1st Platoon, Company L, extended about 35 yards southward

down the slope of the rocky hill toward the 3d Platoon, but a gap of 200 yards existed between the two.

In the meantime, Company K remained on the high ground until the French Battalion came on line about 1630. It then moved to Kudun, where the men ate supper while the platoon leaders with the company commander reconnoitered the valley to the northeast. When the men returned, Lt. Col. Charles Kane, 3d Battalion Commander, ordered Company K to defend the high ground splitting the road junction. Company K's sector extended from the right flank of Company I on Hill 333 southward to the road junction. The 1st Platoon, Company K, tied in with Company I, and the 3d Platoon was in the center of Company K's sector. The 2d Platoon guarded near the road junction, and two of its squads acted as a security force for attached tanks, guarding against a possible enemy attack from the northeast. As Company K was going into position, it passed the bodies noticed by Company I.

Organization of the positions on the high ground surrounding the tunnels continued through the night. Colonel Freeman would have preferred not to occupy Hill 453 because it stretched the defensive line far beyond that which normally could be held by two battalions. However, because Hill 453 dominated the area, one French company was positioned there. The remaining two French companies occupied the north-south ridge west of the 3d Battalion, 23d Infantry, sector. Large gaps remained in the perimeter, especially the 500 yards between Companies I and L. The night was unsettled, as Lieutenant Mewha relates in his narrative.

The men in all the companies were very uneasy and on edge. "We took the terrain too damn easy," one man said. Sgt. James Jones, Company I, said that when Lieutenant Roberts spotted the two men on the way to the twin tunnels area, a rumor started that an enemy company was on the high ground to the east. Shortly after dark, the men at Company I's CP spotted a small searchlight to the extreme left flank of the French Battalion on the left side of the road. This was reported to the 3d Battalion CP by the company. The men in the 3d Platoon, Company L, spotted small lights—similar to pencil flashlights or small tips of phosphorous—flickering on and off on the high ground to the southeast. The range was too great for 81mm mortar fire, and for some unknown reason artillery fire was not placed on the area. "We had a feeling we were going to get it," one man in Company L said. As the men in the 2d Platoon, Company L, were digging in, thirty-five to forty men were seen in the village of Ch'och'on-ni, and the 2d Platoon placed small arms and mortar fire on them. Harassing mortar and artillery fire was placed on the village all night.

The night was extremely quiet other than the intermittent mortar and artillery fire, and the men in the companies were placed on a 50 percent alert—one man asleep in a foxhole while the other remained awake. At 2400–0100 a bugle was heard to the northeast and another answered it to the east. However, there was no enemy attack. About 0200, small arms fire was heard in the French sector on Hill 279, about 2,000 to 3,000 yards to the rear of Company L's positions. PFC Cecil Eide remarked that when the shooting started, he had diarrhea but wouldn't leave his foxhole. "I just dropped my drawers and let it fly," he said. During the firefight, the French were heard yelling: "Banzai, Vive La France." Approximately fifteen to twenty flares were dropped in the French sector by the Air Force, and friendly artillery (37th FA Battalion) supported the French defense. Intermittent fighting lasted throughout the night in the French sector.

About 0315 bugles were again heard in the east, northeast, and northwest. The men were immediately placed on a 100 percent alert. About forty-five minutes later, men in the 1st Platoon, Company K, heard movement near the railroad bridge in the valley to the northeast, and red and green flares were being sent up from the high ground to the east.

No enemy attack came until just before dawn, when a Chinese regiment, later identified as the 374th Rifle Regiment of the 125th Division, hit the northeast sector of the perimeter manned by Companies I and L. The French Battalion on the southeast sector was attacked about 0600 hours by the 373d Rifle Regiment. Lieutenant Mewha describes the initial fighting of Company K and the fierce struggle of Company L to hold its positions.

At 0420–0430, the enemy attacked the 3d Battalion from two and possibly three different directions. An unestimated number of enemy opened fire with .51-caliber and .30-caliber machine guns on the tanks supporting Company K at Kudun. Approximately twenty minutes later, an enemy group of 75 to 100 was seen by Company K on the high ground to the east, and artillery and 4.2-inch mortar fire was placed on them with undetermined results. This was the only contact with the enemy Company K had with the exception of the 1st Platoon, which later assisted Company I.

Simultaneous with the attack on Company K, a column of approximately 500 enemy troops marched south from the general direction of Ch'och'on-ni and were spotted by a guard on the tanks and flak wagons near the 2d Platoon, Company L. The tanks fired on the column, but it never broke formation. Some of the leading elements approached close enough to throw a grenade into one of the flak wagons, and the vehicles withdrew to the 3d Battalion CP at Ch'owang-ni. The guards returned to the 2d Platoon. When the vehicles withdrew, the enemy deployed and attacked the French to the left of the road, and placed small arms, automatic weapons, and mortar fire on the 2d Platoon, Company L. The enemy mortar position was later silenced by counter-60mm mortar fire.

The enemy bypassed the 2d Platoon, Company L, and went eastward up a draw leading to the north-south ridgeline. An outpost of the 1st Platoon, Company L, saw approximately 500 enemy approaching the ridge on the double in a "column of deuces hub to hub." When the enemy failed to halt when challenged, the outpost guard fired a clip of BAR [Browning automatic rifle] ammunition into their ranks, but the enemy never faltered. Three other BARs in the platoon fired six or seven clips at the enemy, but they never broke formation. They did return fire with automatic weapons but kept approaching the rocky hill held by the 1st Platoon, Company L. Suddenly they echeloned to the right around the hill, and the 1st Platoon fired into their flank for ten to fifteen minutes; however, they never slackened or broke formation. An enemy soldier shouted a command, and several whistles and bugles started to blow a tempo similar to "Taps" or "Adjutant's Call." Firing was then heard in the 3d Platoon's sector.

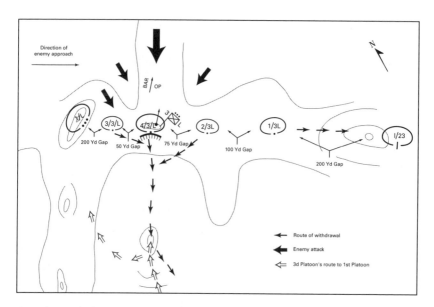

Attack on 3d Platoon, Company L (based on a sketch by M. Sgt. Henry Bagley; not to scale).

The 3d Platoon, Company L, had a 600-yard front to cover, and there were gaps of 50 to 100 yards between squads. The saddle defended by the 3d Platoon had three little rises of ground, each about ten to fifteen feet high, and in the center of the saddle, a ridge finger extended in an eastward direction. The 4th Squad covered the finger with a machine gun, the 3d Squad was on its left, and the 2d was on the right. The 1st Squad was to the right of the 2d Squad, but a gap of 200 yards existed between the two. The ridge finger was out posted to the east about fifty yards with two men, PFC Philip Nako-moura and Cpl. Alessandrino Buluran, with a BAR.

At about 0530 the men on the outpost were heard throwing hand grenades, and about ten minutes later the men withdrew to the platoon and said "bunches of Chinks were coming up the hill." Some of the men in the 3d Platoon evidently didn't know the men had returned and called: "Hey Philip, what's wrong?" A voice called back in perfect English: "Yes, this is Philip." Nakomoura then said: "That's not me, I'm right here."

About ten minutes later the 3d Platoon, Company L, was hit from four directions by an enemy using small arms, automatic weapons, and grenades. The platoon sergeant tried to contact the company CP for artillery support but was unable to reach it by phone. SFC George F. Bammert, communications sergeant, said Company L was trying to contact the 2d Platoon at the same time to see what was happening in its sector; 2d Platoon was receiving small arms, automatic weapons, and mortar fire from a ridge finger north of its position. The platoon sergeant of 3d Platoon, M. Sgt. Henry Bagley, then called for 81mm mortar fire, but couldn't contact Company M by phone. He then tried Channel 37, Company M's fire channel, but got no answer. Sergeant Bagley said that someone was evidently asleep.

The 3d Platoon's machine gun fired down the ridge finger to the east for about thirty minutes, and 1st Lt. Malcolm Aldrich ordered the 3d Squad behind the 4th to reinforce its fires. The 2d and 1st Squads remained in place. The machine gun then ruptured a cartridge, and Lieutenant Aldrich "lost his head." He ordered the two squads (3d and 4th) to withdraw to the reverse slope and to lay prone on the ground. He wouldn't let them get up. "The men showed outward signs of nervousness knowing the lieutenant was inexperienced," Bagley said. Aldrich and a sergeant then went to the top of the saddle and stood firing carbines at the enemy. A burp gun burst wounded the lieutenant in the leg and the sergeant in the stomach. The sergeant fell forward, but Aldrich ran a few steps to the rear and rolled down the slope about fifteen feet.

In the meantime, the enemy had infiltrated unobserved in the heavy underbrush between the foxholes of the 2d Squad and was firing at the men on the reverse slope. About 0630 someone yelled, "Let's get the fuck out of here." The men then fled to the rear, abandoning two radios, and yelled over to the 1st Platoon: "Don't shoot, it's us—the 3d Platoon." Some of the men grabbed Lieutenant Aldrich and assisted him down the hill. The 2d Squad heard the men running to the rear and pulled out behind them. Because of the gap between the 1st and 2d Squads and the fact that the enemy had infiltrated between them, the 1st Squad withdrew through the 2d Platoon, Company I.

As the 1st Platoon, Company L, heard the men in the 3d Platoon shouting, Lieutenant David Mock, 1st Platoon leader, called the

Company L CP and asked if the 3d Platoon was still in position. At the CP, Capt. Chester T. Jackson, Company L CO, had a radioman contact the 3d Platoon and received the answer that it was all right and was still in position. About five minutes later, Mock called again and said the 3d Platoon was withdrawing to the rear. At the very same time, Sergeant 1st Class Bammert in the company CP was talking to someone using the 3d Platoon's abandoned radio. "It was a normal voice speaking excellent English, and he said: 'No, we're still in position.' They were using our company call signs, too," Bammert said.

At about 0700, the 3d Platoon, Company L, reached a trail that led to the rear of the company CP; and as the men were stumbling and half-running down the trail and were about 200 yards from the CP, a voice with a French accent called out: "American?" As the men in the platoon tried to explain who they were, Aldrich struggled to his feet and started running toward the company CP. He called back to the men: "Boys, I may be hit, but you can see what I can do."

When the 3d Platoon, Company L, disintegrated, the enemy attacked the 1st Platoon, Company L, on the right of the saddle, forcing it to withdraw to the 2d Platoon, Company L's sector. There the enemy was halted. The enemy, however, switched his main attack on Company I. When the 3d Battalion CP, near Ch'owang-ni, learned that the 3d Platoon had given away, the supporting tanks trained their weapons at the draw. Evidently this discouraged the enemy from attacking down the draw.

Colonel Freeman had ordered forward the 1st Battalion, 23d Infantry, as reinforcement when the strength of the Chinese attack was recognized in the early morning. But it would take several hours for them to reach the twin tunnels area. The morning continued foggy and overcast, preventing air support or effective observed artillery and mortar fire. While heavy fighting shifted from Company L to Company I, a crisis point soon was reached in the French sector. About 1030 hours the Chinese reached the top of Hill 453, but a fierce counterattack by the French drove them off. Coordi-

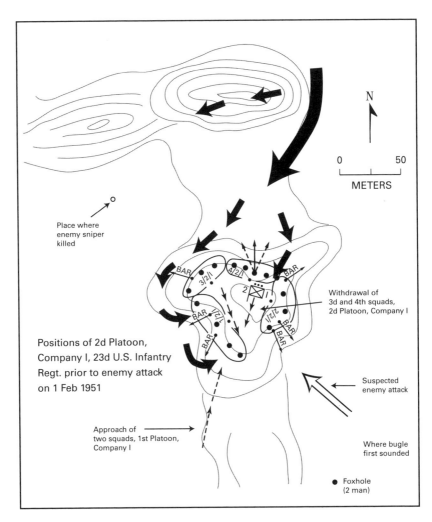

Attack on 2d Platoon, Company I, 23d U.S. Infantry Regiment, 1 February 1951 (sketch 2, Comapny I Interviews, CMH Manuscript, 8–5.1A BA 84, Twin Tunnels).

nated attacks against the French and Companies I and L continued through the morning. By noon the Chinese had seized high ground in the northwest sector and brought direct fire on the regimental CP and trains in the valley. The French 3d Company, under cover of tank and recoilless rifle fire, attacked and drove the Chinese back.

Company I and the French continued to hold their positions, but at a high cost. Lieutenant Mewha continues his narrative of the fighting in Company I's sector.

The 2d Platoon, Company I, occupied a small knoll northwest of the Company I CP. The knoll was separated from the rest of the high ground to the south by a small saddle, and it was thirty feet from the base of the saddle to the top of the knoll. The top of the small hill measured about 50 to 75 feet across and sloped abruptly to the left rear into a draw. Another abrupt draw was to the right rear, and a little finger extended to the northeast. To the north of the knoll, the ground sloped into a saddle approximately 800 yards long (extending in a northward direction and defended by the 3d Platoon, Company L) and then went up to a hill that dominated the knoll. The knoll and the hill to the front were covered with thick underbrush and pines ranging from waist high to head high. Some of the trees were two or three feet apart. The ground was covered with two or three inches of snow.

The 1st Squad, 2d Platoon, covered the left side of the knoll and had two BARs guarding the draw to the left rear. The 3d and 4th Squads protected to the north and had a machine gun strongpoint. The 2d Squad covered the right slope and had one BAR covering the small finger and two others guarding the draw to the southeast. Most of the men had poor fields of fire due to the heavy underbrush and had to break branches from the pines in order to see.

At 0430, a bugle blew directly in front of Company I's CP, and another blew directly west of the 2d Platoon. Sgt. Teeter Rampandahl, 2d Platoon guide, ran over to the 2d Squad and warned them to prepare for an attack up the draw to the right rear. Rampandahl then went to check on the other squads. Just then Company L was attacked in the draw to the north of the knoll, and at about 0545, a squad from the 3d Platoon, Company L, came through the 2d Platoon's Company I positions and passed on to the south. At the same time a squad from the 3d Platoon, Company I, on the finger to the rear of the company CP started to receive small arms and rifle grenade fire; it was thought that it was overhead fire from Company L's sector falling on the position. Some short 81mm mortar rounds fell near the finger.

About 0600, the 3d and 4th Squads, 2d Platoon, started receiving small arms and automatic weapons fire from the hill to the north. It was light enough to see down the saddle a short way, but a heavy mist prevented good observation. M. Sgt. Junior Crayton, 4th Squad leader, said he could hear Americans and Chinese yelling and shouting in the saddle. When the fog intermittently dispersed, the men in the 3d and 4th Squads saw the Chinese coming over the hill through Company L's position in "droves." Crayton said, "They were in a column of deuces hub to hub." Sgt. Teeter Rampandahl immediately reinforced the 3d and 4th Squads with one man out of each of the 2d Squad's foxholes (the men were occupying two-man foxholes). During this time, the 3d and 4th Squads were firing small arms and machine guns on the enemy on the hill to the north. Not many were actually seen, but the pines could be seen moving "all over the hill," and branches could be heard cracking. Crayton was with the gunner at the time, and both were so intent on watching and firing on the hill to the front that they didn't see the enemy crawling up the slope of the knob toward them. When the branches started rattling below, they tried to place machine gun fire on it, but the firing pin broke. Rampandahl came up and said that he would get another, but he never came back. Crayton and the gunner had a rifle and a .45 pistol with them and continued firing on the enemy. Both were wounded by enemy small arms fire within a few minutes but joked about who would go to Japan first with his wounds. After ten minutes Crayton realized that Rampandahl wasn't coming back and yelled to the riflemen on each side to cover them while they withdrew because they were short on ammunition. He received no answer from the riflemen on either side. The two men then got out of the foxhole and ran to the reverse slope.

Prior to this, the 3d Squad Leader, Cpl. Robert E. Logan, was killed by small arms fire. When the men saw Logan fall, they fled to the 2d Squad's positions about thirty-five to forty yards to the rear on the reverse slope. When the fighting started, some of the enemy infiltrated around the base of the knoll and started attacking the 1st Squad. The squad leader shifted his men from the reverse slope around to the west to meet the enemy attack. The 2d Squad then shifted to cover the reverse slope. From the 2d Squad's positions just below the crestline on the reverse slope, the men could see the hill to the north. "The enemy was so thick on that hill that the trees were actually shaking," said Sgt. James Jones. When the men from the 3d Squad and the replacements from the 2d Squad came over the hill, Rampandahl and Jones threatened them with rifles and told them to go back and protect the wounded. Three or four men were lying near their holes, moaning and screaming. It took about five to ten minutes to get the men organized, and in the meantime the enemy had reached the top of the knoll. The three squads then remained together and actually sprayed the top of the hill with small arms and BAR fire. The men saw Crayton and the gunner running toward them and held fire for a minute. One of the men yelled: "They'll use the machine gun on us." Crayton replied, "Oh, no, they won't. The firing pin's busted."

As the men were standing there firing over the underbrush, 1st Lt. Thomas Craig, 1st Platoon leader, came around the knoll from the right on the reverse slope. A rifleman, mistaking him for an enemy soldier, opened fire. Jones grabbed his rifle and said: "If you can't see, get the hell off the hill. You'll kill some of our own men." The men in the three squads were now out of their foxholes, shifting around to avoid concussion grenades that the enemy was lobbing over the forward slope. One of the Chinese who reached the top of the hill started to slide into a foxhole. A rifleman hollered: "Don't shoot him, it's a GI." Sgt. Hubert Lee yelled: "GI, hell," and shot him through the head three times—"to make sure he was dead." The dead enemy soldier had a brown quilted uniform and a GI pile hat. Because of grenade fire, the friendly forces withdrew five feet further down the reverse slope.

The 1st Squad, Company I, never left its positions and kept firing at the enemy, who attempted to infiltrate up the hill and the draw to the left. At 0900 the squad was reinforced by two squads from the 1st Platoon, Company I, and together they set up a small perimeter. A machine gun was placed facing the crest of the knoll to prevent the enemy from attacking down the slope toward them. Fire was also placed on the crest to protect the wounded who lay where they fell and to give covering fire to the 2d Squad.

The Chinese had seen the men on the reverse slope and knew

where to throw their grenades. Every time they threw one, they yelled: "OK, Joe." The men were "damn mad" and "didn't want the Chinks to have the satisfaction of running us off the top" and wanted to banzai them back off. "It was suicide standing there with the grenades (a potato masher–type concussion grenade) coming down on us," Jones said. However, Lieutenant Craig said to hold for a few minutes because mortar fire was coming. The 81mm mortar forward observer would not come close enough to the knoll to observe fire, and when he did, he called for one round of white phosphorous, which landed in the company CP. 1st Lt. Charles Roberts told him not to call for anymore.

At 1015 the men in the three squads charged up the slope about ten feet, firing from the hip. The enemy grenades "sailed" over their heads and landed to the rear, where they had been before. By laying down a steady barrage of small arms and BAR fire, the men forced the enemy to withdraw to the forward slope. When the men reached the crest, small arms and automatic weapons fire was received from the hill to the front and from the little finger that extended to the right off the knoll. About 1030, the men started running low on ammunition, and the enemy, noticing the slackening fire, fixed bayonets and charged the top. The squads withdrew to the reverse slope again.

Rifle ammunition was sent up to the squads, but it was loaded in .03 clips, which necessitated reloading into M1 clips. The company was completely out of carbine ammunition, and the ammunition bearers carried the weapons back to the company CP, where they were stacked. The men picked up rifles from the wounded and continued fighting.

Some Chinese infiltrated to the draw to the left rear and placed automatic weapons fire on the men on the reverse slope. The men on the slope could not see them, but a machine gun burst from the 1st Squad silenced them. Someone, possibly an enemy, could be heard yelling, "Medic." The medical NCO, "who fought with the rest of us," wanted to go down but was restrained by Sgt. Hubert Lee.

At 1045 Lieutenant Craig appeared with a squad of riflemen from Company K. The squad had two BARs, and Craig ordered them to distribute the grenades so that each man had two grenades.

He then told all the men to fix bayonets, every other man to throw a grenade and to charge the crest. The other men were then to throw their grenades. However, most of the men threw their grenades the first time and, when they reached the top, met heavy small arms fire from the hill to the front and from the forward slope of the knoll. Some of the men said that the order was not practical—that the range was too great and the underbrush too thick to throw grenades. They thought they should have waited until they reached the top of the crest before throwing them. Some of the enemy were seen taking the 4th Squad's old positions, and fire was placed on them. Sergeant Jones remarked: "I wasn't scared right then and killed several gooks with my rifle; then I caught a slug in my leg and got scared as hell. Then I knew they were playing for keeps." The men had to stand to fire over the underbrush, and two or three were wounded by enemy automatic weapons fire coming in about two or three inches off the ground. At 1110 ammunition again ran low, and the men withdrew to the reverse slope, firing only at the enemy as he appeared on the skyline.

About 1130 the men were reinforced with two more squads from Company K. The men formed a close skirmish line and charged to the top again, forcing the enemy to withdraw to the forward slope. While on top, five or six were hit by effective sniper fire that seemed to be coming from a group of trees in the draw about 300 yards to the left front. This sniper also wounded several men in the 1st Squad, which still remained in position. Finally the sniper was located and killed with a BAR burst. After twenty minutes, the men were again forced to withdraw to the rear slope because of a shortage of ammunition. They were resupplied on the reverse slope. Mortar fire was not used again because of the close proximity of the friendly troops to the enemy.

At noon, approximately twenty-five rounds of friendly artillery landed beyond the hill to the north. The day was very misty and foggy, and observation was poor. Artillery was called for and received three times during the course of the battle, but the fire was very ineffective.

At 1300, on the third charge up the slope of the knoll, some men from Company M brought up a water-cooled machine gun and left it near the crest to the rear of the 1st Squad; the machine gunner was killed. Sgt. Richard Bass, Company K, whose weapon had been destroyed by small arms fire, manned the machine gun and raked the top, shifting the gun whenever men called for close fire support. During the entire time he was firing, he griped about not having enough pipe tobacco. Finally he was given some more and sat behind the gun "smoking up a storm." The water-cooled machine gun was hit by a burst of enemy burp gun fire that also stunned Bass. A man in the 2d Squad covered him with BAR fire while he crawled to safety behind the reverse slope. Again the men were forced to withdraw.

Two more times the men retook the knoll (five times in all) but were forced to withdraw each time when ammunition ran low. About 1630–1700, the men again formed a skirmish line, went to the top, and forced the enemy to withdraw. The men continued toward the forward slope for about ten yards and saw many enemy and friendly dead. By this time the 2d Platoon had lost twenty-eight out of thirty-eight men, but the remaining men were determined to stay and protect the wounded. Ammunition was so low that the men were searching the ground for loose rounds; some fixed bayonets. Enemy soldiers were seen jumping from tree to tree with striplings tied to their backs and waists as camouflage.

Just then, a liaison plane circled overhead. The mist had lifted, and the sky was clearing. Some yelled over the firing, "Air support's coming, and it's going to be close." During the night an air panel had been placed on the forward slope of the knob near the top, and after the fighting started, it was so located as to be between the Chinese and the 2d Platoon, Company I. The enemy evidently knew an air strike was coming when they saw the liaison plane, for they lobbed many more grenades up the slope and attempted to crawl up to seize the panel. However, the men kept them away with small arms fire.

The plane circled low over the panel and fired a yellow flare, to indicate a target to fighter planes, which landed in the middle of the panel about twenty-five yards in front of where the men were fighting. During this time, four jets were circling overhead, and as soon as the liaison plane departed, they came in and strafed the ridgeline to the north. On the second pass, they strafed again, and on the third run, they rocketed the valley to the northeast and the ridgeline to the north. Four Navy Corsairs then came over and strafed "every inch of the ground to the front," flying approximately fifty feet off the ground. The enemy broke and fled to the north, with the remaining men in the 2d Platoon firing after them. After a few minutes all firing ceased. "I was not ashamed to admit tears were in my eyes when I saw those planes," Sergeant Bass said.

After the action ceased, it was found that Company I had expended 23,000 rounds of small arms ammunition, killing an estimated 637 Chinese.

A total of twenty-four fighter sorties struck the Chinese and, combined with mortar and artillery fire, eventually drove the enemy from the high ground. By 1800 hours the 1st Battalion, 23d Infantry, arrived and went into position, allowing the 3d and the French Battalions to pull back to reorganize. During the twelve-hour action, the two battalions lost 45 killed, 207 wounded, and 4 missing. Casualties inflicted on the enemy included 1,300 dead. The estimated total casualties for the enemy were 3,600. The 23d Infantry remained in position the next day without any contact and the following day began their advance to Chip'yong-ni. It became apparent that, because of crippling losses to the 373d and 374th Regiments, the Chinese 125th Division was no longer a combat effective unit. On 2 February, based on the successes at Hill 312, Twin Tunnels, and elsewhere, General Ridgway ordered the ROK I Corps on the eastern UN flank and the X Corps in the center to join the I and IX Corps advance to the north. Operation Thunderbolt would continue.

Chapter 7

OPERATION ROUNDUP

Supporting the ROK Troops

The strong attack on units of the 23d Infantry Regiment south of Chip'yong-ni in the Twin Tunnels area confirmed intelligence reports of a large Chinese buildup between Chip'yong-ni and Hongch'on. From this area the enemy could launch an offensive either south into the Han River valley or down the Wonju road, with both axes of advance directed on the UN lines of communication linking the U.S. I and IX Corps with the supply base at Pusan. To disrupt the enemy preparations for such an advance, General Ridgway approved a plan prepared by General Almond's X Corps, Operation Roundup. The plan called for the two ROK divisions of X Corps, supported by U.S. artillery and armor, to advance on Hongch'on, while simultaneously the ROK III Corps to the east moved forward. The ROK advance in the X Corps area would begin on 5 February, after U.S. units secured forward support positions, including Chip'yong-ni, occupied by the 23d Infantry on 3 February.

Meanwhile to the west, Operation Thunderbolt continued as the U.S. I and IX Corps maintained their deliberate advance toward the Han River, thoroughly searching the occupied area to eliminate all enemy forces. By 11 February resistance in front of I Corps had disappeared, but the enemy facing IX Corps put up fierce resistance and launched powerful counterattacks. By 10 February, it was clear that the Chinese planned to retain a strong fifteen-mile-wide position south of the Han in front of IX Corps to prevent direct observation and artillery fire on their staging area north of the river. Air observers north of the river reported numer-

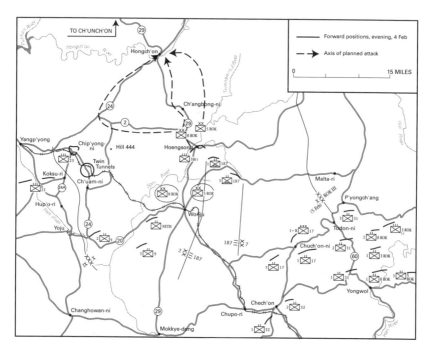

Operation Roundup, the X Corps plan, 4 February 1951 (based on U.S. Army Center of Military History map).

ous enemy forces moving east, but poor weather limited the effectiveness of air strikes. Eighth Army intelligence officers estimated that four Chinese armies, some 110,000 men, were massing in front of X Corps and would be ready to attack as early as 15 February.

Ridgway, on 11 February, recognizing the danger to X Corps, halted the advance to the north and expressed concern over the complex command arrangements Almond had created for Operation Roundup. The 2d Division Command Report for February 1951 describes the situation.

The X Corps plan for Operation Roundup envisaged a double envelopment of the enemy in the vicinity of Hongch'on. The 5th and 8th ROK Divisions were to be employed in the attack. The 2d Division was to support the attack of the 8th ROK Division by artillery and armored support protected by infantry units organic to the 2d Division. Support Force 21 was to consist of the 15th Field Artillery Battalion; Battery D, 82d AAA Battalion; and the 1st Battalion of the 38th Infantry, which was to provide close-in support. Operation Order 23 directed establishment of Support Team A, organized by the 9th Infantry Regiment with Company K and a platoon of its Tank Company, while Support Team B was composed of Company L of the 38th Infantry and a platoon of its Tank Company. Each of these teams was to be further subdivided into smaller teams capable of independent action. The support teams were to operate under the operational control of the commanding general of the 8th ROK Division.

The 38th Regimental Combat Team (RCT) concentrated its forces in the Hoengsong area during the first few days of February preparatory to carrying out its proposed commitments in support of the 8th ROK Division. Operation Roundup commenced on 5 February, the 38th RCT limiting its activities to close-in patrolling to prevent any possibility of fights caused by improper identification of the Korean units during the period that the 8th ROK Division moved through its zone.

The situation along the twenty-five-mile front [of the division] was very fluid during the early period of Operation Roundup. As it was impossible to cover the entire area from fixed defensive positions, the 9th RCT continued its aggressive patrols that combed the central sector in an attempt to wipe out the great numbers of small, infiltrating enemy units. The constant threat to the division sector from enemy along the Han River corridor to the division left flank made it imperative that the 9th be immediately available should this threat develop.

Although the CCF 125th Division withdrew completely from the 23d RCT area after its abortive attempt to drive the regiment from the tunnels area, there were constant probing attacks of North Korean units, which frequently infiltrated to considerable depth. Enemy patrols in the Hoengsong area were particularly active.

The 8th ROK Division ran into trouble shortly after launching its attack, and reports were soon received by 2d Division headquarters of attacks by a CCF division. By the 10th of February, it had become obvious that there was a large enemy buildup north of the 23d RCT, and it became apparent that the enemy was preparing an offensive not only to drive the 23d from its perimeter in the

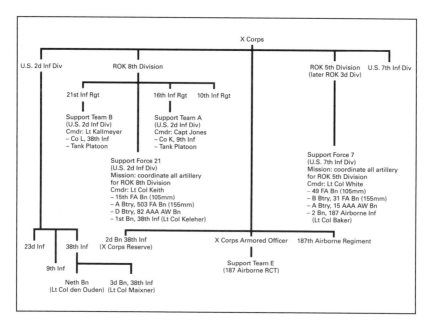

Operation Roundup, ROK support forces (original by author).

Chip'yong-ni area, but also to push back the entire front. Thousands of enemy troops moving south had been observed by planes operating in the area. There had been numerous reports from friendly agents of continuous movements into the area and indications of a pre-assault concentration of troops during the daylight hours on the 10th.

There was little activity along the division front on the 11th. Nevertheless, Eighth Army was anticipating a heavy attack along the entire front, and X Corps was notified that the 8th ROK Division was to remain in position. There was to be no further movement north or west unless cleared by Eighth Army.[1]

As an experiment to increase the combat effectiveness of the South Korean troops, General Almond created temporary American organizations, support forces and support teams, to bolster the advance of the two ROK divisions against Hongch'on. Support Forces (SF) were under the operational control of the 8th ROK Division (SF 21 provided by the U.S. 2d Division) and the 5th

ROK Division (SF 7 provided by the U.S. 7th Division). Each support force had a 105mm field artillery battalion and a 155mm field artillery battery. The mission of these forces was to provide direct support artillery fire to the ROK division and to coordinate all artillery fire, including the ROK artillery assigned to the division, within the division zone. In addition to coordinating artillery, to provide local security each support force had an infantry battalion, augmented with a battery of heavy antiaircraft weapons used for direct fire; the commander of the support force was the artillery battalion commander. On 11 February the 3d ROK Division replaced the 5th ROK Division in the drive on Hongch'on; Support Force 7 switched its support to the new division at the same time. Support teams, consisting of a platoon of tanks and an infantry company, provided support directly to ROK regiments. Two support teams operated with the 8th ROK Division: Support Team A, attached to the 16th ROK Infantry Regiment, and Support Team B, attached to the 21st ROK Infantry Regiment.

Control of the support forces and support teams ran from X Corps to the ROK divisions and, in the case of support teams, to the ROK regiments. Communications were difficult in the mountainous region. In the event that the ROK divisions came under attack and were forced to quickly withdraw, communications with and control of the support forces would be doubtful. The 2d Division and especially the 38th Infantry Regiment were concerned about the vulnerability of their units supporting the ROK troops and their limited ability to influence the situation in the event of a crisis. Moreover, vesting the command of the support forces in the artillery battalion commander, instead of the infantry battalion commander, posed potential problems. Clear-cut command responsibility and unified organization were lacking.

Support Force 21: Action at Ch'angbong-ni

On the evening of 11 February, the 8th ROK Division was deployed across an eleven-mile front with significant gaps between its regiments. The 21st ROK Regiment was astride Route 29, the Hoengsong-Hongch'on road, nine miles north of Hoengsong; to its

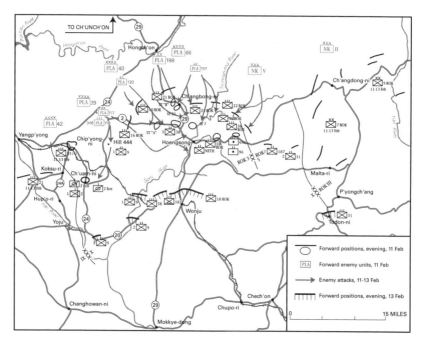

Battle for Hoengsong, 11–13 February 1951 (based on U.S. Army Center of Military History map).

left across a three-mile gap was the 10th ROK regiment; one mile to the left of the 10th was the 16th ROK Regiment astride Route 2, a mountain road connecting Route 29 and Route 24, the main Hongch'on-Chip'yong-ni road. Support Team B was on Route 29 two miles to the rear of the 21st ROK Regiment. Support Force 21 was one mile further back at Ch'angbong-ni. The 3d Battalion, 38th Infantry, was in position as ordered by X Corps at the junction of Routes 29 and 2 at Saemal, and was under corps orders to secure the road junction; Support Team A was two miles west of Saemal on Route 2 at Ch'owon-ni. Lt. Col. William P. Keleher, the commander of the 1st Battalion, 38th Infantry, the infantry protection for the support force, describes the situation at the start of the enemy attack.

On 11 February 1951 Support Force 21 displaced to Ch'angbong-ni. This was the farthest point north that we reached. Hill 930 overlooked this position and had not been cleared of the enemy. The

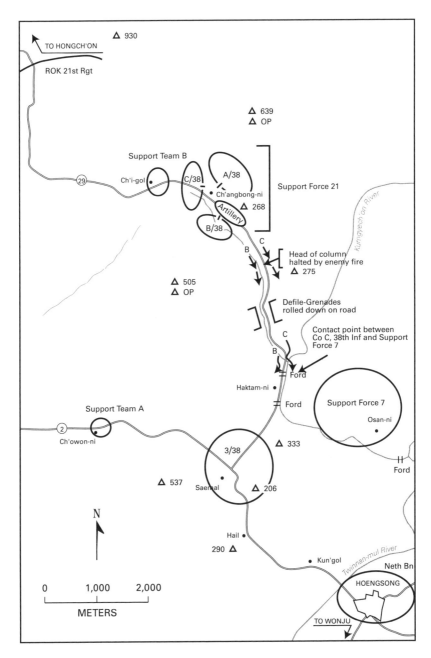

Route of withdrawal on situation night, 11 February 1951 (original map by author).

21st ROK Regiment was still attempting to clear this hill. At about 2130 hours, the 21st ROK Regiment was counterattacked and started falling back. At about 2200 hours, Support Team B [which had been forward supporting the 21st ROK Regiment] joined Support Force 21. Major Blackwell, 1st Battalion, 38th Infantry S-3, contacted the 21st ROK Regiment KMAG [American advisors in the Korean Military Advisory Group] and the Commanding Officer, 21st ROK Regiment, and attempted to get them to stay in position until the 21st Support Force could be loaded up. Lieutenant Colonel Keith [Support Force 21 commanding officer] contacted General Haynes, the 2d Division Artillery CG, to have him contact the 8th ROK Division CO in an attempt to have him get the 21st Regiment to hold until Support Force 21 could load up. These efforts to get the 21st ROK Regiment to remain were unsuccessful.

Lieutenant Colonel Keith ordered Support Force 21 to load up as soon as possible and prepare to move back to the area occupied the night of 10 February [about three miles south near Haktam-ni]. This was about 0200 hours, 12 February. At about this time, elements of the 21st ROK Regiment had begun to stream through the 21st Support Force area, heading generally south.

Support Team B was ordered by me to send one section of tanks and one platoon of infantry to protect the bridge just north of Haktam-ni. Just short of this bridge, the driver of the lead tank was blinded by an enemy hand grenade, and the tank went out of control, ran off the road, and turned over. The other tank was knocked out by bazooka fire. It was off the right side of the road. It is not known what happened to the tank crews or platoon of infantry. The remainder of Support Team B was held in reserve with Support Force 21.

At about 0230, Company A started receiving automatic weapon and small arms fire on its portion of the perimeter [north of Ch'angbong-ni]. No vehicles of Support Force 21 had begun to move south at this time. Mortar fire was falling in the assembly area of Support Force 21. By 0300 Company A was under general attack by an estimated 300 enemy.[2]

Confusion reigned in the ROK 8th Division and Support Force 21. When the initial Chinese attack hit the ROK 21st Regiment, the

This chain of vehicles, lined up bumper to bumper, inches its way along the withdrawal from Hongch'on to Wonju on 3 January 1951. The distance of 36 miles between the two towns took 10.5 hours to cover.

A freehand sketch of Wonju after the battle, made by a representative of the X Corps historical section in April 1951. The destroyed railroad bridge is visible in the background. The highway bridge in the center of the picture has since been repaired. The church building in the left foreground contained small arms ammunition and Korean rifles, which were destroyed by 1st Lt. William H. Champion, Company C, 2d Engineer Combat Battalion.

(Above) Soldiers of Company B, 9th Infantry, stand a "warm" shift in their foxhole overlooking the Wonju area on 19 January 1951. A few nights before, the mercury here dropped to 21 degrees below zero. On the left is Sgt. James McLeroy, and on the right is SFC Nelson Lee. (Right) The men of the 2d Infantry Division used this bypass to enter Wonju.

The battle on 24 January 1951 left Wonju in virtual ruins.

Parachutes carrying vital supplies for the 2d Infantry Division drop from a C-119 and float earthward, south of Wonju. The poor condition of the roads, combined with winter weather, led to an increased reliance on the air delivery of supplies.

The hulk of a C-46 Commando lies on the makeshift evacuation strip near Wonju, after colliding with two other C-46s during landing.

Soldiers of the 9th Regimental Combat Team warm up around
a fire on 26 January 1951 before starting on a patrol north of
Wonju.

(Above) M-4 tanks of the 9th Regimental Combat Team probe the area north of Wonju during their advance against Chinese Communist Forces on 26 January 1951. (Below) An armored patrol of the 9th Regimental Combat Team advances northward from Wonju on 26 January 1951.

Twin Tunnels area. Company L defended the ridge finger, with the 2d Platoon nearest the road, the 1st Platoon occupying the high hill topped with three trees, and the 3d Platoon defending the saddle. One of the railroad tunnels is visible in the background.

Twin Tunnels area. The arrow indicates the probable direction of approach used by the enemy to bypass the 1st Platoon, Company L, and hit the 3d Platoon, Company L, in the saddle. The attack then continued against the knoll occupied by 2d Platoon, Company I (left foreground). The saddle is approximately 800 yards wide.

Twin Tunnels area. Company I defended Hill 333. This picture was taken from a position occupied by Company K. The railroad bridge is in the right foreground.

Twin Tunnels area. A hand-to-hand counterattack drove the Chinese off the hill.

Operation Roundup. 1st Lt. George W. Gardner served as commanding officer of Company A, 1st Battalion, 38th Infantry.

Operation Roundup. Capt. Chester B. Searls served as commanding officer of Company B, 1st Battalion, 38th Infantry.

Operation Roundup. 1st Lt. James H. Jacobs is pictured after he was promoted to captain and became the acting commanding officer of Company C, 1st Battalion, 38th Infantry.

Operation Roundup. 1st Lt. Earle M. Welch of Company C, 1st Battalion, 38th Infantry.

(Above) Operation Roundup. The destroyed village of Ch'angbong-ni surrounded by hills. (Below) Hills in the foreground were defended by Company C at Ch'angbong-ni; Hill 930 can be seen in the background.

Operation Roundup. High ground dominates the road south of Ch'angbong-ni.

Operation Roundup. This destroyed prime mover belonged to the 15th Field Artillery Battalion.

Operation Roundup. 1st Lt. Duncan MacLeod, executive officer of Company A, led a successful attack on this hill, clearing it of enemy forces who were firing on the road.

Operation Roundup. The enemy rolled grenades onto the road at this point on the route.

Operation Roundup. Hills overlook the assembly area of Support Force 21 at Saemal.

Operation Roundup. The enemy dug hasty positions on the high ground near Saemal.

Operation Roundup. Capt. Chester Searls took cover under this bridge near the village of Hail.

Operation Roundup. Massacre Valley, as seen looking north from Hoengsong.

Operation Roundup. Well-concealed enemy emplacements overlook the main supply route in Massacre Valley.

Operation Roundup. A ford is located beside the destroyed bridge at Hoengsong.

An aerial view of Chip'yong-ni's southern perimeter shows Company G's positions atop the dominant terrain south of the railroad.

Chip'yong-ni. Company G's rear area positions are marked: 1. Company G command post; 2. 1st Platoon command post; 3. Battery B, 503d Field Artillery Battalion gun positions; 4. Battery B squad tent.

Chip'yong-ni. Number 5 indicates foxhole positions of the 2d Platoon, Company G, on the main line of resistance. The platoon position, located in rice paddies, provided good fields of fire toward the enemy (indicated as "E"). Company F's position is marked as number 6.

Chip'yong-ni. The village of Masan lies at the base of the main line of resistance of the 3d Platoon of Company G (indicated as number 7). Number 8 and the arrow indicate the direction of Chinese assaults on the nights of 13 and 14 February 1951. The arrow marked "S" indicates that Masan is south of the 3d Platoon positions; the direction of the photograph is looking north from Masan.

Chip'yong-ni. Cpl. Eugene L. Ottesen's squad location on the left flank of the 3d Platoon, Company G, is indicated as number 10a. The arrow labeled number 9 indicates the direction of the Chinese assault, along the ridge leading to the position, on the nights of 13 and 14 February 1951. The direction of the photograph is southeast toward Hill 397 in the distance, not southwest as marked.

Chip'yong-ni. Looking south from the position of Company G: Number 10b shows the direction of the Chinese withdrawal on 14 February 1951; number 11 marks the culvert; number 12 shows the main supply route used by Task Force Crombez; number 13 marks the dead spot in the dry creek bed.

Chip'yong-ni. This view from the dead ground in the dry creek bed looks north toward the positions of Company G. The clump of trees on the high ground (number 15) is the same clump as seen in the previous photo overlooking the dry creek bed. Number 14 indicates a rude Chinese shelter. The arrow marked "SW" indicates that the photographer is looking southwest.

Chip'yong-ni. The knoll on the small hill mass was occupied by the 1st Platoon, Company G, on the right flank of the 3d Platoon. Number 16 indicates holes dug by the Chinese during the attack. Number 17 marks the main line of resistance of the 1st Platoon.

Chip'yong-ni. V cut where the main supply route crossed the 23d Infantry lines. Number 18 shows the machine gun position manned jointly by the artillery and infantry; number 19 indicates the location of a minefield. The area marked by number 20 was covered by barbed wire. Number 21 shows the position of the 1st Platoon, Company G. The French were positioned to the right of the machine gun.

Col. Marcel Crombez (left), commanding officer of the 5th Cavalry Regiment, talks with Maj. Charles Parziale, operations officer of the regiment.

(Above) The 5th Cavalry Regiment crossed the pontoon bridge over the Han River near Korun-ni during its advance to relieve Chip'yong-ni. (Below) The advance of Task Force Crombez began in this low-lying area just north of Sangch'ohyon-ni. The road to Chip'yong-ni traverses the hills in the distance.

(Above) This view from west of Koksu-ri looks southeast toward the southern outskirts of the village and the road to Chip'yong-ni. Task Force Crombez advanced along the road between the village and the hill to the right, and continued on the road to Chip'yong-ni to the left. (Below) After entering the 23d Infantry's southern perimeter, Task Force Crombez moved north to this highway underpass and railroad bridge on the southern outskirts of Chip'yong-ni.

North of the highway underpass, the town of Chip'yong-ni lay in ruins.

8th Division commander, Brig. Gen. Choi Yong Hee, ordered the regiment to fall back a short distance. Soon after, the Chinese 198th Division struck in full force and began moving around both flanks of the 21st Regiment. Communications were soon out between regiment and division, and the 21st was in full retreat. Simultaneously, Chinese divisions struck the 10th and 16th Regiments of the division. General Choi and his staff had their hands full, and by 0100 on 12 February, communications were broken between the division and all of its regiments and within each regiment, with the command posts of the 10th and 16th Regiments being overrun. The 8th Division rapidly disintegrated as an organized unit.

By the time that the seriousness of the situation was recognized by Support Force 21, there was a command vacuum, because the communication link to X Corps through the ROK division was broken. Attempting to communicate through the U.S. 2d Division took time, and it was not until 0245 hours that Colonel Keith received permission from X Corps to withdraw. The column was moving south within fifteen minutes, but by this time the enemy had closed on Support Force 21. Chinese troops penetrated the weakened defensive perimeter. As Battery A, 503d Field Artillery, was preparing to move out, enemy troops entered their position, killed several drivers, and captured others, including the battery commander and first sergeant. The problems of Company B are described by Capt. Chester B. Searls, the company commander.

Company B manned the battalion perimeter on hills south of Ch'angbong-ni. A company outpost was on Hill 505. About 0200–0300, Company B received an order to be prepared to move out, and about five minutes later the order to move came. Upon receiving the order, I notified all of my platoons to assemble in the kitchen area on the rice paddies. Fire was coming from Company A's sector at this time. As I was getting my CP ready to move, the 1st Platoon came down off its position and the 3d Platoon started to move across the rice paddies from its position when it came under heavy fire from the high ground in Company A's sector [Hill 268] and from Hill 505, where the company OP was located. Because of the heavy fire, the 3d Platoon cut south and rejoined the company on the road. When the 1st Platoon left its position, the enemy moved in

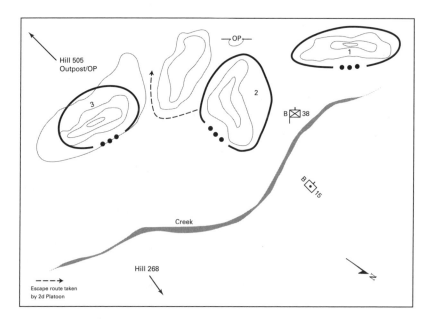

Withdrawal of the 2d Platoon (based on a sketch by SFC Floyd W. Frazier).

and cut off the 2d Platoon. The last I heard from Lieutenant Faulk, 2d Platoon leader, was that he was taking the platoon up into the hills in a southeasterly direction in hopes of cutting back to the road. The platoon never rejoined the company; one sergeant managed to get through.[3]

Sergeant 1st Class Frazier, platoon sergeant of the 2d Platoon, describes what happened to Lieutenant Faulk's platoon.

At 2130 Lieutenant Faulk, 2d Platoon leader, received a call from the company CP placing the platoon on a 100 percent alert for a possible attack. Between 2400 and 0100 another call was received telling the platoon to move back to the company CP, and that the company was moving out. ROK soldiers were then straggling through the 2d Platoon's positions and were going south and west into the hills.

I sent word out to the platoon to pack and to move down to the foot of the hill where the platoon CP was located. At 0210, the platoon had assembled and started to move to the company CP. Small arms fire could be heard in the valley near the artillery position of Battery A, 15th Field Artillery Battalion. As the platoon reached the riverbed and started toward the company CP, heavy machine gun fire forced the platoon to withdraw. Lieutenant Faulk ordered the men to turn back and go up the valley separating the 2d and 3d Platoon's positions. The lieutenant told me that there was a chance to rejoin the 1st Battalion further down the road. The valley ran into another draw extending southward, and the platoon followed it along with some ROK soldiers. From the valley we could see troops skylighted on the hillcrests on the left of the Hongch'on-Hoengsong road and could hear them digging emplacements. I asked an ROK soldier if they were speaking Chinese, but I could not get the ROK to understand; finally he said that they were Chinese. About 0630–0700, the platoon spotted enemy soldiers on the hill to the front and saw a column of troops approaching up the valley approximately a hundred yards away. Visibility was poor, and the enemy did not spot the platoon immediately.

I ordered the men up a hill on the immediate right and told Lieutenant Faulk that I was going to take the men over the hill in hopes of finding another escape route before daylight. When the platoon was halfway up the hill, the lieutenant hollered, "GI?" and the enemy opened up with automatic weapons fire. The platoon reached the other side of the hill and returned fire with small arms, BARs, machine guns, and one mortar belonging to the ROKs. At this time some stragglers from Company L, 38th Infantry Regiment [part of Support Team B that had been with the 21st ROK Regiment], and some Negro soldiers from the 503d Field Artillery Battalion, joined the platoon.

One man was killed and one wounded at this time. Lieutenant Faulk and four men were on a small knoll aiding the wounded man, and the lieutenant ordered me to take the remainder of the platoon over on the right flank of the hill. When I got to the right flank, I saw some enemy soldiers working up the valley and around the hill to the front. I immediately called over to the lieutenant, a distance of about fifty yards, and told him to bring the men over and get out before [we became] completely surrounded. He remained with the wounded man, and I told the men that we would try to escape before it was too late.

When the platoon started down the hill, the enemy opened fire with automatic weapons. At the bottom of the slope was a ditch approximately six feet deep. One man, Private Bowles, jumped into it and ran up the ditch until he got to another valley between the two hills. I followed him. When he reached the valley, he looked back, and the rest of the platoon had stopped. It was too great a distance to call, and so I came out with Private Bowles. I assume that the enemy had infiltrated between me and the rest of the platoon. Private Bowles and I went east over a mountain and reached positions of the U.S. 7th Infantry Division.[4]

The 3d Platoon of Company B was in a similar situation but was more fortunate than the 2d Platoon. The assistant platoon sergeant of the 3d Platoon, Sergeant 1st Class Robert P. Major, describes their experience.

The 3d Platoon went into position on a small hill separated by a draw from the 2d Platoon on the right. When the orders came to pull the platoon back to the assembly area, I was on the platoon OP with Lieutenant Brisbane, 3d Platoon leader. We could not see anything, but firing could be heard from the vicinity of the road to the east of the OP. The company mess tent was designated as the assembly area, and the 3d Platoon had to approach it through a draw. Enemy mortar fire was landing in the vicinity at the time, and friendly machine guns opened up on the platoon thinking that we were enemy troops.

Lieutenant Brisbane called Captain Searls and told him that he could not reach the assembly area because of the intense fire, and the captain told him to take the platoon to the road and rejoin the company at that point. Firing was coming from the vehicular column on the road, and the men had to jump and run between the ridges of the rice paddies, hollering, "GI." When the men approached to within thirty feet of the road, the firing ceased.[5]

Support Force 21: Fighting Withdrawal to Saemal

In the midst of confusion from the enemy attack and the ROK withdrawal through the positions of Support Force 21, the vehicle column began moving south on the Hoengsong road with the artillery units in the lead. Their short progress is described by Lieutenant Colonel Keleher.

At about 0400, the vehicles of Support Force 21 began moving south. The 1st Battalion, 38th Infantry, was deployed in a column of companies, Company B leading, followed by Company C, Headquarters, Company D, with Company A fighting the rearguard action. The head of the column had moved less than a mile and was just west of Hill 275 when it met very heavy small arms and automatic weapons fire. Several of the lead vehicles were knocked out, and drivers and other personnel on the vehicles were killed by bayonets or taken prisoner. In a few cases, they were stripped of their valuables and released.[6]

Meanwhile Company A, hit hard early on, was desperately fighting to hold off the enemy. First Lt. George W. Gardner, the company commander, describes the action.

Company A was on high ground north of the town [Ch'angbong-ni] with lines extending to the northwest toward Hill 930. The 2d Platoon was on the left flank crossing fire with Company C. The 1st Platoon was in the center of the company sector, and the 3d Platoon was on the right tied in with Company B. All crew served weapons and two M-16s [quad 50 half-tracks] from the 82d AAA Battalion were emplaced with the 1st Platoon. The mission of Company A was to supply local security for the 15th Field Artillery Battalion supporting an ROK attack on Hill 930. Battery A, 15th FA Battalion, was in the immediate rear of Company A. At this time the ROKs were continuing the attack. Patrols from ROK units were passing through the position of Company A's 1st Platoon. During the day [11 Feb] I, together with an ROK liaison officer, went out to check ROK positions in front of the 3d Platoon. I wanted to be sure they were ROK soldiers. Just prior to darkness I established a combat outpost on Hill 639; the artillery and 60mm and 81mm observers were located on the hill along with riflemen.

Sometime between 0100 and 0200, Major Blackwell, 1st Battalion S-3, called me and told me that the support force would withdraw and for Company A to load out our kitchen and supplies.

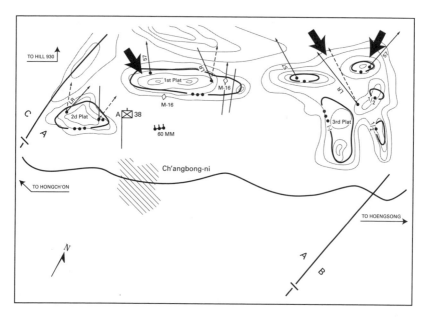

Company A, 38th Infantry (drawn by Lt. Duncan A. MacLeod).

Company A was to prepare to fight a rearguard action. Company A had experienced no enemy contact at this time.

A short time later several flares of various colors (amber, red, and light pale green) were observed to the north of Company A's positions. Immediately after the flares, the 3d Platoon received small arms and automatic weapons fire from the north. After a brief firefight, the 3d Platoon outposts were overrun, and the 3d Platoon leader, 1st Lt. Robert Novak, notified me that hand-to-hand fighting was taking place on the platoon's position. At this time approximately a reinforced company of Chinese troops attacked the 1st Platoon from the northeast, coming from the high ground overlooking the platoon's position. Mortars, automatic weapons, and grenades were used by the enemy, and bugles could be heard over the area.

I ordered the OP on Hill 639 to withdraw when the fighting first started. The group talked all the way in on SCR 300 radio to where the fighting was going on, and then said that they couldn't get through. I then instructed them to go east and south and to rejoin the company later. A "roger" was heard, but the group was never contacted again.

The enemy got on the 1st Platoon's position by destroying one squad. The remainder of the 1st Platoon and the 2d Platoon were able to contain the enemy on the high ground but suffered heavy casualties in doing so.

During this time the artillery, supply trains, and kitchens had moved on the road and started to withdraw toward Hoengsong. The column started to move south about 0400. In the meantime Company A withdrew from the high ground and established a perimeter defense in Ch'angbong-ni. At this time the company was receiving small arms fire from the southwest and heavy automatic weapons fire, mortar fire, and grenades from the high ground from which they had withdrawn. In returning the fire, all available ammunition was expended. Some riflemen went over and manned .50-caliber machine guns on abandoned equipment of the 503d Field Artillery Battalion. When the column began to move, some of the men had a few clips of ammunition and one machine gun had one box left.

I loaded the wounded on jeeps, the M-16s, and the tanks. Because of the time involved in doing this, contact with the enemy could not be broken. Consequently more men were wounded.[7]

First Lt. Duncan A. MacLeod, the executive officer of Company A, provides more details of their fighting withdrawal.

At 2400 Lieutenant Gardner received a call from the 1st Battalion alerting the company to the fact that the Communists were counterattacking; in essence it was a message to get ready to fight. Company A had an outpost on Hill 639 and had radio contact with them. An artillery forward observer from the 15th Field Artillery Battalion, an 81mm mortar forward observer from Company D, and one rifle squad in the charge of Sgt. Kenneth J. Gorman were manning the outpost.

Small arms fire started coming into the area at approximately 0100 and increased in tempo until approximately 0200. At this time intense small arms, automatic weapons, and mortar fire hit the company. Lieutenant Owens, 1st Platoon leader, was the first to report his positions under attack. Shortly after that, the 3d Platoon, commanded by Lieutenant Novak, also reported that they were under attack from the north and east. The 2d Platoon never came under attack until it left its original positions. The artillery forward observer, who was in charge of the OP, called in when the firing first commenced and asked permission to return to the company area. He was told to remain in position, but later when he said it was impossible to return to the area because enemy troops had infiltrated around the OP, Lieutenant Gardner told him to stay away from the road and to head south. The men never reached the company.

The 1st Battalion notified Company A that they were to hold and fight a rearguard action. During this time, the small arms fire kept increasing in tempo, and I saw an unbelievable number of tracers coming into the company area. The platoons were reporting time to time of their progress, and notified the company CP that they were suffering numerous casualties. Lieutenant Owens, 1st Platoon leader, was killed in about the first fifteen minutes of fighting.

Finally at approximately 0400 Company A received orders from the 1st Battalion to withdraw from their positions as soon as Battery A, 15th Field Artillery Battalion, had cleared their area and moved onto the road. Company A was to continue to provide rearguard protection for Support Force 21.

After Battery A moved out, Company A moved to positions astride the road in Ch'angbong-ni, exactly west of their original defensive positions. It took approximately thirty-five minutes to assemble what was left of the company and to organize them to move as a tactical unit. Part of the company with me held in the town for approximately thirty minutes while the rest had crossed the creek and joined two tanks from the 72d Tank Battalion. They were attached to us by the 1st Battalion to assist the company in the rearguard action. At this time word was received from Lieutenant Gardner for the men to move on southward, fighting a rearguard action, until they rejoined the remainder of the company. During this withdrawal, the 3d Platoon, which had been cut off, rejoined the company on the road. Lieutenant Novak had been wounded. When Sergeant Copenhaver and I rejoined the company with the men, we found that the support force had bogged down and was not moving. During this time the column was drawing heavier and heavier fire from the east and northeast. ROK stragglers were scattered throughout the column trying to find a place to hide. The column remained halted until shortly after daybreak.[8]

Maj. Jack Rodearme, 1st Battalion executive officer, describes the conditions in the convoy.

I directed the vehicles on to the Hoengsong road in proper order. The column proceeded about 1,000 yards south and came under heavy small arms fire from the high ground to the east of the road. The 1st Battalion commander had instructed me to keep the [infantry] vehicles slightly to the rear of the foot troops. When the column halted I went forward to the head of the column to see what had happened.

Upon reaching the head of the column, I found that the lead vehicles from Battery A, 15th Field Artillery Battalion, and a prime mover of Battery A, 503d Field Artillery Battalion, had been ambushed. Some of the drivers from the 503d FA Battalion had established a small perimeter near the road. At the time, a warrant officer (name unknown) came up thoroughly frightened and stated that he had been captured by the Chinese and released. All of his valuables had been taken. The warrant officer told me that the Chinese had captured some of the men and had bayoneted others. No bodies could be seen, however. When I tried to get someone to drive the wheeled vehicles and the prime mover, the men around said they couldn't drive. Drivers for the wheeled vehicles were obtained from Headquarters Company, 1st Battalion, and a driver for the prime mover was finally located. During this time, the entire column on the road was receiving intense small arms fire. Colonel Keleher ordered the 105s to go into position and fire point-blank. Four guns went into action and fired approximately seventy-five to a hundred rounds at ranges varying from 150 to 600 yards.[9]

To clear the road so that the support force could continue withdrawing, Lieutenant Colonel Keleher ordered Companies B and C forward. Company B was to attack on the west side of the road while Company C attacked on the other side. Company C met the stiffest resistance; the company commander, Capt. Leonard Lowry, describes the action.

About 0415 the company was on the road and heading south with the leading elements just south of Ch'angbong-ni. At this time, Colonel Keleher held up the company to allow some artillery pieces of the 15th Field Artillery Battalion to pass through to the south. Firing could be heard approximately a mile to the south, and word came back that the enemy had established a roadblock. During this time, Company C was still experiencing small arms and automatic weapons fire from the hills to the northeast. Colonel Keleher also instructed me to release the two tanks to Company A, which was to fight the rearguard action. Company C was ordered to attack down the left of the road, clearing the high ground, and Company B was to attack on the right in an attempt to remove the roadblock. The time of the attack was to be 0645. During the time the convoy was halted, four guns of the 15th Field Artillery had dropped their trails and were firing white phosphorous rounds point-blank at enemy positions to the left of the road and on the high ridges at an estimated range of 400 to 500 yards.

At 0645 the fire was lifted, and Company C jumped off in attack to the left with two platoons abreast—the 1st Platoon on the right and the 2d on the left. The 3d Platoon was in support near the road. Visibility was poor, due partially to the haze created by the artillery fire. The advance was very slow up the steep terrain, and when the platoons reached to within twenty-five yards of the crest, they came under small arms, heavy machine gun, and grenade fire. The 2d Platoon eliminated one machine gun when Corporal Wall threw a hand grenade, forgot to pull the pin, and hit the gunner on the head, knocking him unconscious.

During this time the column on the road was moving forward. I was with the 3d and 4th Platoons at this time, and ordered the 3d Platoon to follow the road paralleling it on the left. Contact with parts of the 1st and 2d Platoon was lost when elements became split due to smoke, casualties, and poor visibility. The 3d and 4th Platoons continued approximately one and one-half miles down the road, receiving enemy fire from hills to the left. I instructed Lieutenant Teets to stay with the vehicles while I went back to see what had happened to the 1st and 2d Platoons. It was now approximately 0800, and I thought that we were clear of the roadblock. On the way back I met the platoons and immediately started south. There was no enemy fire at this time on Company C, but firing could be heard to the rear.[10]

Other members of Company C provide additional details.

The company started to move down the road [near Ch'angbong-ni] when they came under enemy automatic weapons fire. Captain Lowry ordered the men off the road into the rice paddies and told them to march south toward the head of the vehicular column. Before reaching the front, the column moved about three-quarters of a mile and stopped. Word reached the company that the Chinese were up to the trucks and captured men from the 15th Field Artillery Battalion. At this time some 105mm artillery pieces dropped their trails and were firing WP [white phosphorous] point-blank into the hills at a range of 100 to 300 yards.

At about 0530 Colonel Keleher called for all the company commanders and gave them the order to clear the hills of the enemy. Company C was to clear the hills on the extreme left of the road. The attack was to begin at 0610.

Artillery and Company C's 60mm mortars gave the company close support in the attack. The men reached the crest of the hill before being fired upon. BARs and grenades knocked out the enemy positions. One machine gun was captured and another silenced on the next ridge. Company C remained on the ridgeline for approximately one and one-half hours until the vehicular column moved. The column during the attack was under heavy small arms, automatic weapons, and machine gun fire from a high hill to the right of the road. The company moved down to the road and assisted in loading the wounded and dead on the vehicles.[11]

Company B had an easier time clearing the right of the road, as members of the company recall.

Captain Searls, commanding officer of Company B: When I reached the head of the column, Colonel Keleher told me to take the company and clear the high ground to the right of the road.

Major Blackwell and I took some riflemen up the hill, but the enemy had withdrawn by this time. Some 105s of the 15th Field Artillery had dropped their trails on the road and had been firing point-blank on the enemy prior to Company B's assault. The company then returned to the road and got the dead and wounded drivers out of the vehicles. Drivers were furnished by Company B. About 0800, approximately a company or more of ROK troops came streaming out of the hills in a disorganized mob with no officers or NCOs. I forced some down the road as a point for the column. At any little fire, they ran to the hills and ditches, so Company B took over as point.

As the column moved out again, I observed the enemy on a high cliff on the left overlooking the road [about 1,000 yards south of where the column was first halted] throwing grenades down into the path of the column. Small arms and BAR fire was placed on the cliff, dispersing the enemy and permitting the column to move forward.

SERGEANT 1ST CLASS MAJOR, ASSISTANT PLATOON SERGEANT, COMPANY B: Upon reaching the road, I tried to locate the company but could not find it. About 0600–0630 a colonel, whom I did not recognize, came along the road and ordered me to move the platoon down along the edge of the road and place fire on the hills to the left. The platoon advanced approximately 800 to 900 yards when Captain Searls caught up with us. Artillery was firing point-blank on the hills to the south. The platoon remained in a skirmish line along the road until daylight, receiving some small arms fire from the hills to the left.

The platoon leaders regrouped their men, and a plan of withdrawal was worked out. The 3d Platoon was to put two squads on the hill to the right of the road as a flank guard for the column. The weapons squad and one rifle squad were to take from the creek to the bottom of the hill, and the 1st Platoon was to take from the road to the creek in a skirmish line. The company moved out in a skirmish line formation at 0700, and there was no enemy fire at the time. About 0730, the two squads on the hill came under enemy small arms and automatic weapons fire. I was with the two squads at the time and ordered the men to a higher ridge to the left; and from there, the two squads came down from the hill and rejoined the company near a bridge.[12]

Colonel Keleher describes the effort in getting the convoy moving again.

On the east side of the road C Company met stubborn resistance, while B Company on the west initially met light sporadic resistance. C Company was successful in eliminating their resistance and continued sweeping the high ground.

Considerable time was spent finding drivers for the leading twelve or fourteen vehicles. Most difficulty was found in trying to obtain drivers for the prime movers for the 155mm howitzers [M5 Tractors]. Disabled vehicles were pushed aside, and the column moved on, keeping abreast of B and C Companies. After moving about 1,200 yards, the column received extremely intense heavy mortar fire. After C Company swept the high ground on the east side of the road, the enemy moved back on the high ground above the road and placed intense automatic weapons fire on the motorized column. Headquarters Company of the 1st Battalion was committed and was successful in eliminating this fire. Disabled vehicles were pushed aside and the motorized column continued.[13]

The column was halted again near a bridge north of Haktam-ni by fire from the surrounding high ground. Company B deployed west of the Kumgyech'on River, while part of Company C cleared the enemy from the high ground east of the river. Several officers of the battalion describe the action.

LIEUTENANT COLONEL KELEHER: The concrete bridge was covered by automatic weapons fire from the south, west, and east. Intense heavy mortar fire was also falling at this point. Company B covered the bridge while the motorized column crossed the bridge. As Company B covered the bridge and high ground, the rest of the 1st Battalion fought their way through and continued toward the 3d Battalion.

CAPTAIN SEARLS, COMPANY B: I took my company across the bridge at the end of the defile and deployed it across the valley on the right. Small arms, 57mm, machine gun, and BAR fire was placed on a high nose of a hill on the left while Company C was attacking it. This was done to permit the convoy to cross the bridge. The bridge was only capable of handling light vehicles, while the heavier equipment had to ford the stream. From the bridge to the 3d Battalion assembly area [around Saemal], the convoy only halted once because of enemy small arms fire.

CAPTAIN LOWRY, COMPANY C: When I reached the place where the 3d Platoon had been before, I was informed by Colonel Keleher that another roadblock had been encountered and that he had ordered the 3d Platoon to the high ground to the left in an effort to reduce the roadblock. I took the remainder of the 1st and 2d Platoons up to join the 3d, encountering light sniper and sporadic mortar fire from the northeast and to the west of the road. Upon reaching the 3d Platoon, I regrouped my company and found that the 1st and 2d Platoons were in fairly good shape, but that the 3d Platoon had lost approximately 50 percent of its men. A lieutenant from the 2d Battalion, 17th Infantry Regiment [infantry protection for Support Force 7 supporting the 3d ROK Division, which was in retreat], contacted the company at this time and wanted to know what was going on. He stated that the 17th Infantry had encountered no enemy but that the ROKs were moving south through their positions. The 2d Battalion, 17th Infantry Regiment, was in position east of Company C at the time.

A short time later, the company went back to the road and followed Company B south to the 3d Battalion, 38th Infantry Regiment, assembly area, arriving there around 1030–1100.

FIRST LT. JAMES H. JACOBS, EXECUTIVE OFFICER, COMPANY C: At 0900 the column was abruptly halted again by heavy mortar, machine gun, and automatic weapons fire from the hills to the left front. I was at the rear of the company on foot, and Colonel Keleher ordered me to gather what men I could and to clear the hills. I gathered approximately thirty men from various companies and formed a skirmish line in depth to assault the hill. One enemy machine gun was destroyed, and enemy soldiers (who were not entrenched) fled before the advancing troops. The men pushed on over the rugged terrain approximately 300 to 500 yards when the convoy started to move ahead. I ordered the men back to the column, joining it at the tail end. Sporadic mortar and grenade fire was hitting the column at this time. From this point until Company C reached the 3d Battalion assembly area at Saemal, very little fire was received.[14]

Company A meanwhile had broken through the encirclement and had closed with the column of vehicles about halfway between Ch'angbong-ni and Saemal. The head of the column began arriving at Saemal around 1000 hours, and the remainder of the vehicles of Support Force 21 closed into the area by 1100.

Initially many members of Support Force 21 believed that they had reached safety, but they soon learned that the Chinese attack had spread to Saemal. After destroying the ROK 8th Division and dealing a heavy blow to the ROK 3d Division in the east, the enemy was now intent on cutting off the American support units. The ordeal had just begun.

Chapter 8

OPERATION ROUNDUP

Escaping the Trap

The collapse of the ROK 8th Division and the ROK 3d Division to the east placed their American support units in extreme peril. The enemy rapidly moved south to block the escape of Support Teams A and B and Support Forces 7 and 21. Successful withdrawal depended on the defense of critical points on the escape route, such as Saemal and Hoengsong. The enemy first turned its attention to the elements of the 38th Infantry holding Saemal.

Defense of Saemal

When Support Force 21 arrived at Saemal, the 3d Battalion, 38th Infantry, guarding the road junction there, had been defending against an attack that had begun before dawn on 12 February. Although having only Companies I and K (Company L was part of Support Team B), they had held their positions. Captain Tate, the battalion S-3, describes the action.

At approximately 0130 hours enlisted personnel from Company K, 9th Infantry Regiment, started to arrive in the area occupied by Company K, 38th Infantry. The 9th Infantry men were members of a task force [Support Team A] that was attached to the 16th ROK Regiment, 8th ROK Division, which was now engaged to the front of the 3d Battalion perimeter. The wounded were taken to the 3d Battalion aid station for treatment, with all able-bodied men taking positions on the Company K, 38th Infantry, perimeter. Within a few minutes Company K, 38th Infantry, reported that the company

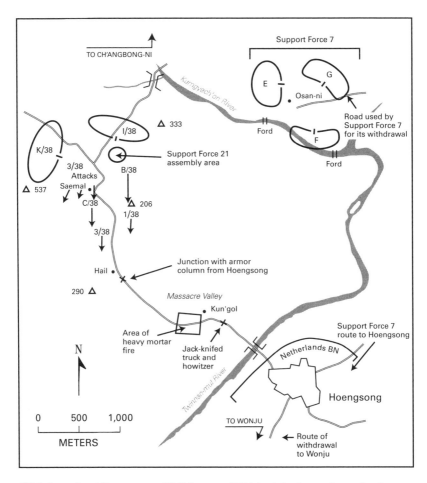

Withdrawal to Hoengsong, 12 February 1951 (original map by author).

commander of Company K, 9th Infantry, had arrived in their area slightly wounded and that he was being forwarded to the battalion aid station. Upon his arrival he was questioned by the battalion commander regarding the situation of the 16th ROK Regiment. Captain Jones stated that the 16th ROK Regiment had been overrun and that his company had been badly mauled. During the action he had lost most of his company and did not know where the remaining elements were located.

At approximately the same time, it became apparent that the 8th ROK Division was in full rout to the rear. Members of the division were streaming past the 3d Battalion CP moving south. Immediately Lieutenant Colonel Maixner [3d Battalion commanding officer] ordered a checkpoint be established at the Y junction in Saemal, where it would be possible to collect members from all friendly units who were retreating. Inasmuch as Colonel Maixner had no command control over the retreating ROK units, he directed that all ROK troops be held until contact could be made with KMAG officers. All other able-bodied men were utilized on the perimeter.

At 0200 hours, Company K reported observing concentrations of enemy in the vicinity of Ch'owon-ni. Immediately Colonel Maixner ordered his artillery liaison officer to request fire on this area. This fire was not received for hours due to the 8th ROK Division commander's reluctance to give the artillery clearance. It was apparent that it would be some time before the 3d Battalion would receive any artillery support; accordingly Colonel Maixner ordered Company M and Company K to fire all available mortars, machine guns, and automatic rifles on known enemy locations.

At 0300 hours the 3d Battalion was notified by the 1st Battalion, 38th Infantry, that they were given orders to withdraw. At the same time, Company K, 38th Infantry Regiment, reported that small arms and mortar fire was falling to their front in the vicinity of the east-west road. However, the company was not receiving any fire at this time. At 0330 hours Company I was receiving fire from Hill 333.

At the same time numerous individuals started to arrive at the 3d Battalion CP. Included in the arrivals were members of KMAG, 16th ROK Regiment, a liaison officer of the 82d AAA AW Battalion, and one artillery officer attached to Support Force 21. At this time the KMAG officers gave Colonel Maixner permission to use the retreating ROK units as he saw fit. Accordingly orders were given to use the ROK troops to hold the line. As the ROK men were being assembled, word was received from Company K that a ROK engineer unit, presumably a unit that was to attack to relieve the pressure on the 16th ROK Regiment, had taken up defensive positions with the right flank platoon of Company K. Colonel Maixner ordered that the commanding officer of this unit be sent to the 3d

Battalion CP to receive orders concerning the disposition of his unit on the perimeter. Upon arrival at the CP, the ROK officer stated that the 16th ROK Regiment CP had been overrun, whereupon Colonel Maixner ordered him to use his unit on the perimeter alongside Company K. To insure proper coordination, he was ordered to report to the company commander of Company K.

At 0500 hours the 3d Battalion was receiving medium caliber mortar fire. This fire was dropping in the vicinity of Company I and the 3d Battalion CP. At daylight Companies I and K were receiving heavy small arms fire, and by 0630 Company K was heavily engaged. Some of the enemy succeeded in getting into the perimeter by following close behind the retreating ROK troops. A few moments later an unidentified artillery officer arrived at the CP and stated that the enemy had set up a roadblock south of the 3d Battalion perimeter, thereby cutting the Saemal-Hoengsong road. Companies K and M were under small arms fire, and at approximately 0700, both CPs were overrun.[1]

The actions of Sgt. Charles R. Long of Company M, 38th Infantry, were instrumental in helping to hold the perimeter. Sergeant Long's heroism is described by members of the unit in their recommendations for award of the Medal of Honor.

COMMANDING OFFICER, COMPANY M, 38TH INFANTRY: At approximately 0300 hours, 12 February 1951, several thousand enemy troops attacked the 3d Battalion, 38th Infantry, in rugged mountain terrain in zero weather. Sergeant Long was serving as forward observer for the mortar platoon with a rifle company. When the unit was ordered to withdraw, Sergeant Long, deliberately and in the face of certain death or capture by the enemy, remained on his observation post in order to continue directing the fire of the mortar platoon while the rifle troops were withdrawing. All alone and with the enemy almost on top of him, he steadfastly and calmly relayed his observations and directed the fire over his radio, while holding the attacking enemy from his own position by firing his carbine and hurling grenades at them.

CPL. JOHN G. ZOELLER, COMPANY M, 38TH INFANTRY: I was listening to the radio in the company command post when Sergeant

Long called the company commander and reported the enemy was coming in several groups in large numbers. He reported he was going to direct mortar fire so the riflemen could withdraw and reorganize as they had been hit very hard. All the time he was calling the mortar fire closer to his position. Several minutes later he reported he was firing his carbine and throwing grenades at the enemy, which could be heard over the radio. His last report was that the enemy had closed in on him and all his ammunition was gone. He then called for fire on his position.

SERGEANT KILNER, COMPANY M, 38TH INFANTRY: On 12 February I had the 1st Section of the 81mm mortars, and Sergeant Long was on the forward OP. At approximately 0300 hours I received a radio call from Sergeant Long that the enemy was advancing in several groups in large numbers. He called for mortar fire on several targets and then would wait and observe, and in a few minutes call for more fire. This he did for a period of time, and then he reported that the enemy had broken through and was disorganizing the riflemen. He continued to observe and direct the mortar fire until the riflemen had fallen back to a fairly safe position. He reported to me on the radio that all the riflemen were clear now, and then he began to call for more fire. He then reported that the "Chinks" were very close and that he was out of grenades and carbine ammunition. A few seconds later he called to fire forty rounds high explosive rapid fire; then his radio went silent. Checking the map I discovered that he had called for the concentration to be fired on his position. Sergeant Long was killed in action.[2]

Captain Tate continues his account of the action in the 3d Battalion area.

At 0722 the battalion was notified by Support Force 21 that they were going to attempt to join the 3d Battalion by attacking south down the road. This information was passed down to the 38th Regiment [at Hoengsong] along with a request that Colonel Maixner be allowed to use Support Force 21 to strengthen his lines. Although K and M Company CPs were overrun, the perimeter was still holding fast and countermeasures were being taken to wipe out the enemy that was now in the perimeter.

At approximately 0730 hours the left flank of the 3d Battalion perimeter was heavily engaged; however, frontline positions were still intact. Mortar fire continued to be received by all elements of the 3d Battalion, and it appeared that the enemy was slipping around to the rear; the rear was then supplemented with more headquarters personnel. No sooner had the CP been strengthened than it started to receive small arms fire from the south. All indications pointed to the battalion being completely surrounded.

Sometime after 0900 hours, advance elements of Support Force 21 and Support Team B started to arrive in the 3d Battalion perimeter. Upon arrival Colonel Maixner ordered the artillery elements to place their guns in firing positions in the vicinity of the road junction. As soon as each gun had been set up, they started to fire direct fire on the hills to the east, south, and west. When remaining elements of Support Force 21 and Support Team B closed into the 3d Battalion perimeter, Colonel Maixner received a message from regiment stating that division had ordered Support Force 21 to return to Hoengsong. Regiment ordered the 3d Battalion to stay in position in the vicinity of Saemal until further notice.

During the period 0950 to 1200 hours, pressure on the right flank of Company K and the left flank of Company I was considerably relieved. The main threat to the battalion was from the south in the vicinity of the CP. During this period, the high ground [to the south of Saemal] was twice taken by the enemy, but on both occasions direct artillery fire and vicious counterattacks by personnel of Company K, 9th Infantry [Support Team A], artillery personnel, ROK forces, and headquarters regained the hill. In an effort to tighten the perimeter, the left flank of Company K was pulled in from Hill 537 about 900 yards to the east. Enemy activity in the vicinity of Hill 537 and the ridgeline running to the south commenced to increase. Simultaneously, the volume of fire from Hill 206 to the southeast was mounting. Both areas were taken under direct fire by artillery and AAA weapons (M-16s and M-19s).

The 3d Battalion aid station was overflowing with wounded. It was decided that the wounded be loaded on all available transportation and placed at the head of the vehicle column of Support Force 21. Upon reaching Hoengsong the wounded would be turned over to the Medical Clearing Company. At this time a helicopter landed near Saemal amid a rain of small arms fire to evacuate a seriously wounded soldier. In the process of helping the wounded man on the helicopter, two men were killed by small arms fire. Nevertheless, the helicopter was successful in evacuating the wounded man.[3]

Earlier in the morning an infantry and tank patrol moving north from Hoengsong discovered that the enemy had blocked the road just north of the town. The War Diary of the Tank Company, 38th Infantry Regiment, describes the patrol.

At approximately 0730 hours, the 1st Platoon, Tank Company, 38th Infantry Regiment, with 2d Lt. James Howden commanding, along with two tanks of the 9th Infantry and the security platoon of the 38th Infantry under command of 2d Lt. Francis Uzzo, were ordered to move north, clear the road, and effect a linkup with the 3d Battalion.

This force crossed the river and proceeded approximately 1,000 yards, where they were confronted by approximately 400 Chinese standing in a large group in the middle of the road. This force offered no resistance, and by their actions, such as laying down their weapons, waving white slips of paper, and so on, indicated their desire to surrender. The tank platoon leader radioed for instructions and was told not to take any chances, but to give them an opportunity to surrender, if that is what they desired. At this time another force of what was believed to be enemy was observed on the hills on both sides of the road, just as the warning of the presence of this possible enemy was radioed to the platoon leader. The enemy closed on the tanks, and the "surrendering" force on the road also opened. Lieutenant Uzzo was killed and SFC Jack Rogers, one of the tank commanders, was wounded while attempting to rescue the lieutenant.

The tank platoon engaged the enemy, inflicting heavy losses, which were estimated at 200 to 300 killed and wounded. The platoon was ordered to withdraw, as its position was untenable. At that time, the platoon leader's tank was hit by an undetermined weapon, slid off the road, and turned over. The platoon leader was pinned under the gun; Sgt. Freddie Clark and Cpl. Arthur Lockrem subjected themselves to intense enemy fire, but succeeded in extracting the platoon leader and returned him to the comparative safety of their tank.

The balance of the platoon then withdrew back across the river into Hoengsong. The tank that turned over caught fire and burned completely. Second Lt. William Todd was ordered to assume command of the 1st Platoon and place his tanks in a defensive position along the river astride the road leading out of Hoengsong.[4]

Cpl. James Lee, a member of the Headquarters Security Platoon, provides additional details of the patrol's combat action.

On the morning of 12 February, at approximately 0800 hours, the Security Platoon, of which I was a member, was acting as close-in security for six tanks from the 38th Infantry Tank Company. We had been given the mission of making contact with friendly forces that had been cut off in the vicinity of Saemal.

As we were crossing the river just west of Hoengsong, we observed one Chinaman walking toward us. We did not open fire on him, for we expected him to surrender; however, upon meeting up with him we discovered that we were wrong. He went through the motions of bringing his hands up in a fighting fashion, indicating that he wished to fight our platoon leader, Lieutenant Uzzo. He then went for his weapon, which was slung over his shoulder, in an effort to bring fire on Lieutenant Uzzo. Before the Chinaman could get his weapon down, Lieutenant Uzzo pulled his pistol and killed him. We continued on toward Saemal, and after crossing the river we observed five more enemy who quickly fired on us and then attempted to withdraw over a hill. We brought fire on them and killed them all.

Again we started forward, and after advancing 500 yards we observed approximately 200 men to our front. As soon as they saw us they started waving their hands, indicating that they were friendly. ROK units had passed through this area all night long; consequently we accepted them as ROK troops and allowed them to approach us. As they came within six yards of us, one of them said in English, "We are friends." This brought on an exchange of handshakes, for now we thought they were our ROK allies. As all of this was taking place, Lieutenant Uzzo noticed that many more men were appearing on the hills to our right, left, and front. At this time, the sixth tank, last in the column, opened fire at a group of men who had gotten around to our right rear, and was now holding this group under .50-caliber machine gun fire so they could not move in any direction. In the meantime one of the group that we had been talking to threw Lieutenant Uzzo a piece of paper which read: "Surrender, give up your arms and cartridge belts, and we will allow you to keep your personal effects. We will give you safe passage to your lines." This was the first indication we had that we were faced by enemy and not friendly forces. Lieutenant Uzzo told the platoon sergeant to withdraw the men and put them in a position ready to fire. Simultaneously, the lead tank, which was two feet from the platoon leader and six feet from the enemy, opened fire on the group with its machine gun.

Immediately, a bugle call was heard, and on this signal the enemy started to pour fire at the lead tank and Lieutenant Uzzo. Individual Chinamen attempted to drop grenades through the hatches of the two leading tanks, but were not successful because the tankers had closed their hatches. The tanks were unable to turn around on the road, so they started to move to the rear with all tanks going in reverse. The second tank misjudged the side of the road and turned over. We were now firing furiously, and the enemy force had built up to approximately 500. One burst from the enemy machine gun hit Lieutenant Uzzo in the back, causing him to fall in the ditch alongside the first tank. The members of the tank attempted to rescue him, but he stated that he was badly hit, and that they should continue to withdraw. It was impossible to get Lieutenant Uzzo at this time, for the enemy was completely covering the area that he was in. Soon Lieutenant Uzzo was hit in the chest with another burst of machine gun; however, he was still firing his weapon at the enemy when I last saw him.

The third tank attempted to get the CP by radio but was not successful. The enemy on the hills continued to move to the southeast in an attempt to encircle our group, but as we withdrew to the vicinity of the river, one of our tanks had already reached the east bank of the river and was delivering heavy fire on the enemy. Simultaneously, the Netherlands Detachment, in position on the northwest outskirts of Hoengsong, was able to take the enemy under fire and allow us to withdraw without further fire.[5]

In Hoengsong, the commanding officer of the 38th Infantry Regiment, Colonel John Coughlin, had few available options. Soon after 1100 hours, he received word that General Almond had returned control to him of the 1st Battalion, and a short time later, Almond ordered the 1st Battalion to withdraw to Hoengsong. However, his 2d Battalion was still guarding Wonju under 2d Division orders; his 3d Battalion was still under attack at Saemal with orders from corps to remain in place; and his only remaining unit, the Netherlands Battalion, was needed to secure Hoengsong. An enemy force had cut the road between Hoengsong and Saemal, and there was no force available to assist the 1st Battalion, already weakened by casualties incurred in their withdrawal from Ch'angbong-ni. Air strikes and artillery were placed on enemy positions between Saemal and Hoengsong, but Colonel Keleher's 1st Battalion troops would have to fight their way through the likely firetraps and roadblocks along the road by themselves. Additionally, any chances for the 1st Battalion to reorganize and recover somewhat before resuming the withdrawal were cut short by the enemy. Members of the 1st Battalion explain what happened upon their arrival at Saemal.

FIRST LIEUTENANT GARDNER, COMMANDING OFFICER OF COMPANY A: Upon reaching the 3d Battalion assembly area I immediately established security around Battery A, 15th FA Battalion, and resupplied the company with small arms ammunition. While the company was resupplying, the enemy attacked from the northwest and destroyed a squad outpost within 200 yards of Battery A; 120mm mortar fire and automatic weapons fire was received from the southeast and northeast. At this time Company A had approximately forty men and two officers.

FIRST SERGEANT COPENHAVER, COMPANY A: The forward elements of the company reached the 3d Battalion assembly area about 1030 and established security outposts to the north, east, and west. An outpost of fifteen men was sent to an outpost on the high ground about 600 yards east of the road junction, and as soon as they reached the knoll, about thirty to forty enemy troops were observed closing in on them. Hand-to-hand combat resulted for approximately five minutes. Artillery of the 15th FA Battalion, not knowing friendly troops were there, opened up with point-blank fire, forcing the enemy to withdraw.

FIRST LIEUTENANT MACLEOD, EXECUTIVE OFFICER, COMPANY A: The company commanders were summoned to the 1st Battalion CP, and I assisted in regrouping the remainder of the battalion. Approximately one-half hour later the area came under heavy mortar fire from 60mm, 81mm, and 120mm mortars; the heaviest concentrations were in the artillery area.

CAPTAIN SEARLS, COMMANDING OFFICER, COMPANY B: Everyone thought the action was over. The 1st Battalion arrived in the assembly area between 1030 and 1100. About 1130, enemy small arms fire and 120mm mortar fire fell into the assembly area. The fire was coming from the high ground on three sides: from the southwest, from Hill 333 to the northeast, and from Hill 206 to the southeast.

SERGEANT 1ST CLASS MAJOR, 3D PLATOON, COMPANY B: The company was in the assembly area approximately fifteen minutes when Captain Searls ordered the platoons to spread out among the rice paddies. Each squad was to be in one paddy. I was dispatched to draw ammunition, and when I returned, mortar fire hit the entire area. Simultaneously, small arms and automatic weapons fire came in from four sides, forcing everyone to scatter. Captain Searls tried to regroup the men and managed to round up eight out of the 3d Platoon. When the rest of the men regrouped, the company was broken down into two platoons.

CAPTAIN LOWRY, COMMANDING OFFICER, COMPANY C: The company followed Company B south to the 3d Battalion assembly area near Saemal, arriving there around 1030–1100. Colonel Keleher issued instructions for the companies to resupply, regroup, and to report the number of men left. Company C had 121 enlisted men and three officers capable of fighting. The entire assembly area was quite congested, with many vehicles being in a small area. While reorganizing, Company C came under 120mm mortar fire, killing three men and wounding twenty. The rest scattered out and took cover.

FIRST LIEUTENANT JACOBS, EXECUTIVE OFFICER, COMPANY C: Upon reaching Saemal, the company reorganized and waited on instructions. ROK soldiers were on the surrounding hills as a perimeter guard. A medical aid station had been set up, and the wounded were being attended when intense, accurate mortar and small arms fire fell in the area. The small arms and automatic weapons fire seemed to be coming from all directions, but primarily from the high ground to the left (Hill 206). I noticed the enemy setting up a machine gun; I manned a .50-caliber machine gun mounted on a three-quarter-ton vehicle and placed fire on the enemy.

FIRST LIEUTENANT WELCH, 3D PLATOON LEADER, COMPANY C: When the opposition on the right was overcome, the column moved to the 3d Battalion assembly area at Saemal, going into positions on both sides of the road. The vehicles crowded into the area bumper to bumper, causing much congestion and confusion. Company C had lined its men up in a company formation to count the number of missing when a mortar shell landed to the right, killing and wounding several men. ROK and GI troops were on a low hill to the right, and I heard firing on the hill. When I looked up, I saw the men running down. Almost immediately small arms and automatic weapons fire hit the assembly area. The men in the company scattered and took cover.

PRIVATE 1ST CLASS REED, HEADQUARTERS PLATOON, COMPANY C: After losing a lot of men, we finally got to an assembly area about five miles away. We stopped there, and nobody knew the score. All the men thought we were going to stay there. They lined us up and started counting. There were about seventy-two of the company there. While the counting was going on, a mortar round lit right in the middle of us, and small arms opened up. We all scattered and took cover.[6]

38th Infantry: Saemal to Hoengsong

Unable to remain any longer in the 3d Battalion area because of the heavy fire, Colonel Keleher ordered his 1st Battalion to attack south along the Hoengsong road. Company C was to be on the west side of the road, Company B on the east in the hills; Company

A was to follow along the road in reserve with the vehicles of Support Force 21. Major Jack Rodearme, executive officer of the 1st Battalion, describes the preparations for the continued withdrawal and the attack.

The vehicles and foot elements arrived in the 3d Battalion area between 1015 and 1030. The companies immediately began to reorganize, turn casualties in, and set up perimeter defenses. I contacted the battalion commander who was with the Support Force commander and the 3d Battalion commander at the 3d Battalion CP. I was informed by Colonel Keleher that the Chinese had cut the road between the 3d Battalion and Hoengsong and that the 1st Battalion was to clear the road.

At 1130 the assembly area came under heavy 120mm mortar fire. An enemy OP was seen approximately 2,500 yards away, and Battery B fired on it along with the men of Company C. The men from Company C manned the .50-caliber machine guns of the 15th Field Artillery Battalion. After the artillery fired a few rounds, the mortar fire into the assembly area ceased. In spite of this, the battalion commander gave the attack order. Company C was to attack up the road on the right, clearing the high ground, with Company B on the left, and Company A in support on the road. At this time, Lieutenant Kelly returned from the 2d Battalion, 17th Infantry Regiment, and stated that they had no enemy contact and were awaiting instructions as to what to do. Later, the 17th managed to get out on another secondary road that the 1st Battalion did not know was useable. The battalion jumped off in attack at 1230. Colonel Keleher instructed me to organize all indigenous personnel and to keep the vehicle column moving as the foot troops progressed.

The battalion CP was set up on the road by a radio truck, and communication was established with the headquarters of the 38th Infantry Regiment [in Hoengsong]. An artillery forward observer was provided to the 1st Battalion whose mission was to adjust artillery fire capable of supporting Support Force 21 from south of Hoengsong. He was placed in the radio truck, given the channels and call signs, but was never seen again by me. At this time, however, the 1st Battalion was under the orders of Support Force 21. The Support Force commander, Colonel Keith, was wounded in the cheek, and Colonel Keleher took over command; the situation called for strong leadership.[7]

The attack of Company C is described by members of the unit.

CAPTAIN LOWRY, COMPANY C COMMANDER: I was instructed by Colonel Keleher to attack the ridgeline southwest of the assembly area. At this time, Company C was badly disorganized due to mortar fire and small arms fire, but I succeeded in gathering about sixty men and made a composite platoon. The men fixed bayonets and went up the ridge, capturing two machine guns and killing about fifteen Chinese. The attack was launched at 1300 amid mortar, small arms, and machine gun fire. I was shot during the attack and evacuated to an aid station. Lieutenant Jacobs, Company C, executive officer, took over the company.

LIEUTENANT WELCH, 3D PLATOON LEADER, COMPANY C: Colonel Keleher called for the company commanders and ordered them to attack. Company C was to take the hills on the right going southward, Company B on the left, and Company A in support. Captain Lowry succeeded in collecting about half the company, and a few ROK soldiers were forced to fight at pistol point. The captain led the company up the hill, receiving no fire until they crossed the ridgeline. Then the enemy opened fire with automatic weapons from another ridgeline to the front. Lieutenant Jacobs and I cleared a nose to the front where enemy troops were firing on the road. Captain Lowry took approximately twelve men and started over toward the enemy positions on the next ridge when he was wounded. The company was pinned down on the ridge by heavy automatic weapons fire until 1700.

LIEUTENANT JACOBS, EXECUTIVE OFFICER, COMPANY C: Captain Lowry told me that the company had been given the mission of clearing the high ground to the right of the road from which the assembly area was receiving small arms and automatic weapons fire. Approximately two platoons of men were assembled, and the plan was for Captain Lowry to take part of the men to the right, and Lieutenant Welch and myself to take the remainder of the men to the left of the hill. The high ground was taken, with several Chinese killed and wounded.

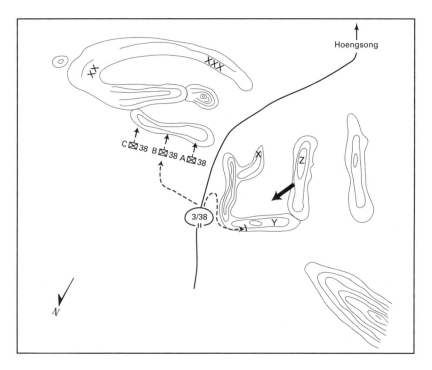

The 38th Infantry attempts to clear the high ground (based on a sketch by 1st Lt. James H. Jacobs).

I then sent a runner to tell Captain Lowry that I was going to take a small nose of the hill (X on map above). Approximately eight to ten Chinese were taking cover behind a burial mound, but BAR fire killed several, and the others fled down the hill. A quad fifty killed them as they crossed a rice paddy. I remained on the ridge for approximately one hour, and then left a small holding force with Lieutenant Welch while I went to check on the situation. Upon reaching the vehicular column, I was notified that Captain Lowry had been wounded.

Colonel Keleher instructed me to attack with Company C down the ridge on the right side of the road (Y on map above) at 1515. The men in the company were scattered and disorganized because of the intense mortar and small arms fire, and control was poor. I found the first sergeant and told him to send a runner to Lieutenant Welch on the point telling him to rejoin the company. Lieutenant Welch never showed up. I never knew the reason; the runner said he conveyed the message.

At approximately 1445 I moved up the hill with thirty men and a few ROK soldiers, but with no platoon leaders or platoon sergeants. Just as the company was to attack, a lieutenant colonel, whom I did not recognize, came to the foot of the hill and ordered me not to attack. I told the colonel that I had orders from Colonel Keleher to jump off at 1515 hours. At this the colonel said, "I'm a colonel from the 38th, and you will not go into attack." I then tried to contact Colonel Keleher on the radio but was unable to do so. Failing in an attempt to relay the message through Company B, I decided to move out in attack.

As Company C jumped off, friendly troops could be seen on the high ground on the left of the road. As the company advanced down the ridge (Y on map, facing page), enemy automatic weapons fire was received from the other finger of the hill (Z on map, facing page). When the company reached a small knoll on the ridgeline, I deployed the men and succeeded in grenading the enemy. Approximately ten were wounded or killed, and several others fled to the west. One man from Company C was killed and two wounded in the attack.

I had difficulty getting the men to advance to the knoll. They just froze, forcing me to hold and consolidate the position. At this time, approximately a platoon of enemy counterattacked, wounding one and killing one. I sent a runner to Colonel Keleher stating the situation.

PRIVATE 1ST CLASS REED, HEADQUARTERS PLATOON, COMPANY C: We got up on another ridge with most of the company and were going to push off to another when a lieutenant colonel came down the valley. He hollered up, "Hold that hill." Lieutenant Jacobs said, "My orders are to push off in ten minutes." Every man on the ridge heard the colonel say not to jump off. Lieutenant Jacobs asked him who he was, and he replied, "I'm a colonel from the 38th, and I got orders for you not to jump off."

When the time came to jump off, the company attacked. There were not many NCOs at the time, and the men were hesitant about jumping off after what the colonel said. There were quite a few enemy on the next ridge, and in the attack four men were wounded. We withdrew to the hill where we jumped off.[8]

On the other side of the road, Company B's attack had also stalled as described by members of the unit.

CAPTAIN SEARLS, COMMANDER OF COMPANY B: I was ordered by the 1st Battalion commander to attack the high ground to the left of the road. Company C was to attack on the right. About 1200 the attack jumped off, with Company B advancing in a skirmish line: the 1st Platoon on the right and the 3d Platoon on the left. The heavy weapons platoon was in support of both rifle platoons. The company advanced over the hill to the forward slope and came under small arms and automatic weapons fire from the front and left flank. Machine gun fire seemed to be coming from both flanks. At this time, Company C on the right of the road was not up with Company B, and the fire from the right flank was coming from their sector. About this time a quad fifty and a twin forty from the 82d AAA under the command of Lieutenant McCoy came down the road. I went down to the road and pointed out the machine gun in his sector, which was giving Company B trouble. Fire from the quad fifty destroyed the gun. I remained with the section from the 82d AAA, and as they advanced, enemy machine guns and small arms opened up from the right flank again, wounding four or five men. Lieutenant McCoy literally covered the ridge with fire; this was the ridge that forced Company C to hold up.

SERGEANT 1ST CLASS MAJOR, 3D PLATOON, COMPANY B: When the rest of the men were regrouped, the company was broken down into two platoons. One platoon was given the mission of taking a hill on the left of the road by the assembly area, and the other platoon was to attack near the road. I was with the platoon on the left flank clearing the hill, and noticed Company C attacking on the other side of the road. Captain Searls was on the road directing fire of a quad fifty and a twin forty on enemy positions in both companies' sectors. Lieutenant Brisbane and twenty-three men were with me in the attack on the first and second hills. During the assault on the third hill to the direct front, all but six men were wounded by small arms fire. The quad fifty and the twin forty were approximately fifty yards behind at the time, supporting Company C. In the meantime, Lieutenant Brisbane had gone to the road to try to get supporting fire. I withdrew the six unwounded men to the adjacent hill and ordered them to hold while I went down for reinforcements. On the road I contacted the first sergeant of Company B, who told me that Lieutenant Brisbane had taken approximately thirty men to the right flank in an effort to take the hill. I then contacted Lieutenant Hobson, 4th Platoon leader, and asked for Captain Searls. Before he could answer, a mortar round exploded behind the two, injuring Lieutenant Hobson and four other men. I assisted in getting the men back to the medics by the side of the road. Approximately fifteen minutes later, at 1430, a sergeant from Company A came with two rifle squads to relieve Company B. I withdrew my six men to the road.[9]

Meanwhile Captain Searls had advanced down the road using the antiaircraft automatic weapons from Battery D, 82d AAA AW Battalion, to blast a path. He describes what happened.

I got orders to hold where we were, but the order didn't come out of the 1st Battalion. I was under the impression that Company C was still advancing, and so we kept going. What was left of the heavy weapons platoon and I advanced down the road behind the quad fifty and the twin forty. Around 1330 to 1400 a bazooka round hit the quad fifty injuring two cannoneers but not damaging the guns. Two volunteers from the heavy weapons platoon manned the guns, and the two vehicles proceeded to within fifteen to twenty yards of a concrete bridge [near the small village of Hail]. At this point a 3.5 rocket hit the quad fifty, putting it out of commission and killing Lieutenant Hobson, 4th Platoon leader, Lieutenant McCoy, and several others.

The two platoons of Company B on the hills to the left ran into stiff resistance and could not advance because of heavy enemy fire. I led the twin forty south of the bridge about 200 yards in an effort to knock out the enemy position. The gunner then told me that they were out of ammunition, and the vehicle took off toward Hoeng-song, leaving me exposed to the heavy machine gun fire. I was forced to take cover in a ditch beside the rice paddies.

In the meantime, the convoy had advanced 600 to 700 yards out of the 3d Battalion assembly area and was pinned down by fire from the right flank. From where I was I could hear the firing to the rear. I worked my way back to the bridge and found some wounded men taking cover under the bridge. Many dead were around the area. I looked down the road toward Hoengsong and saw approximately fifty to seventy-five Chinese soldiers coming down the hills into the valley. I noticed that they had large strips of white cloth hanging down their backs to their waistlines. There was snow on the hills and rice paddies at the time, and when the enemy lay on the ground, they were camouflaged from the air and the ground.

When the enemy started toward the bridge, I ordered the men to follow me or be captured, and started toward the convoy. The enemy set up a machine gun on the road and fired on us. A few men and I finally reached the head of the convoy about 1630 and waited there until dusk.[10]

The remnants of Company A were committed to the fight to open the road. The company commander and executive officer describe the action.

FIRST LIEUTENANT GARDNER, COMMANDING OFFICER, COMPANY A: At 1330 Company A was ordered to join Company B and to support the attack by passing through Company B. The company had to fight its way up to Company B's position through sniper and machine gun fire. The enemy had hidden until Company B passed, then opened fire on the column. By the time Company A reached Company B's position, I could muster only thirteen to fourteen men and one officer. Company A was unable to drive the enemy from the high ground dominating the road. At approximately 1500, an esti-mated company counterattacked from the east and northeast, sup-ported by four machine guns laying a base of fire. Company A was forced to withdraw approximately 500 yards. The high ground to the flanks and left front was secured, and a skirmish line was established from the high ground on the left, down across the road, and to the high ground on the right.

FIRST LIEUTENANT MacLEOD, EXECUTIVE OFFICER, COMPANY A: The attack started successfully at first, but both Company B and Company C were unable to advance very far due to excessive losses and the nature of the terrain. Between 1300 and 1400 the column halted after advancing approximately 1,200 to 1,500 yards. Some of the enemy had infiltrated between Company A, which had advanced farther down the road, and the remainder of the column.

Company A was committed to clear the enemy, which was holding up the column's advance from a hill to the east of the road. Company A took the hill after a brief firefight and secured it until dark. The reason Company A could not advance any farther was the excessive loss of personnel. Company B had joined Company A shortly before dark, and the total personnel in both companies came to twelve enlisted men and three officers.

I noticed that the enemy entrenchments on the hill were dug facing northward to fire on the road to Hongch'on. I estimate that they had been dug at least forty-eight hours before, indicating that the 21st ROK Regiment had not swept the high ground in its advance northward.[11]

While the fight to clear the high ground continued, the convoy also took casualties. The situation is described by the Company A first sergeant and the battalion executive officer.

FIRST SERGEANT COPENHAVER, COMPANY A: I was near the rear of the column with battalion headquarters when the column was stopped in a draw in the hills. Approximately eleven Chinese came off the high ground to the right of the road and started approaching the column. GIs were in the ditches along the roadside and refused to fan out to protect the column. I had heard that ROK troops were coming to join the column and held up fire, and one ROK soldier in a nearby ditch said that the approaching troops were friendly soldiers. One Chinese actually reached the part of the column where I was standing, and the Korean in the ditch started yelling and pointed to the man's white armband. I then shot the enemy soldier. Personnel from Headquarters Company, 1st Battalion, killed the others.

MAJOR RODEARME, EXECUTIVE OFFICER, 1ST BATTALION: As the foot troops progressed, the vehicles were fed on the road. A little later, the troops were held up, forcing the column to halt while approximately one-half the vehicles were still in the assembly area. The vehicles were moving out in the order of the 1st Battalion, 38th Infantry Regiment; 15th Field Artillery Battalion; Battery A, 503d Field Artillery Battalion; and Battery D, 82d AAA AW Battalion.

After Company A had moved down the road, the enemy moved back into positions upon the hills and placed fire on the remainder of the column, causing many casualties. As the attacking companies again proceeded, the motor column resumed its forward movement. After a very short time, Company C met heavy resistance and could advance no farther. I ordered the 81mm mortars from Company D to fire in direct support of Company C, which they did, using up all of their basic load.

The ammunition situation was becoming acute at this time. Because of the impending shortage, I contacted the 3d Battalion about 1600 and received additional small arms, .50-caliber, and mortar ammunition. I further requested a resupply of ammunition by airdrop. The 3d Battalion CP notified me that the airdrop could be expected by 1730, but it never came off, even though the plane came over. No air markings were out; it was impossible to do so because of the intensity of the enemy fire. However, the 1st Battalion never did completely run out of ammunition.

Throughout the afternoon I assisted in gathering casualties and placing them on vehicles. This soon posed an acute problem, because of the lack of litter space.[12]

The ROK troops in the area were remnants of 8th Division units that had been hit hard and suffered heavy casualties. Shaken and leaderless, they provided little help. First Lieutenant Gardner, commander of Company A, 1st Battalion, was particularly critical about their conduct. Writing soon after the withdrawal, while his memory was fresh and his anger was raw, he told Colonel Keleher:

As was previously stated, the ROK troops were only in the way; they would not fight. They bunched up around our troops and drew fire. Most of their officers were dead or wounded (or had fled), and try as we did, we could not get them to fight.

As we moved along, C Company was held up, and at the same time B Company was meeting stiff resistance, so that Company A had to go to help them. However, A Company was strongly engaged before it could get to B Company, and had another real fight on its hands, with heavy mortar and automatic weapons fire raking us. At this point I again found the area swarming with ROK troops who would not fight; with the help of my first sergeant, I put some of them in position by beating them and by forcing them at gunpoint. I located the regimental commander of the 21st ROK Regiment and told him forcefully to get control of his cowardly soldiers and get them to fighting. He tried but was unsuccessful, because he could find no subordinate officers. With the help of Headquarters Company, I was able to secure the high ground on our flanks and establish two outposts. At this time the "valiant" ROK troops became very "bold and brave," and fired upon my men from the rear, causing them much consternation.

The ROK troops were the worst, most ineffectual troops I have ever seen. Had they fought before they faded, we wouldn't have been left holding the bag; had they fought with us, at any time, our operations would have rolled along smoothly, and we could have damaged the enemy much more than we did.[13]

Lieutenant Gardner was equally critical of the American artillerymen, suddenly thrust into an unfamiliar role as fighting infantry under extremely difficult circumstances. He vented his frustration and disgust in the same letter to Colonel Keleher:

The skirmish line that I established approximately thirty yards ahead of your OP was receiving heavy fire, so I sent a runner back to seek any type of reinforcements. When he returned, he reported that there were many artillerymen to the rear: some sitting in their vehicles, some securing their flanks, but most of them were cowering in the ditches. I walked back up the column and organized them into groups, sending them up to the skirmish line and up to our west, where there was a fight going on on the hill. Some of them actually went where I sent them, and gave a good account of themselves; but most of them only moved to a more secluded area, and cowered some more, waiting for the enemy to come and get them; and hoping that one of the officers wouldn't find them and make them fight (real, red-blooded, American soldiers). I was actually informed by five artillery soldiers that they were not fighting men, and had no desire to fight as infantry.

The artillery troops were relegated to four categories: the panicky (15 percent), the lazy and indifferent (20 percent), the let-the-infantry-do-it slackers (40 percent), and the brave (25 percent).[14]

At 1430 hours General Almond, after a meeting with General Ridgway, removed the restrictions on use of the 3d Battalion, 38th Infantry, and an hour and a half later Colonel Coughlin received the welcome news. He immediately ordered the 3d Battalion to leave Saemal and join the 1st Battalion in a coordinated attack to open the road so that all American forces could withdraw to Hoengsong. Colonel Maixner's 3d Battalion began to disengage at Saemal and reposition itself for the attack to open the road. Captain Tate of the 3d Battalion describes the action.

At approximately 1600 hours Colonel Maixner received a message from regiment ordering the 3d Battalion to assist the 1st Battalion in its fight to Hoengsong. Colonel Maixner was contacted by Colonel Keleher, and they coordinated the attack. The plan was to have Support Force 21 on the left and the 3d Battalion on the right. Boundaries and the axis of attack would be the Saemal-Hoengsong road. It was further decided that each battalion would sweep the high ground as the men advanced. The 3d Battalion plan was to attack in a column of companies, Company K leading, followed by Company I. As each hill was taken, one platoon would remain on the hill to keep it secured until all friendly elements had cleared. Headquarters, 3d Battalion, personnel, along with the remnants of Company L [formerly part of Support Team B], formed the rear guard. The 3d Battalion vehicles were to follow close behind those of Support Force 21. The 1st Battalion's plan was to have Company A and Company B attack abreast of each other. Company C, which was in the 3d Battalion area, was ordered by Colonel Keleher to move across the road and join the rest of the battalion after the 3d Battalion passed through them.

Soon after 1600, the 1st Battalion jumped off in the attack on the left of the road. Two of the tanks, which were with the 3d Battalion, were committed to move down the road to make a junction with a force that was moving up from Hoengsong. The 1st Battalion was successful in securing the next high ground, knocking out six machine guns and killing approximately ninety enemy troops. As they went over the high ground and started down the valley, they came upon two enemy groups, of approximately twenty-five each, eating supper; these two groups were quickly eliminated, and the advance continued.

Just after 1600 hours Company K jumped off, followed by Company I and then Company M. Company K passed through elements of Company C and continued the attack, securing the nose of a hill near the road, where they left one platoon for security. By 1700 hours another platoon had secured a hill [Hill 290] about 800 yards farther south. At this time two tanks of Support Team B were sent forward to support the advance of the 1st Battalion. It was later learned that these two tanks were of tremendous help in assisting the battalion to fight its way forward. Other tanks had gone out on their own [toward Hoengsong] leaving the column at the mercy of murderous small arms and automatic weapons fire.

At approximately 1730 the lead platoon of Company I was ordered to advance to the nose of another hill [next to the road about 500 yards east of Hill 290] and secure it. The enemy was delivering very heavy fire from this point. The platoon moved out toward the objective, but some time later it was discovered that they never did secure the hill. However, they were successful in denying the enemy its use, and consequently enemy fire from this point ceased.

At approximately 1800 hours, the vehicular column started slowly down the road to a point to where the road had been cleared of enemy fire.[15]

Members of the 1st Battalion provide additional details of their renewed attack on the east side of the Hoengsong road.

FIRST LIEUTENANT JACOBS, ACTING COMMANDER, COMPANY C: When Company K arrived at 1700, Company C reported to the 1st Battalion commander on the east side of the road. The company was instructed to make another clearing attack down the east side of the Hoengsong road. Company A had been unable to advance in their sector, and Company B was to go to the left of Company A; Company C was to sweep the higher ground on Company B's left flank.

Company C had approximately fifty men, two officers, and twelve ROK soldiers at this point. The ROK men were forced to fight by their sergeant at the point of a .45-caliber pistol. At 1800 the company moved up on the high ground with two platoons moving forward and one echeloning to the right; Lieutenant Welch was in charge of this platoon. I followed the platoon on the left with the 4th Platoon, which was being used as riflemen. The company advanced to within fifty yards of the ridgeline when the enemy opened fire with automatic weapons and two machine guns. The men went in with bayonets and yelling at the top of their voices. One machine gun was destroyed, and all the enemy riflemen killed. Lieutenant Welch, in advancing down the ridge to the left [see XX on map, page 198], bypassed one machine gun, which fired on the vehicular column. I took eight men and succeeded in destroying the position. Lieutenant Welch's platoon went on and surprised approximately eight to ten Chinese with mortars huddled around a fire eating chow. Automatic weapons fire killed or wounded everyone. The platoon went on and took the next ridge without any opposition [see XXX on map, page 198].

Because of darkness I took my men and returned to the road and met Captain Searls, Company B commander, and his men. A runner was sent out in an effort to locate the rest of the company, but they had moved on beyond the ridgeline to the next higher ground.

PRIVATE 1ST CLASS REED, HEADQUARTERS PLATOON, COMPANY C: When we were relieved we went back down to the road again and came under heavy small arms fire from the surrounding hills. Many of the men who were wounded were just careless and never followed what they were taught. They just huddled in groups and wouldn't take cover. Lieutenant Jacobs got the rest of the company together and went up and drove the enemy off. They were all over the place. Lieutenant Jacobs was a good combat leader.

FIRST LIEUTENANT WELCH, 3D PLATOON LEADER, COMPANY C: Lieutenant Jacobs reassembled the company on the road and received orders to proceed down the road to the village of Hail to contact the 1st Battalion commander. The column had halted before reaching the village, and Colonel Keleher was waiting at the head of it for Lieutenant Jacobs.

At approximately 1745, Company C was ordered to join with Companies A and B in sweeping the high ground to the left of the road, and to keep going southward. The 3d Battalion was to sweep the hills on the right of the road. From the road to the left, the 1st Battalion lined up in the order of Companies A, B, and C.

The attack jumped off prior to dark amid sporadic mortar and intense small arms and machine gun fire. Approximately five minutes after the attack started, Companies A and B were unable to attack further, because of heavy casualties. The men in Company C climbed to within fifty yards of the top and then rushed the enemy positions. Two automatic weapons were destroyed with grenades. In the advance my platoon missed one automatic weapon, which did not open fire, but it was destroyed by Lieutenant Jacobs and his men.

By the time my platoon reached the next ridge, it was dark and all firing had ceased. In order to maintain control, I ordered the men to the base of the hill near the road. A skirmish line was set up around the base of the hill.[16]

Meanwhile in Hoengsong, efforts were under way to send relief forces up the road to the 1st and 3d Battalions to help them in their fight. X Corps ordered a reserve battalion of the ROK 3d Division with Support Team G, consisting of Company G, 187th Airborne Infantry Regiment, and a platoon of the 72d Tank Battalion, to move north from Hoengsong at 1400 hours to open the road for the column moving south from Saemal. The ROK advance stalled after half a mile, and upon learning of this, X Corps ordered Colo-

nel Coughlin to assume command of all American forces in the
Hoengsong area. With this new authority, Coughlin quickly ordered Support Team G, reinforced with additional tanks from the
Tank Company, 38th Infantry, to immediately move north, break
through the enemy blocks, link up with the Saemal column, and
help them in their move to Hoengsong. The War Diary of the Tank
Company, 38th Infantry, provides details of the attempt to reach
the battalions moving toward Hoengsong.

At 1745 hours word was received that the platoon of tanks from
the 72d Tank Battalion and Company G of the 187th Airborne were
attached to the 38th Infantry. The regimental commander, Colonel
Coughlin, placed this task force under command of Captain Hinton, company commander of the Tank Company, 38th Infantry.
Upon arriving at the river to assume command of this aforemen-
tioned task force, Captain Hinton discovered that the task force was
returning to Hoengsong. The force was reorganized and turned
around at approximately 1830 hours.

In the meantime the battalion from the 3d ROK Division had
pulled back off of the high ground astride the road and immediately
across the river. The task force proceeded north for about 1,000
yards and then was subjected to machine gun, small arms, and intense mortar fire. The force pressed forward for approximately one
and one-quarter miles, and by this time it had sustained fifteen seriously wounded and fifteen lightly wounded. The mortar fire was so
accurate and intense that it was impossible to move but a few feet at
a time. Captain Hinton at this time requested permission to withdraw and was told to make one more attempt. At approximately
2230 hours the linkup was effected [most sources indicate the
linkup was between 2000 and 2100 hours].[17]

*The arrival of the small task force from Hoengsong provided
little relief for the column. Heavy losses ensued as the troops continued to fight their way south through the night. Members of the
1st and 3d Battalions describe the fighting.*

LIEUTENANT COLONEL KELEHER, COMMANDER OF THE 1ST
BATTALION: Two of the tanks of the 3d Battalion were sent down the

road to make a junction with the force moving north from Hoeng-song. The two tanks from the 3d Battalion made contact with the force moving north, and the 1st and 3d Battalions continued fight-ing to the south. About 1,000 yards from the river, we received the heaviest mortar barrage I have ever witnessed. At the same point the enemy had cross- and plunging fire from the west side of the road. Near this point approximately thirty to forty enemy were attempting to close in on the road but were eliminated to a man by point-blank small arms fire. Apparently the force moving north from Hoengsong did not clear the high ground on either side of the road; also the en-emy did not fire on this force as it moved north. Junction was made with the foot elements of the force moving north.

Our two tanks were placed just off the road to furnish addi-tional cover to the motorized column that was moving along the road. M-16 fire was placed on the enemy machine guns firing from the high ground on the west of the road. The column continued to move down the road toward Hoengsong.

It is estimated that there were two enemy battalions dug in be-tween the 3d Battalion area [at Saemal] and Hoengsong. This plus the extremely rugged terrain made the mission a slow and costly process.

MAJOR RODEARME, EXECUTIVE OFFICER, 1ST BATTALION: A junc-tion was made with Company G, 187th Airborne, and two tanks. The ROK soldiers on the hills, seeing the junction, left their posi-tions and returned to the road, permitting the enemy again to close in on the rear of the column. Personnel from Headquarters Com-pany killed twenty enemy by firing point-blank. Many of the drivers in the column were wounded and killed at the time, and I thought that the enemy had closed in with sufficient numbers to kill the men with small arms fire and grenades.

After the junction heavy fire came from the high ground on both sides of the road. As the column advanced behind the tanks and foot troops southward, the intensity of fire from the high ground and lower slopes increased. In the darkness, small groups would come up to the column before they were destroyed. Small arms, automatic weapons, and machine gun fire of all descriptions (plunging, grazing, interdictory) was placed on the column, causing many casualties, which further slowed the advance. As a vehicle was disabled it was removed, and the column proceeded.

CAPTAIN TATE, S-3, 3D BATTALION: The leading elements of the 3d Battalion made contact with the task force moving up from Hoengsong. It was believed that the road to Hoengsong was now clear of enemy. Accordingly, the relief column and elements of Company I were started down the road. In the darkness, contact with friendly units became very difficult. As the leading elements of the convoy started down the road, they encountered heavy mortar, small arms, automatic weapons, and machine gun fire from points that had previously been secured. It became necessary for the column to run the gauntlet of fire the remaining distance to Hoengsong. The fire was being delivered at point-blank range. In numerous instances, friendly troops would hold one side of the road and the enemy the other. Hand grenade duels were fought all along the route.

FIRST LIEUTENANT GARDNER, COMMANDER OF COMPANY A: When Company G of the 187th RCT reached us, they turned around and started fighting out with us. Again, the enemy was unrelenting and cut the company to ribbons. More vehicles were knocked out. I put a security force on the high ground to the left of the road with M. Sgt. Ruby L. Denton in charge and told him to deny the ground to the enemy until the column had passed, which they did, but the enemy had too many other strong points.

CAPTAIN SEARLS, COMMANDER OF COMPANY B: The junction was made with the tank relief column and a company from the 187th RCT. I succeeded in getting their five tanks turned around and had them headed southward down the valley in a skirmish line with the troops and the remainder of the convoy behind. As the tanks moved forward, they fired on the enemy machine gun positions. For five or ten minutes the foot troops were able to follow the tanks, but then the tanks pulled away. The foot troops followed the road, avoiding the vehicles, which were drawing heavy mortar and .50-caliber fire. The troops were also aiding in loading the wounded on the vehicles. Several ROK soldiers had to be beaten as they tried to drag the wounded off the trucks and climb aboard. From then on out to Hoengsong, we were running a continuous gauntlet of fire from the hills on both sides of the road.

FIRST LIEUTENANT WELCH, 3D PLATOON LEADER, COMPANY C: The company commander of Company G, 187th RCT, told me that his company had suffered heavy casualties, and he expressed doubt if the relief column could push back to Hoengsong alone.[18]

Near Hoengsong, just north of the river, a disabled truck led to disaster for the vehicles trapped behind it.

CAPTAIN TATE, S-3, 3D BATTALION: At this point an enemy mortar round struck a prime mover, causing the 105mm howitzer it was towing to jackknife, forming a block on the road and making vehicle movement past this point impossible. All vehicles behind this prime mover were forced to be abandoned. This and other delays enabled the enemy to pinch off portions of the column. Company L and Headquarters Company at the rear of the column were receiving murderous fire, and their casualties were mounting very fast. In order to get them through, some of the men broke up into small groups and fought their way across country. Others bulled their way through, fighting and firing their weapons at point-blank range. Even though most of them knew they were fighting against terrific odds, they were fighting superbly. Finally the column arrived at the river west of Hoengsong; however, they were still subjected to mortar fire.

FIRST LIEUTENANT MEYER, P&A PLATOON LEADER, 1ST BATTALION: The column would move and stop at intervals but never stopped for more than a few minutes at any one time, until after passing two tanks on the road that were firing to the left and right of the road near Kun'gol. About two hundred yards beyond the tanks, the column stopped. There was intense small arms fire and a few mortar rounds. The column started to double, then the tanks moved past the column through rice fields. Then approximately a hundred men started running down the road. I asked where they were going. One of the drivers told me that they were ordered to abandon the trucks. I went forward about fifty yards to see why the convoy stopped. I found a two-and-a-half-ton truck with a 105mm howitzer jackknifed across the road. A machine gun was firing into the cab of the truck, thus preventing anyone from trying to start the truck and clearing the road. Consequently, this caused the loss of all vehicles behind it.[19]

About 2200 hours the leading elements of the 1st and 3d Battalions began to arrive at Hoengsong, passing through the defensive perimeter of the Netherlands Battalion. They moved to an assembly area just south of town, where they were met by trucks that carried them south to Wonju. Confusion reigned in Hoengsong as the two infantry battalions and the other remnants of Support Force 21 moved through the streets simultaneously with Support Force 7, which had escaped from the Chinese who had struck the ROK 3d Division.

Support Force 7 / Task Force White

Support Force 7, also called Task Force White after its commander, Lt. Col. Barney D. White, was organized with forces similar to those of Support Force 21. It was more fortunate than Support Force 21 because it had more time to react to the Chinese attack and plan the withdrawal to Hoengsong. The recommendation for award of the Presidential Unit Citation describes the action.

From prepared positions at Osan-ni, about 4,000 yards north of Hoengsong, the mission of the artillery element of the task force was to support the 3d ROK Division, which was operating to the north, while the infantry elements protected the artillery by occupying a perimeter defense around the artillery positions.

At 0130 hours, 12 February, the task force commander received information from X Corps artillery that one unit of the 8th ROK Division to the northwest was under heavy attack and was giving ground. The S-3, 49th Field Artillery Battalion, called the artillery liaison officer, who was working with an infantry regiment of the 3d ROK Division, at 0145 to ascertain the situation in his unit's sector. Fifteen minutes later the same liaison officer called and reported that the regiment was withdrawing. This same liaison officer was killed during the withdrawal.

After learning that the enemy had passed south of the task force's left flank, the task force commander called X Corps artillery to ascertain whether or not the task force should link up with the 38th Infantry's right flank. While the task force was being told to wait for daylight, a heavy firefight was reported slightly northeast of the perimeter. Company G was receiving long-range machine gun fire from due north, and both E and G Companies reported heavy small arms fire 2,000 yards to the north. Due to the rapidly changing situation, X Corps artillery advised the task force commander to use his own judgment in selecting the best route to Hoengsong.

Realizing that contact with the 38th Infantry Regiment could be made only by suffering many casualties, the task force commander ordered his engineer unit to improve the southeastern escape route leading into Hoengsong. The task force commander directed that two serials be organized for the motor march, with one light battery and one medium battery of field artillery in the first serial. The two serials were organized so that the first serial could support, from Hoengsong, the withdrawal of the second serial. After the final engineer work was completed on the road leading southeast from the right flank, the first serial departed the area at 1531. The fighting elements of the infantry, minus one company, one reconnaissance platoon, and a section of AAA AW Artillery, remained to protect the two firing batteries of the artillery and cover the route out until the task force was completely withdrawn. The perimeter itself was evacuated without incident, although movement was slow and impeded by difficult, icy roads.

Lead elements of infantry and artillery arrived in Hoengsong at 1730. Considerable mortar and sporadic small arms fire was falling in the town at this time. Battery A, 49th Field Artillery, and Battery B, 31st Field Artillery [in the first serial], cleared the town and went into firing positions south of Hoengsong. From these positions the rear guard could be supported by artillery fire. Company G, reinforced with most of Company H, was deployed in Hoengsong itself to protect the withdrawal. Also in the town were withdrawing elements of the 38th Infantry, fleeing ROK soldiers, innumerable enemy who had infiltrated with the ROK soldiers, and a Netherlands Battalion acting as rear guard for the 38th Infantry. The situation was confused to the extent that friends rubbed shoulders with enemies and neither recognized the other.

At about 2045 enemy fire was already heavy upon the road in and south of Hoengsong. The town was literally lighted with the flash of tracer, bursting mortar fire, burning vehicles and trailers, and illuminating shells from friendly artillery units to the south. At this moment, Batteries B and C of the 49th Field Artillery entered the town from the north end. The enemy, in desperation to capture the guns and vehicles, made frantic attacks with grenades and burp guns at point-blank range, but fell in scores on the edges of the roads and at the sides of the trucks as the artillerymen shot them down with their individual weapons. In this manner the two firing batteries progressed until they finally broke through the enemy positions south of town.

As the column turned south from the crossroad in Hoengsong, Chinese and American soldiers were fighting hand to hand. Notwithstanding the presence of his own soldiers in the town, the enemy was dropping mortars on the road with such accuracy and intensity that they were actually falling inside the vehicles.

One-half mile south of town it was necessary to bypass a long concrete bridge across a wide streambed. Because of the delay at this point, plus the fact that many stops were necessary to collect wounded or remove knocked out vehicles from the road, the enemy was keeping abreast of the head of the column. By the time the tail of the column had bypassed the bridge, the head of the column, still another one-half mile to the south, was attacked in force by enemy using hand grenades, automatic weapons, and mortars. The remainder of the column was under heavy fire from enemy occupying positions in the hills 200 yards to both flanks. The road at this point was straight, level, and elevated some three feet above the rice paddies that flanked it.

The attacking enemy found a break in the column, and a sharp battle ensued at hand grenade range until finally the Chinese were momentarily repulsed. About twenty vehicles then got through the block. At this point, however, the enemy renewed his attack and succeeded in knocking out a heavy truck of Company A, 13th Engineer Combat Battalion. With the column thus blocked, the enemy pressed his advantage and destroyed the next seven vehicles. Among these was an ammunition truck, which caught fire and began exploding with heavy detonations that threw flaming particles on the vehicles in front of it and ignited four of them.

With more than fifty vehicles trapped behind this flaming barrier, the enemy began again to close in with grenades and automatic weapons. Mixed elements of the rifle battalion, consisting mainly of Company G men plus volunteers from the other units in the column, dismounted under the fierce fury of the enemy fire and attacked astride the road. With hand-to-hand combat the rearguard troops destroyed about fifty enemy who had occupied positions on and astride the road at the head of the column.

The time then was about 0200 13 February. The enemy, constantly advancing, was now about a mile south of the head of the column as well as to the rear and on the flanks. The tremendous volume of fire that developed within the column was keeping the enemy at bay, but the column itself was enfiladed by fire and was suffering terribly under a heavy crossfire.

The plight of trapped elements was reported to the commander of that part of the task force that had already escaped to safety. Two tanks from the 7th Reconnaissance Company were sent back to assist in removing the roadblock. These tanks arrived about 0300 hours 13 February. The commander of the trapped elements immediately employed the tanks to pull, push, or butt the flaming vehicles off the road. The enemy, with the target clearly illuminated in the glare of these burning vehicles, increased and concentrated the volume of his fire to discourage this final effort to escape. Again and again the tanks pushed and butted at this flaming, exploding tangle of vehicles. About 0430 the road was reopened, and the column began moving again. Still there remained a mile-long gauntlet of fire. The column was not again stopped, however, and moved steadily, maintaining a constant volume of fire until the last enemy was left behind.

Arriving in Wonju, there was hardly a vehicle that did not contain dead or wounded. Almost every vehicle was repeatedly pierced by small arms fire. Yet, there was not a vehicle abandoned that would still operate, and many came in with from one to four flat

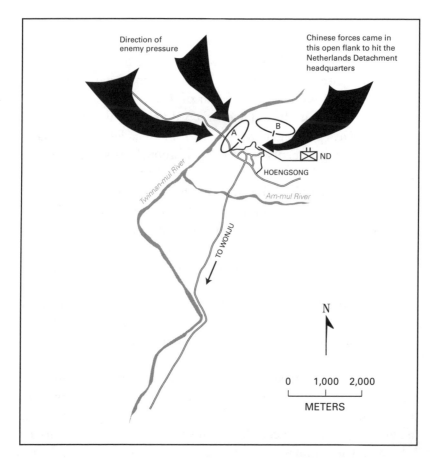

Attacks on the Netherlands Detachment (Netherlands Detatchment, Award Case File, RG 500, NA).

tires. The task force suffered 191 personnel casualties: 14 killed, 51 missing, and 126 wounded. The task force also lost forty-six vehicles. It is estimated that the enemy suffered at least 1,150 personnel casualties.[20]

Hoengsong: The Netherlands Battalion

The Netherlands Battalion defended the northern outskirts of Hoengsong as Task Force White, Support Force 21, the 3d Battalion, 38th Infantry, and assorted ROK troops passed through the town en route south to Wonju. Their task was made more difficult be-

cause of the confusion among the withdrawing units, which allowed
the enemy to infiltrate into the town. The account of the Nether-
lands Battalion fight to hold Hoengsong is provided in the recom-
mendation of its regimental commander, Colonel Coughlin, for
award of the Presidential Unit Citation.

On the night of 11–12 February, the Netherlands Detachment,
consisting of two rifle companies, a heavy weapons company, and a
headquarters group, was disposed on high ground, forming an arc
of approximately 2,100 yards north, northeast, and east of Hoengsong, where the command posts of the 38th Infantry Regiment and
the 8th ROK Division were established. Because of the Chinese attack on the 8th ROK Division north of Hoengsong, the Netherlands
Battalion in the course of the night shifted the rifle company on the
east flank to extend the west flank of their defense to place this unit
squarely in front of the advancing enemy. The task now fell to the
Netherlands Detachment to defend the approaches to the important
road junction of Hoengsong and, at all costs, to hold its position
until the friendly forces had cleared the town.

By noon the enemy had concentrated a large force in the vicinity
of Hoengsong and was bringing small arms, automatic weapons,
and mortar fire on its defenders. After darkness had fallen, a company of enemy troops infiltrated with the withdrawing ROK forces
from northeast of Hoengsong, under the ruse of being friendly ROK
elements, and succeeded in passing around the open right flank of
the Netherlands positions and gaining the location of the Netherlands command post. Recognizing the enemy and shouting warnings to his troops, the commander of the Netherlands Detachment,
Lieutenant Colonel den Ouden, rallied his headquarters personnel
and led his small group in a charge against the enemy until he himself fell mortally wounded. His gallant example and self-sacrifice so
inspired the staff personnel that they shortly routed the enemy, killing many of them in fierce hand-to-hand combat.

The courageous Netherlands troops steadfastly held their blocking positions against ever-increasing hostile fire until finally, by approximately 2300 hours, the last of the friendly forces had broken
through the enemy lines and rejoined the regiment.

The enemy meanwhile had infiltrated to the southwest and established a roadblock on the Wonju road. Ordered gradually to fall back from their semi-perimeter defense and fight a rearguard action against the enemy, who was now making his most desperate efforts to enter the town and overrun the friendly forces there, the tired and battle-weary Netherlands companies doggedly fought their way back, thus effectively covering the rear of the regiment until the latter could penetrate the roadblock.

With the elimination of that resistance, the Netherlands Detachment successfully broke contact with the enemy under cover of darkness and retired to new positions north of Wonju, where the rest of the UN forces were now located.[21]

The cost had been high. Of the 765 men in the 1st Battalion, 38th Infantry, on 11 February, 489 were casualties by the 13th. Total losses for all 2d Infantry Division troops involved in the operation were 1,769. Twenty artillery pieces, 6 tanks, and 280 vehicles were also lost. Support Force 7 accounted for an additional 191 personnel casualties and 46 lost vehicles. But the 38th Infantry Regiment and its attached Netherlands Battalion and Support Force 7 were still effective combat units, which they would soon demonstrate in their stubborn defense of the new line established just north of Wonju. Meanwhile to the west, the other prong of the Chinese attack rolled forward and soon engulfed the 23d Infantry Regiment, which was holding a key crossroads at Chip'yong-ni.

Chapter 9

HOLDING THE CHINESE

Chip'yong-ni and Wonju

On 13 February, as the remnants of Support Forces 7 and 21, along with the 38th Infantry Regiment, reached the new defensive line above Wonju, the Chinese closed in on the 23d Infantry Regiment at the key crossroads of Chip'yong-ni. Because the 23d Infantry was separated from other UN forces by a twelve-mile gap and could easily be isolated and possibly overwhelmed, General Almond planned to withdraw them south to the Yoju area. However, General Ridgway feared that if the 23d Infantry gave up Chip'yong-ni, the enemy could continue its drive south into the Han River valley, thereby threatening the entire UN position. He ordered the 23d Infantry to hold while the British 27th Brigade and the 6th ROK Division were quickly transferred from IX Corps to reinforce X Corps and to plug the gap on the left flank of X Corps. Almond was ordered to attack to relieve the 23d Infantry if they were cut off by the Chinese. The X Corps commander believed that the main enemy attack would come at Wonju. However, the first blow fell at Chip'yong-ni, followed quickly by other attacks seeking to overwhelm the units holding the defensive lines west of Wonju.

Chip'yong-ni: 23d Infantry Regiment, Night of 13–14 February

The Chinese moved rapidly, and by late night on 13 February, the 23d Infantry was surrounded. That night the enemy attacked with four regiments from four different divisions, representing three

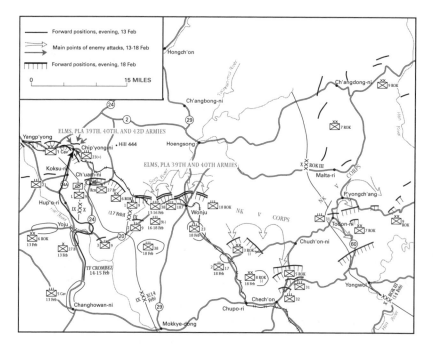

Defending the Wonju Line, 13–18 February 1951 (based on U.S. Army Center of Military History map).

Chinese armies. An overwhelming force had been concentrated around Chip'yong-ni, and it appeared that the Chinese were determined to take the position. The 23d Infantry Regiment's After Action Report, a part of the recommendation for award of the Presidential Unit Citation, describes the situation of the unit and the initial fighting.

Six hills, which were desirable to occupy—345 to the northwest, 348 to the northeast, 506 to the east, 319 to the southeast, 397 to the south, and 248 to the west—dominated the area around Chip'yong-ni. A perimeter formed on these hills would have required more troops than were available. Therefore, a smaller perimeter had to be established on lower, less desirable ground. To accomplish his mission and still maintain a reserve, the regimental commander placed the rifle companies of the 23d RCT around the perimeter in a clocklike fashion: Company C at 12:00, A at 1:00, L at 2:00, I at 3:00, K at 4:00, E at 5:00, F at 6:00, G at 7:00, 1st French Com-

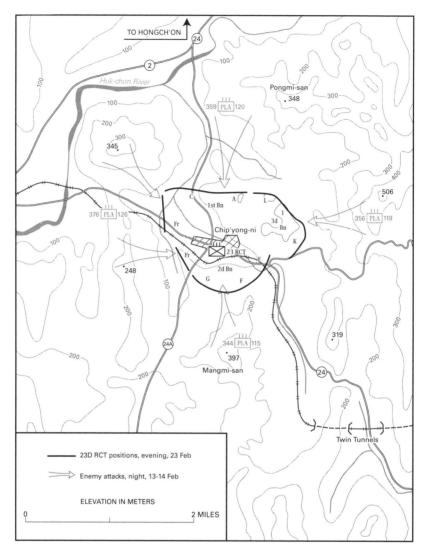

Chip'yong-ni, 13–14 February 1951 (based on U.S. Army Center of Military History map).

pany at 8:00, 3d French Company at 9:00, French ROK Company at 10:00, and 2d French Company at 11:00. The regimental commander retained Company B and the 1st Ranger Company as regimental reserve within the perimeter behind A and C Companies. With the units in these positions, the night of 12–13 February passed with no enemy contact. However, units on all sides of the perimeter reported intense flare activity.

Normal patrols for the daylight hours of 13 February reported increased enemy activity close to the perimeter in three directions, north, east, and west. Air observers reported enemy groups to the north and east moving toward the perimeter, and the TACP directed forty flights of aircraft against the enemy when it was not possible to place artillery upon them. The 2d Recon Company, reinforced by Company L, 9th Infantry Regiment, reported enemy moving from southeast of Chip'yong-ni westward toward the MSR [the road from Chip'yong-ni through Ch'uam-ni to the south]. They engaged the enemy in a firefight and were forced to withdraw [to a position south of Ch'uam-ni]. Observers on all sides of the perimeter again reported flare activity during the late afternoon and early evening. Between 2200 and 2300 hours enemy small arms and mortar fire began to fall on the perimeter from the northwest, north, and southeast. Shortly thereafter, enemy troops attacked the 1st Battalion, which was occupying the northern sector of the perimeter. Heavy mortar and artillery fire preceded this attack. As midnight approached, activity spread in other directions until the 3d Battalion on the southeast of the perimeter was the only unit not in contact with the enemy. Mortar and artillery fire also fell on the regimental command post, field artillery, and heavy mortar company areas. As at the Twin Tunnels area, the enemy frequently blew on whistles, horns, and bugles.

As the activity subsided somewhat after midnight, a quick check revealed that a portion of the 1st Battalion CP was burning, and an M-16 half-track on the southeast part of the perimeter had been damaged.

At 0100 hours on 14 February, the enemy launched another strong attack from the north and then from the northwest. The defending troops of the perimeter repulsed these attacks, but the enemy could be heard digging in. Observers noted much activity to the north, where they also detected enemy mortar positions. At about 0215 hours the enemy launched new attacks from the southwest and southeast, with the enemy from the southeast making a desperate frontal assault against the positions of Company K. At 0245 hours friendly troops were still holding in both areas; therefore, the enemy launched another heavy attack from the northwest against the positions held by the French Battalion. Fifteen minutes later, the enemy hit C Company again, but the defending troops held. By 0530 hours most of the pressure was off the troops in the perimeter, except for the French, who were still receiving attacks from the northwest, which they repulsed. Company G had regained its positions, but Company K was fighting fiercely to hold its sector. The stubborn enemy launched another attack from the north against Company C's positions at 0545 hours but was repulsed. In the south, the enemy had made unsuccessful attempts to infiltrate the lines.

At 0630 hours the fighting flared up again, and the 2d Recon Company and Company L, 9th Infantry, both reported that they were being attacked on three sides. The enemy attacked the perimeter from the southeast again, but was driven off by K and I Companies. Elsewhere on the perimeter, the enemy was feinting at the lines and withdrawing. At 0730 hours Company K on the southeast was still fighting, and the French Battalion on the northwest was hit again, but shortly thereafter, the enemy broke physical contact on the entire perimeter.[1]

Chip'yong-ni: Company G, 23d Infantry, Night of 13–14 February

Some of the heaviest Chinese attacks fell on the section of the perimeter held by Company G, 23d Infantry Regiment. Capt. Edward C. Williamson, a combat historian who visited the battlefield and interviewed members of the unit, describes the unit's position at Chip'yong-ni and the night action.[2]

Company G, commanded by 1st Lt. Thomas Heath, held the 500-yard right flank arc of the 2d Battalion sector, tying in with the French Battalion at the MSR on the west and with Company F in a rice paddy on the east. Heath's CP was located in a small Korean hut 50 yards east of the MSR. Communication wire was laid to the platoons, which were generally 150 yards to the south. Taking advantage of the steep south slope of a small group of hills 600 yards south of the town, 1st Lt. Paul J. McGee's 3d Platoon keystoned the

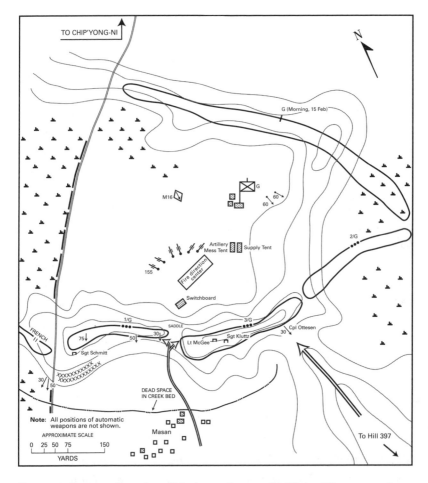

Company G sector (based on U.S. Army Center of Military History map).

MLR in the Company G sector. First Lt. Kenneth Finn's 2d Platoon on the left was in a rice paddy. The 3d Platoon CP was in the center of its MLR. The 2d Platoon CP was in a cave 75 yards to the rear of the platoon MLR. Lt. Carl F. Haberman's 4th Platoon had its three 60mm mortars set up on the gentle reverse north slope 75 yards behind the 3d Platoon.

The 1st Platoon, also located on the forward slope of the small group of hills, held the right flank. The platoon commander, M. Sgt. Emery S. Toth, had his CP in a Korean hut 5 yards from the company CP. Without informing Heath, Toth remained in the hut and did not establish a forward CP after the fighting began. He did maintain wire communication with SFC Donald R. Schmitt of the 1st Platoon, who was up on the hill.

In taking defensive measures, Heath had the men prepare two-man covered foxholes and set up flares and trap expedients in front of the positions. The 2d Battalion A&P Platoon mined the MSR with nine antitank mines at the Company G–French Battalion contact point, where the drop to the MSR forms a V in the small hill mass. The A&P Platoon also set up two fougasses: the first on the MSR and the second in front of the 2d Platoon. Fougasses were improvised explosives consisting of 55-gallon drums of napalm mixed with gasoline placed in front of defensive positions. When detonated from the rear, ten yard-wide flames shot out almost forty yards. Under A&P Platoon supervision, Company G men strung wire on the MSR and in front of the 1st Platoon. The company was at all times on a 50 percent alert; this means that during the night one man was awake and one asleep in each foxhole. The 2d Platoon in the flat rice paddy had good fields of fire; however, the 1st and 3d Platoons up on the small hills lacked a satisfactory final protective line. From the 3d Platoon's hilltop McGee had excellent observation to the south, with one exception, a dead spot in the dry creekbed just below the 3d and 1st Platoons.

Battery B, 503d Field Artillery Battalion (155mm howitzers), was in position 100 yards behind the 1st Platoon of Company G and 200 yards behind the 3d Platoon. In preparation for the defense of the sector Capt. John A. Elledge, artillery liaison officer of Battery B, came to the Company G CP and furnished Heath with a list of all of his battery's weapons and ammunition. Elledge, Heath, and Haberman worked out a plan for defense, taking into account the use of artillerymen as riflemen in the event the position was penetrated. The coordinated defense provided for skeleton crews to man the howitzers. An infantry-artillery machine gun post was set up on the side of the MSR at the Company G–French Battalion contact point. Here a four-man crew manned a .50-caliber and a .30-caliber machine gun.

At around 2000 [the night of 13 February], as PFC Donald E. Nelson of the 2d Squad, 2d Platoon, Company G, was sitting in his foxhole arguing with Pvt. Jack Ward over who would pull guard first, both men heard the sound of digging 600 yards to the south. A shrill whistle caused them both to jump out of their hole and grab their bazooka.

What had happened? Two squads of Chinese were attempting to envelope the 3d Platoon position. By 2220 one squad had succeeded in crawling 75 yards up the small spur to the vicinity of Cpl. Eugene L. Ottesen's machine gun. The enemy threw three grenades and opened up on Ottesen with small arms fire. Ottesen returned the enemy fire. At the same time another enemy squad 200 yards to the west took advantage of the dead spot in the creekbed, climbed the hill, and attacked the foxhole of the BAR man in Sgt. Franklin H. Querry's squad.

Hearing the firing, PFC Herbert Ziebell of the 1st Squad, 3d Platoon, awakened his foxhole buddy, PFC Roy F. Benoit, and said, "There is some firing going on. Get up and get ready." Ziebell did not fire immediately because he could not see anyone to fire at, and he felt that the flash of his M-1 would draw enemy fire.

Pvt. Kenneth C. Green in the 3d Squad, 3d Platoon, also heard the firing on his left. He awakened his foxhole partner, Pvt. Henry Heimerl, and both men sat in the darkness awaiting the Chinese.

When Lieutenant McGee [3d Platoon leader] heard Ottesen's machine gun open up, he immediately phoned Lieutenant Heath [Company G commander]. He then called the other squad leaders by sound-powered telephone and informed them that Ottesen's squad was under attack. In order to conserve ammunition, he ordered the men to fire only when they could see the enemy.

To the east of the 3d Platoon, Pvt. Andrew C. Warf of the 2d Platoon opened up with his machine gun. Pvt. Jack Ward threw a round into the rocket launcher and fired at flashes that appeared to come from rocks 800 yards to the south. He continued to operate the rocket launcher until on the third round he had his face burned by powder when the back blast came out the side. The rocket launcher was not fired again until morning.

Around 2300 a Chinese squad succeeded in penetrating Cpl. James C. Mougeat's squad sector, which lay twenty yards to the west of the 3d Platoon CP. One Chinese tossed a grenade in

Mougeat's foxhole, wounding him. Mougeat crawled out of his hole and, shouting, "Lieutenant McGee, I'm hit," started for the CP. Two Chinese closed in for the kill. They threw several grenades at Mougeat. One grenade knocked Mougeat's rifle out of his hand and tore the stock off. Fortunately for Mougeat, two men from his squad shot the Chinese. Recovering his damaged rifle, Mougeat ran to the CP. McGee calmed him down, and then Mougeat decided, "I'm not hit bad," and returned to his squad.

Lieutenant McGee observed several men about 20 yards below the platoon position. One of them called his name. "Who is that?" McGee asked his BAR man. "It's a Chink," the BAR man said. McGee tossed a grenade down the hill. Wounded, the Chinese fired his rifle at McGee as he rolled down the slope. McGee borrowed the BAR and finished off the enemy.

The Chinese, blowing whistles and bugles, attacked the 3d Platoon four times that night. All attacks were repulsed.

As dawn was breaking on 14 February, platoon sergeant Bill Kluttz in the foxhole next to McGee spotted five Chinese in the creekbed. He fired several tracers at them. Suspecting the presence of other Chinese, McGee ordered him to have the rocket launcher fired at the creekbed. Kluttz was unable to get the rocket launcher men oriented on the target; therefore, he took the weapon and fired a round himself. The rocket hit a tree, making an airburst over the creekbed. About forty Chinese came out of the creekbed and began walking across the rice paddies. The 2d Squad and the 1st Platoon opened fire on the withdrawing enemy.

In the night's fighting Company G lost three men killed; four wounded were evacuated.

At 0900 Lieutenant McGee took out a patrol that captured five Chinese hiding in a culvert and seven more who were wounded and lying in the rice paddies south of the company position; McGee counted eighteen enemy bodies. Near the village of Masan, McGee walked up to a small haystack near an abandoned enemy machine gun. A wounded Chinese rose up in the haystack to shoot McGee; Sergeant Kluttz shot and killed him. Another Chinese, although handicapped by a badly wounded leg, was still attempting to operate a Russian burp gun when Corporal Sander bayoneted him.

While McGee was out with the patrol, Capt. Stanley Terrell, Lt. Charles F. Heady, and Lt. Leonard Napier from Company F made a reconnaissance of Company G's defensive positions. It was planned that either Napier's 1st Platoon or Heady's 3d Platoon would reinforce any sector of Company G in case of a penetration, since it was apparent that the enemy would launch a stronger attack on Company G that night.[3]

During the daylight hours of 14 February, the fighting around Chip'yong-ni died down as the Chinese dug in and hid from UN air strikes. To the south, the 2d Division Recon Company and Company L, 9th Infantry, suffered heavy losses as they withdrew south from Ch'uam-ni in the face of strong attacks, further isolating the 23d Infantry.

Wonju: 2d Infantry Division and 187th Airborne Infantry Regiment, 14–15 February

Meanwhile to the east, the Chinese forces that had captured Hoengsong the night of 12–13 February had closed on the defenders of Wonju. In the predawn hours on 14 February, the Netherlands Battalion, still attached to the 38th Infantry, and the 3d Battalion, 38th Infantry, came under attack. The Command Report of the 2d Infantry Division describes the situation.

As the defense of the road hub, supply points, and C-47 landing strip at Wonju was vital to the success of the defense against the attacking forces, the assistant division commander, Brig. Gen. George C. Stewart, was directed to take charge of all units in the Wonju area and organize the defense. His orders were to hold Wonju, whatever the cost.

Arriving on the evening of 12 February, General Stewart called together all commanders of local units and instructed them that defenses were to be established and that they would be held—there was to be no withdrawal, no evacuation. In order to provide the maximum disruption of the advancing CCF units, supporting artillery was placed in positions from which it could mass fires on every

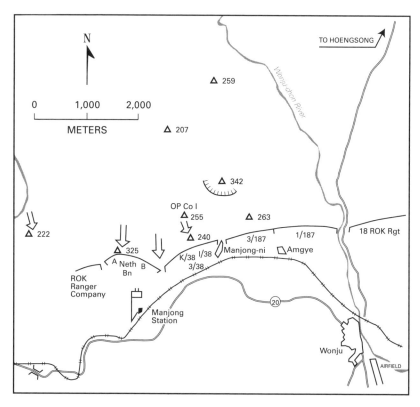

Initial UN positions and enemy attacks, 14 February 1951 (original map by author).

approach to the Wonju defenses. Liaison pilots were instructed to remain in the air throughout the daylight hours, with the mission of keeping the closest possible surveillance of enemy movement to prevent surprise attack or massing of enemy troops.

The primary defense line established by General Stewart followed the high ground approximately 4,000 yards north of Wonju. The Netherlands Detachment (which had lost its commanding officer during the desperate fighting on the previous day) was on the left, with a battalion of the 38th RCT and the 3d and 1st Battalions of the 187th Airborne RCT to the right, in that order. The 2d Battalion of the 187th Airborne was the reserve force. The 18th ROK Regiment established defensive blocks to the east, and an ROK

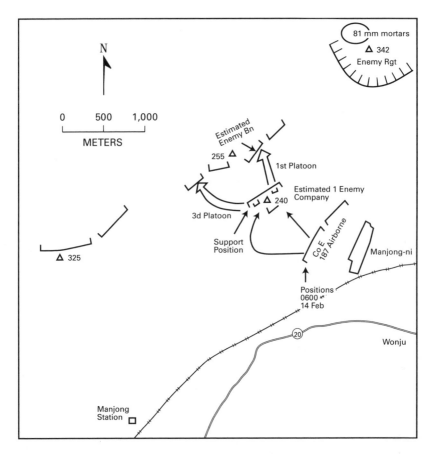

Company E, 187th Airborne attack on Hill 255, 14 February 1951 (original map by author).

Ranger Company established defensive blocks to the west. The enemy was strangely quiet on the 13th, and the defenders worked feverishly to prepare for the assault they knew would soon come.[4]

The beginning of the attack on 14 February is described in the Command Report of the 38th Infantry.

At 0345 hours the right flank of Company K was under heavy attack and a breakthrough by hundreds of enemy was reported. Company I reported considerable activity to its front, but no enemy contact; however, it was later discovered that the I Company OP, located on Hill 255, was engaged in a firefight and was forced to withdraw about 400 yards to the south. At 0710 hours, Company B, Netherlands Detachment, was under heavy attack.[5]

The Netherlands Battalion's position on Hill 325 was lost in the fighting, but the major threat was the penetration of the lines of the 3d Battalion, 38th Infantry. The 2d Battalion, 187th Airborne Infantry, the sector reserve force, received orders to relieve the 3d Battalion, 38th Infantry, and restore the frontline positions. Company E was to recapture Hill 255. Capt. Jack B. Shanahan, the commander of Company E, and 1st Lt. William J. Dolan, an officer of the same company, describe the ensuing action.

CAPTAIN SHANAHAN: At 0430 hours on the 14th of February, I was assigned the mission of repulsing a Chinese Communist attack, which had penetrated and overrun defending elements of the 38th Infantry Regiment. Sending a patrol to my right, I established contact with the 3d Battalion, 187th RCT, and stood by for further instructions from our battalion commander.

While awaiting these instructions, the necessary administrative details, essential to the successful pursuit of the assigned task, were attended to. This included the organization of ammunition and food carrying parties, which were to be composed of mess personnel and drivers. The importance of the mission and critical strategic and military value of the terrain was emphasized to the platoon leaders.

At 0830 hours orders were received to attack and secure Hill 240, which was located about three and one half miles northwest of Wonju. I assigned this mission to the 2d Platoon, attaching a 57mm recoilless rifle as additional support. The other two rifle platoons were designated as flank protection to the left and right of the assault element. The attack progressed without incident until the 2d Platoon reached a point approximately 100 yards from the topographical crest. At this time, the defending American troops [elements of the 3d Battalion, 38th Infantry] were trying to withdraw, but the attacking 2d Platoon, moving up the hill, succeeded in turning part of them around and carrying the attack to the topographical crest of the hill. Here they met face to face with Chinese troops and by employing hand grenades and small arms fire succeeded in overrunning their position.

Reorganizing the entire company on Hill 240, a base of fire was established and counterfires were placed on Hill 255, which was the next high ground, located 600 yards to the front of the newly won company position. The enemy was deployed in strength on Hill 255, so a napalm strike was requested from friendly air support. The enemy attempted an envelopment movement around our left flank but was dispersed by the left flank platoon. Artillery and mortar concentrations were laid upon Hill 255 both as a defensive measure and in anticipation of further attack orders. Hill 240 was secure at 1300 hours.

Upon receipt of the additional orders, a terrain analysis by visual reconnaissance was made and an attack plan formulated. Assigning the administrative details to the company executive officer, I assembled the platoon leaders and the commander of the base of fire and issued my attack order. The 1st and 3d Platoons were to be the assault elements, with the 1st on the right and the 3d on the left. Line of departure (LD) and time of attack was set at 1430 hours.

A planned artillery concentration was laid on Hill 255 at H minus 5 minutes, also supported by small arms fire from the attached heavy weapons company and the company base of fire on Hill 240. The assault platoons crossed the LD at the appointed time to begin the attack. Progress was slow on the right flank due to the advantageous positions occupied by the defending Chinese. Although suffering many casualties as a result of the numerically superior and positioned enemy, the 1st Platoon pressed relentlessly forward in an attempt to establish itself in a final assault position.

Meanwhile the 3d Platoon, assaulting up the left half of the company objective, had reached a point about 50 yards from the military crest, where they were subjected to heavy enemy fires, which included a terrific hand grenade barrage. The intense enemy fires had resulted in the loss of about twelve men from the 3d Platoon, thereby decreasing their combat potential. An enemy automatic weapons emplacement on their left flank was making it exceedingly difficult for them to organize and carry the final assault. I dispatched a rifle squad from the base of fire platoon to their assistance. With this additional aid, the platoon leader was able to continue the assault, and after three attempts against the fanatically determined enemy, gained his objective.

On the right of the company sector, the 1st Platoon had advanced through withering enemy fires to the military crest of Hill 255. At this time I lost radio contact with the platoon and could see they were receiving both frontal and enfilade fires from the enemy. I immediately sent the platoon leader another radio of the SCR 300 type. Upon reestablishment of radio contact, the platoon leader notified me of an enemy bunker on the top of Hill 255. By employing a 75mm recoilless rifle, it was possible to temporarily silence this position. At this time it was noted that after seemingly neutralizing an enemy position, they would replace the dead and wounded with a concentration of troops from the reverse slope of the hill. By withdrawing the 1st Platoon back to the military crest, it was possible to lay high-angle artillery fire and a fighter plane strike on the enemy occupying the reverse slope defensive positions.

Company G of this regiment arrived on Hill 240 and was deployed to support the attack by fire. At this time the remainder of the 2d Platoon and the Weapons Platoon, acting as a part of the base of fire, displaced forward and joined the 3d Platoon on their objective. With a combination of fires and a determined assault by the 1st Platoon, it was possible for them to gain the topographical crest and rout the tenacious Chinese from their holes with white phosphorous, fragmentation grenades, and point-blank rifle, carbine, and pistol fire.

The Chinese forces attempted at this time to disengage from the firefight. By employing a combination of mortar and artillery concentrations and adjustments, it was possible to kill many of them as they fled in disorder to the north. The objective was secure at 1800.

To cope with possible enemy counterattack, the company was reorganized and placed in a forward slope defense. Artillery and mortar concentrations were registered as an additional factor in the defense. Throughout the night maximum utilization of artillery and mortar shell was employed.

Throughout the course of the attack, Company E sustained 63 casualties, whereas the Chinese Communist Forces suffered losses of 451 known dead and an unknown number of wounded.

1st LIEUTENANT DOLAN: Company E seized Hill 240 from an enemy considered to be of company size. Company E had one man KIA and two men wounded in action. Five enemy dead were counted on Hill 240 and an unknown number of wounded had retreated.

In the attack on Hill 255 the company commander decided to use the 2d Platoon as a base of fire, utilizing the 1st and 3d Platoons as the assault elements. The assault platoons crossed the line of departure at 1430 hours, the 1st Platoon to take Hill 255 proper and the 3d Platoon to take the high ground to the left of Hill 255. At approximately 1545 hours the 3d Platoon, with supporting fire from the 1st Platoon, was able to occupy its objective. Once the 3d Platoon was in position on the objective, the remainder of the company moved to its position and took up supporting positions to assist the 1st Platoon. The 1st Platoon by this time had reached the position from which the troops were going to make their final assault.

Because of the devastating fire from the enemy on Hill 255 proper and Hill 342, the 1st Platoon was forced to assault three times before finally seizing Hill 255 in bitter hand-to-hand combat. The enemy consisted of one battalion on Hill 255 and surrounding ground, dug in on the reverse slope. The remainder of an enemy regiment supporting them from Hill 342 was also using the reverse slope defense. Positions occupied by the enemy were mutually supporting in that the enemy on 342 could support major positions on Hill 255, and positions on Hill 255 were capable of engaging by fire all surrounding terrain, including the village of Manjong-ni. The enemy machine guns were tied in final protective fire being fired along the topographical crest of Hill 255 and surrounding ground. The enemy automatic shoulder weapons covered dead space in the final protective line and likely avenue of approach. The enemy mortars appeared to be firing prearranged close, accurate fire on all dead space and likely assault approaches.

By count on Hill 255, the enemy had 451 dead. Patrols to the north on the following day found additional dead, a number of bloody trails, and numerous bloody bandages, leading us to believe the enemy had approximately 1,060 wounded. The 40th Chinese Division was reported by American intelligence to be no longer effective.[6]

Brig. Gen. Frank S. Bowen Jr., the commander of the 187th Airborne Infantry Regiment, comments on the action of Company E, for which the company was awarded the Presidential Unit Citation.

In this attack on Hill 255, Company E pressed a relentless attack against an enemy who was numerically superior and had the advantage of prepared positions for defense. The unparalleled determination displayed by the company's repeated attacks on this objective in the face of such odds represents the most daring act performed in mass in this command. Bold, aggressive action coupled with great courage and a keen desire to close with the enemy and destroy him enabled Company E to rout this decisive number of the enemy, which was identified as elements of the 40th Chinese Division. Intelligence reports indicated that this Chinese division had the mission of seizing and holding Wonju at all costs. The unusually heavy casualties inflicted on the Chinese Communist Forces by Company E broke the back of their main effort to seize Wonju and dampened their enthusiasm for combat with our forces.[7]

To the west on Hill 325, the Netherlands Battalion also came under heavy attack. The 2d Battalion, 38th Infantry, received orders to reinforce the Netherlands Battalion to secure the vulnerable left flank of the UN line. However, the main threat remained Hill 325. The Periodic Operations Report of the Netherlands Battalion describes the battalion's situation and the beginning of the fight for Hill 325.

The Netherlands Battalion CP opened at Manjong Station [three miles west of Wonju on Route 20] at 1145 hours on 13 February. A and B Companies were in position by 1145 hours on the high ground on Hill 325 about one mile north of the CP, manning almost a mile-long defensive line. The Heavy Weapons and Headquarters Companies formed a close perimeter of defense and guarded all routes of approach around and toward the CP. Various intelligence sources reported enemy concentrations north and northeast of our position.

Furthermore it was reported that Chinese forces tried to infiltrate UN positions by mingling with the retreating ROK soldiers.

In the Netherlands sector everything remained quiet until 0400 hours on 14 February, when a message was received that on our right flank, the enemy had attacked the Company K, 38th Infantry, positions and had broken through. Immediately every one of the Netherlands Detachment and its supporting weapons was on the alert. Communications within the battalion were not too good after the loss of commo equipment the previous day at Hoengsong.

At 0730 hours, Company B reported that there were about 1,000 enemy in front of their positions and infiltrating through their lines. The hazy dawn enabled the enemy to approach the B Company positions to within 25 yards without being seen. Company B could not hold its positions and was ordered back about 400 yards to the next high ground. A source of trouble was communication with the company, since this was done only by sound-powered telephone, and as soon as the company withdrew, no communications were possible. Two platoons could not keep in contact with their company commander.

The enemy did not persist in his attack because artillery and mortar fire was immediately placed upon the enemy. At 1200 hours the frontage of the Netherlands Detachment was shortened by maintaining Company A in a front position and Company B in a second line as a reserve.

For the rest of the day it remained fairly quiet in the Netherlands area. Communication with the adjacent units was also a very weak point, and it was not quite clear what the actual picture was. At 1235 the north side of Hill 325 was in enemy hands, and Company A of the Netherlands Detachment and Company F, 38th Infantry, were trying to make their way to the top. At 1747 hours Company A reported that aircraft strafed and napalmed the enemy positions on the other side of the hill. At 1758 hours Company A reported it was being strafed and napalmed by its own airplanes, although its panels were exposed. In various ways, everyone tried to stop the strafing. For instance, the soldiers on the hill exposed their bare chests and stood in a cross in the open [to signal the aircraft]. The TACP near the 2d Battalion, 38th Infantry, CP passed the message to the planes, and the 38th Infantry Regiment CP was informed by phone so they could also try to call off the planes.

Notwithstanding the strafing, Hill 325 fell into enemy hands. One platoon was ordered to evacuate the dead and wounded. Two platoons remained in position on Hill 200 about three-quarters of a mile south of Hill 325. One squad of Company F, 38th Infantry, remained with our left flank platoon.[8]

While the UN forces fought for Hills 325 and 255, air strikes were crippling enemy forces seeking to turn the flank of the Wonju defensive position. The Command Report of the 2d Infantry Division provides details.

At first light [14 February], the liaison pilots took off and soon reported an enemy column of troops, estimated at two divisions, moving down the Som River, evidently to encircle the positions. As they moved down the river, segments would leave the column to move toward Wonju. The order was given to bring all available supporting fires on the advancing troops. Enemy losses during the hours that followed were staggering, and the pilots reported that the stream literally ran red with the blood of the dead and dying Chinese. Still the column advanced. The carnage continued until the afternoon, when the pilots reported that the advance was breaking up and that what appeared to be leaderless bands of survivors were attempting to escape to the north.

It had been a decisive victory, the enemy abandoning Wonju as a primary target and shifting his main effort to the west.[9]

However, the air strikes did not end the fighting in front of Wonju. The enemy still had to be rooted out of their footholds on the hills. The Operations Report of the Netherlands Battalion describes the battalion's struggle during the night of 14–15 February to retake Hill 325.

At 1900 hours Company A was ordered to make the necessary arrangements to retake Hill 325. At this time Company A had only two small-sized platoons ready for combat, and so Company A's lines were reinforced with one platoon of Company B and one platoon of the Heavy Weapons Company. Fox Company of the 2d

Battalion, 38th Infantry, on our left was also strengthened by a platoon from one of the other 2d Battalion companies. The remainder of the Netherlands Battalion was on the alert, and with the available troops a second line was formed behind the task force. Preparations continued until 0200 hours, and by that time coordination between the adjacent units was arranged as well as possible. Our four platoons were in line at the foot of Hill 325.

At 0235 the attack was started. Artillery was placed on the top of Hill 325, but it was not as effective as was expected because of the pointedness of the peak. High trajectory weapons were clearly indicated, but at that time the 4.2-inch and 81mm mortar forward observers were not in a favorable position to be able to see the target clearly. So the Netherlands forces as well as Fox Company could not attain the objective. Machine gun fire was extremely accurate and mortar fire was also received. The whole attacking force was compelled to fall back to the dead ground once more.

At 0345 the 4.2-inch and 81mm mortar FOs were placed in an improved position, and before the second attack was launched, mortar and artillery fire was placed on Hill 325. While the troops were advancing, the mortar and artillery fire was correctly moved to the northern slopes of Hill 325. When our men and those of Company F had advanced to within 300 yards of the objective, one of our platoons and two F Company platoons were pinned down by heavy and accurate machine gun fire from the top. By means of fire and movement the three platoons were able to withdraw to the position of the respective main bodies.

At 0555 hours, although these troops were exhausted by the Hoengsong fighting, had gone three nights practically without sleep, were strafed by friendly aircraft, and had already carried out two previous unsuccessful attacks, they were ordered to try once more to take the hill. This order had to be given because as soon as daylight would arrive, a matter of half an hour or so, the enemy would be in such a favorable situation that our troops would have made obvious targets, and the only way out would have been a costly and dangerous withdrawal.

At this time the artillery liaison officer attached to the Netherlands Detachment had a splendid idea to put white phosphorous and high explosive mortar fire on the target in order to get the enemy out of its foxholes by means of the WP and to kill him with the HE. This first was put on the target and was so accurate, both the 4.2-inch and the 81mm, that the friendly troops saw the enemy running in all directions. This sight boosted morale sky high and irresistibly our men went forward with bayonets fixed, shouting their "Van Heutz" battle cry.

Mortars and artillery again moved to the reverse slope of the hill, and by 0705 hours the first eight men reached the top, killing the remainder of the enemy with bayonets. The rest of the force was about fifty yards behind. Immediately they dug in, consolidated their positions, and prepared for a counterattack. But once more the artillery and the mortars did their work, and although mortar and small arms fire was received, the enemy launched no counterattack on Hill 325.

In the actions mentioned above the following persons distinguished themselves especially:

First Lt. J. Anemaet, who was the leader of the Netherlands Forces that participated in the taking of Hill 325. He encouraged his men by setting an example of bravery and prudence. Careless of his own safety, he was always in front of his men during the attacks, and together with the first men he reached the objective with fixed bayonets.

Sgt. J. H. Van Abbe, who was a squad leader. He acted with outstanding valor during the first attack on Hill 325. He remained in position under heavy enemy fire, although the left flanking platoon of Company F, 38th Infantry, had to fall back, until he was ordered to relinquish his position. He exposed himself to the enemy and kept his ground, covering the retreat of the remainder. When ordered to attack, he stood up under heavy enemy fire, assembled his squad, and fulfilled his order without having adequate cover.

Pvt. J. F. Ketting Olivier acted outstandingly by volunteering for various dangerous messenger missions, as no wireless communication was possible. He covered the Netherlands commander during the attack and was the first man to reach the enemy objective with fixed bayonet. Somewhat later he was killed while acting as a messenger while the rest of the force was consolidating.

Cpl. J. J. Swart as an 81mm mortar FO guided the fire of his

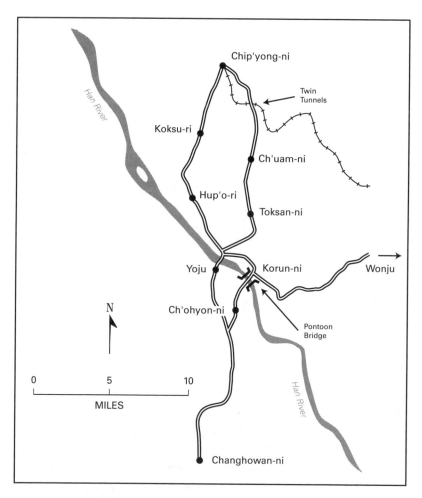

Area south of Chip'yong-ni (original map by author).

mortars quietly and efficiently while he was without cover and under heavy enemy fire. Calling mortar fire so close that he endangered
himself, and going forward with the infantry in the attack with
fixed bayonet, he showed outstanding heroism. Corporal Swart was
killed by hand grenades during this attack.

Pvt. A. Kruyning was a member of Sergeant Van Abbe's squad
and set an example in the exercise of fire discipline, always remain-

ing quiet and cool. Twice he covered the retreat of his squad with his machine gun and remained in position until the last moment.[10]

With their initial attacks on the Wonju line contained, their main enveloping force severely damaged by air strikes, and their positions on the heights captured, the Chinese pulled back from Wonju. However, their assault on Chip'yong-ni continued.

South of Chip'yong-ni: 5th Cavalry Regiment, 14 February

The strong attacks on the 23d Infantry at Chip'yong-ni the night of 13–14 February caused concern among higher commanders. During the day General Ridgway met with General Almond. As a result, Ridgway ordered the 27th British Brigade, which crossed the Han River into the X Corps sector at 0600 hours, to advance north on the road through the Twin Tunnels area and reopen the supply route to Chip'yong-ni. Moving forward in the afternoon, the brigade's advance soon met heavy opposition and ground to a halt seven miles south of Chip'yong-ni. Meanwhile, Ridgway visited General Moore, commander of IX Corps, to discuss plans to use the 5th Cavalry Regiment, in IX Corps reserve south of Yoju, to reopen the more westerly road through Koksu-ri to Chip'yong-ni. When the British advance stalled, Ridgway immediately ordered the 5th Cavalry Regiment to move at once. Col. Marcel G. Crombez, the commanding officer of the 5th Cavalry Regiment, recalls receiving the order.

On 14 February the 5th Cavalry Regiment was in corps reserve when Major General Moore, Commanding General IX Corps, notified me by telephone at 1500 hours that it looked as if I would have to go to the relief of the 23d Infantry, surrounded by enemy forces at Chip'yong-ni, and that I should start planning such an operation along the Koksu-ri axis. The corps commander telephoned again at 1700. General Moore said, "You'll have to move out tonight, and I know you will do it." The British on the other axis to Chip'yong-ni, the better and more direct road, were finding enemy forces heavily entrenched along the route and thus were unable to make a rapid advance.[11]

The initial move is described by Maj. James M. Gibson, executive officer of the 1st Battalion, 5th Cavalry Regiment, whose unit led the move.

On 14 February the 5th Cavalry Regiment moved to an assembly area just south of Yoju, and the 1st Battalion guarded the pontoon bridge over the Han River at Korun-ni. At 1800 the 5th Cavalry Regiment received the mission of relieving the 23d RCT in Chip'yong-ni via the Koksu-ri–Chip'yong-ni axis. The reason the axis was specified was that the 27th British Brigade was using the main Yoju–Chip'yong-ni axis through Toksan-ni and was encountering resistance, which made it seem likely that the British would not be able to relieve the 23d RCT rapidly enough. I understood that the 27th British Brigade had had the original mission of relieving the Chip'yong-ni garrison, but due to the heavy enemy resistance encountered, the 5th Cavalry Regiment was committed on the left.

The 5th Cavalry Regiment made a night march the evening of 14 February and followed the trail to Ch'ohyon-ni in order to reach the Koksu-ri–Chip'yong-ni axis. Starting at 1800 the 5th Cavalry Regiment crossed the bridge at Korun-ni with the 1st Battalion, 2d Battalion, Regimental Headquarters, and 3d Battalion, in that order. Company B, the leading element, halted at 2300 because of a blown-out bridge in the vicinity of Hup'o-ri, and Company A, 8th Engineer Combat Battalion, constructed a bypass for tanks during the night.[12]

Chip'yong-ni: 23d Infantry Regiment, Night of 14–15 February

When the 5th Cavalry Regiment halted for the night about ten miles south of Chip'yong-ni, the Chinese had already begun their second night of attacks on the 23d Infantry. The action is described in the 23d Infantry Regiment's After Action Report.

The first enemy action of the evening occurred at 2030 hours, when Company K received a mortar barrage. At 2130 hours Company C reported sounds of the enemy digging in to their front. The regimental commander ordered conservation of all types of small arms ammunition as the supply was critically short in spite of the airdrops in the afternoon. There were no reserves of 8-round clips for the M-1 rifles other than those in the company stocks at this time.

Simultaneously with an attack from the south on the 2d Battalion area, the enemy brought the regimental CP under heavy self-propelled gun, mortar, and small arms fire. This continued for approximately an hour, and the impact area spread out to include the Heavy Mortar Company and the French Battalion trains area. Fighting increased around the perimeter until the 2d and 3d Battalions to the south and southeast were engaged in fierce close combat. Bugles sounded on the hills to the north and 120mm heavy mortar rounds began to fall in the regimental CP area. The fighting abated for a short period, but the action swelled again when K and A Companies were attacked at 0130 hours, the 15th of February; G Company repulsed two enemy attacks, while pressure increased on the south and southwest against G Company.

At 0230 hours the enemy penetrated Company I but were driven out with the aid of Company L after vicious close-in fighting.[13]

During the fighting in the Company I sector, SFC William S. Sitman performed actions for which he was later awarded the Medal of Honor. Members of the unit describe what happened.

First Lt. Charles E. Dalton, Company M: Sergeant 1st Class Sitman was the section leader of a machine gun section attached to Company I. During the night of 14 February the machine gun section Sergeant Sitman was under constant grenade attack from the enemy. One of the grenades knocked the machine gun Sergeant Sitman was with out of action. A light machine gun squad from Company I was sent to the position where Sergeant Sitman's gun had been knocked out. Sergeant Sitman and the squad stayed in the position to give security to the machine gun crew.

Cpl. John G. Larkin, Company I: I was ordered to take my machine gun and occupy a position formerly occupied by Sergeant Sitman of Company M. Sergeant Sitman's heavy machine gun was knocked out of action, and the sergeant and his crew remained in the emplacement to give us security as there were several defilade approaches leading in. Our position came under hand grenade attack. After some time a lone grenade was thrown into our position. Sergeant Sitman fell on the grenade, shielding the other five members from the grenade with his body, and was killed instantly. Three other members received very light fragmentation wounds, only one being evacuated; the other two returned to duty the same day. I was the gunner in the emplacement and received no wounds at all. Sergeant Sitman's heroic action, I feel sure, saved the lives of the other comrades in the emplacement and enabled us to deliver machine gun fire from our position throughout the attack.

M. SGT. CALVIN A. KEENE, COMPANY M: At that time I was 2d Section leader in the Company M machine gun platoon, which was attached to Company I. Sergeant Sitman was platoon sergeant and was in one of my machine gun emplacements the night of 14 February when we were attacked by the enemy. While under a heavy hand grenade and small arms barrage, the machine gun that Sergeant Sitman was manning was knocked out of action. As I was moving up to the emplacement where the machine gun was knocked out, I was immediately pinned down by machine gun fire. While I was moving toward cover, I heard Sergeant Sitman shout, "There's a grenade in our hole!" and he threw himself down on top of it just before it went off. In throwing himself down he pushed both of the other men toward a safer position and took the full impact of the explosion, resulting in his death. This heroic action saved the lives of the men with him.[14]

The continuing action is described in the 23d Infantry Regiment's After Action Report.

The overwhelming number of enemy forced the Company G line to withdraw at 0315 hours with heavy losses. The regimental commander ordered counterattacks to retake the lost ground. A composite force of Rangers, one platoon of Company F, and the remaining troops of Company G were assembled to accomplish this mission. While they were forming, Companies A and C repulsed another severe attack from the north.

Ammunition stocks in the companies had become so low that commanders ordered their men not to fire unless they could easily see and hit the enemy. At this time the supply trains contained less than 140 rounds of 4.2-inch mortar and 90 rounds of 81mm mortar ammunition. The commitment of the Ranger Company left only Company B in regimental reserve.

The counterattack to retake Company G positions commenced at 0615 hours. At 0800 hours the enemy repulsed the counterattacking composite force with heavy losses to the friendly troops. The regimental commander ordered Company B to the Company G area to retake the vital lost ground, and thus secure the integrity of the perimeter. Heavy small arms and automatic weapons fire from the reverse slopes of Company B's objective prevented them from taking and holding the position. Supporting tanks were unable to gain positions for assault fire because the roads were heavily mined. At 1400 hours Company B was still unable to move, so the TACP brought in air strikes and napalm drops that routed the enemy and enabled Company B to proceed to its objective.

Meanwhile the regimental commander notified Company B of the 2d Engineers that they were now the regimental reserve. With the coming of full daylight, the activity on the remainder of the perimeter ceased and airdrops began to resupply the almost completely exhausted stocks of ammunition. An enemy mortar fired into the drop zone and the regimental CP area throughout the morning, inflicting heavy casualties on the crews that were recovering the supplies. Counter-battery fire by mortars and artillery silenced this enemy mortar at 1130 hours.[15]

Chip'yong-ni: Company G, 23d Infantry Regiment, Night of 14–15 February

Company G on the south side of Chip'yong-ni bore the brunt of the night attack and eventually was pushed off its position. Capt. Edward C. Williamson, a combat historian who studied the action and interviewed members of the units involved, describes the fighting on the southern perimeter.

Company G had a quiet day [during the daylight hours of 14 February]. Hot meals were served. Some of the men thought that perhaps the Chinese had withdrawn.

Enemy activity early that night quickly shattered that hope. Soon after darkness at 1800, the men heard bugles and saw flares. Twenty minutes later Sergeant Otteson's [3d Platoon, Company G] machine gun position was hit, and the gunner was wounded. Otteson took over the gun and found himself in contact with a squad of Chinese who were getting overhead support by a machine gun at the base of Hill 397.

Down at the kitchen the mess heard the firing. They had failed to dig foxholes, and the only place they could find protection was the garbage pit. Cpl. Bernard Jack and the seven other members of the mess crowded into the sump. No one made any funny remarks about the smell.

Up on the hill Lieutenant McGee [3d Platoon leader] had his hands full. Two enemy squads succeeded in penetrating the company position at the contact point on the knoll between the 1st and 3d Platoons. The line was further weakened when aggressive Chinese, gaining a foothold on the hill, planted pole charges in two 1st Platoon holes. The resulting explosions killed three American soldiers and one Korean volunteer who had attached himself to the company and had been furnished a rifle. The Chinese, now in control of the left side of the 1st Platoon sector, set up a machine gun and started firing across the 3d Platoon's right flank. A BAR man was hit, and Lieutenant McGee placed the BAR in his hole.

Because of the enemy fire coming from the 1st Platoon area, Lieutenant McGee began to wonder whether or not the platoon was holding. Phoning Lieutenant Heath, he asked, "Heath, is the 1st Platoon still in position?" Heath was in contact with Sergeant Toth, who had contact with Sergeant Schmitt up on the hill. Sergeant Schmitt was holding in the right sector of the 1st Platoon, and so Toth reported to Heath that the 1st Platoon was still up on the hill. He did not explain that the left sector of the 1st Platoon had collapsed. Heath, thinking that the 1st Platoon was still tied in with the 3d Platoon, relayed Toth's information to McGee. McGee, however, was in doubt. He and Sergeant Kluttz shouted over to the 1st Platoon area, "Anyone from the 1st Platoon?" There was no answer.

Activities in his own area now took up Lieutenant McGee's interest as Chinese soldiers overran a foxhole to his right. On the extreme right flank of his platoon sector, he could see four Chinese soldiers, with shovels strapped on their bodies, crawling on hands and knees fifteen feet above and behind Sergeant Querry's hole. By this time the sound-powered telephone to Querry was out, and McGee shouted to Querry, "There are four of them at the rear of your hole; toss a grenade up and over."

A burst from the enemy machine gun in the 1st Platoon area prevented Querry from rising and lobbing the grenade. Lieutenant McGee and the other occupant of his foxhole, runner Pvt. Cletis D. Inmon, firing a BAR and M-1, respectively, killed the four Chinese. The time was now 2210.

Querry's troubles were not yet over. McGee looked down the slope and saw fifteen or twenty Chinese crawl out of the dry creek-bed and start up the hill toward Querry's hole. McGee called to him, "About fifteen or twenty are coming up to your right front." Querry would not stick his head up. McGee and Inmon with BAR and M-1 fire attempted to pin down the advancing Chinese. The Chinese continued to crawl toward Querry. They threw several potato masher–type grenades at Querry's hole. Querry and a sergeant in his hole climbed out and ran to McGee's hole. They jumped in on top of McGee. The sergeant was hit on the way over. The Chinese then threw a satchel charge into Querry's old hole and killed a private who had remained there.

With Querry on top of him, McGee could not fire. He said, "Get the hell out of here and get back with your squad." Querry did not budge, and McGee repeated the order. Querry then jumped out and was immediately shot through the shoulder. McGee called for a litter team, and the two sergeants were evacuated under enemy fire.

Chinese soldiers started to crawl up the slope toward McGee's position. One threw three hand grenades at McGee before McGee cut him down with the BAR. The BAR was now jamming on every tenth round, and McGee was using his penknife to evacuate the shell. Finally, he dropped the knife, and in the darkness could not find it. Inmon offered his mess kit knife; however, it would not work in the slot. Therefore, McGee abandoned the BAR and attempted to fire his carbine at a Chinese who had crawled up to within ten feet of the platoon CP. As the Chinese rose up on his knees, McGee pulled back the bolt. The cold oil prevented the bolt from going home; a carbine will not fire unless the bolt is completely closed. McGee grabbed the operating handle and pushed it with the palm of his hand, slammed the bolt in, and fired four rounds at the Chinese. McGee killed him. Three other Chinese were also killed by the CP group at this time.

Wire communications were out after 2300. Lieutenant McGee ordered platoon runner PFC John N. Martin, who shared a foxhole in the platoon rear with the 60mm mortar observer, to return to the company CP and inform Lieutenant Heath that the platoon badly needed men, ammunition, and a litter team. Martin delivered McGee's message and returned to the platoon at 2350 bringing fifteen men from the 503d Field Artillery Battalion. As the field artillery men crossed the crest of the hill, they were taken under fire by enemy who had infiltrated the platoon sector. McGee watched with a sinking sensation thirteen of the reinforcing group take off. Of the two remaining, a mortar round killed one and wounded a second.

Private 1st Class Martin then returned to the rear area and guided the company wire team carrying ammunition up to the platoon.

At 2300, shortly after an eight-man carrying party had arrived with ammunition for the two machine guns, an enemy mortar shell scored a direct hit on the company contact point on the right flank. Two men were killed and eight wounded. Cpl. Russell M. Stiltner, who was not hit, continued to man one of the machine guns.

By 2400 the 356th Chinese Regiment had made two unsuccessful assaults on the Company G position. At 2400 the 1st Battalion, 344th Regiment, 115th CCF Division, jumped off in an attack on the southern sector of the 23d Regimental Combat Team perimeter. This attack also failed. The Chinese suffered heavy casualties in the attacks.

As the 1st Battalion, 344th Regiment, began its assault of Company G, an enemy machine gun, firing from a position in the former sector of Company G's 1st Platoon, sent a bullet through Private Inmon's left eye. Inmon started shouting, "I'm hit in the face. I'm hit in the face. I don't want my mother to see me this way. Get me back off this hill." Blood spurted from his eye as Lieutenant McGee attempted to calm him down. McGee said, "Lay down; I can't take you out now." Two Chinese behind the CP prevented Inmon's evacuation. McGee then called to his platoon sergeant, "Hey Kluttz, send the medic over. Inmon's been hit." The aid man came over in two or three minutes and bandaged Inmon's head. McGee now asked Inmon if he could still fire his M-1. Inmon replied, "No, I can't see." McGee said, "Can you load the magazines for my carbine?" Inmon said he would try, but he didn't know. Inmon then went ahead loading the magazines as McGee was firing.

At about 0020 on 15 February, Lieutenant McGee asked the aid man if Inmon got over the crest of the hill, could the aid man walk him to the rear. Inmon's right eye was now cleared, and the runner thought he could make it all right. The aid man and Inmon got over the crest of the hill, and McGee observed the aid man start running and begin to drag Inmon. The two made it to the company CP. The aid man did not return even though Lieutenant McGee had asked him to.

At 0030 two Chinese succeeded in enveloping Ottesen's hole. These Chinese tossed two grenades in the hole and knocked out the machine gun. Corporal Ottesen has since been listed as missing in action. No longer hearing the machine gun, Lieutenant McGee called to Sergeant Kluttz, "What's happened to the machine gun? It's stopped firing." Kluttz replied that Ottesen's position had been overrun and the machine gun knocked out. He reported that Chinese were coming through between Ottesen's squad and Cpl. Raymond Bennett's squad. Bennett, holding the left flank of the platoon, had not been attacked. McGee called him on the sound-powered telephone and ordered him to send several men to fill the gap caused by Ottesen's having been overrun.

Lieutenant McGee then sent Private Martin back to the company CP to find out whether the 1st Platoon was still in position. Lieutenant Heath called Sergeant Toth, who replied that they were still there since Sergeant Schmitt with one squad was holding on the extreme right flank. Martin returned to McGee with this information.

Below the 1st Platoon was an eight- to twelve-foot-high cliff with barbed wire between the cliff and the road. The CCF had penetrated the barbed wire using bangalore torpedoes and satchel charges, climbed the hill, and occupied the left flank of the 1st Platoon sector. Lieutenant McGee sent Private Martin to the CP a second time, and McGee finally convinced Lieutenant Heath that these Chinese were there and were firing at the 3d Platoon. McGee requested ammunition and replacements because the platoon had quite a few wounded and was getting low in personnel.

At 0045 Lieutenant Heath contacted Lieutenant McGee and informed him that a squad was on the way from Company F. Kluttz was now firing the machine gun, giving protective fire to Corporal Bennett's squad, which had succeeded in closing the gap caused by the penetration in Ottesen's sector. The Chinese here had a bugler with them, whom Bennett shot as he tooted his second note. In the melee, however, Bennett was first hit by a hand grenade, which blew part of his hand off. Then he was wounded in the shoulder by a bullet, and a piece of shrapnel struck him on the head. The sound-powered telephone went out, and McGee lost touch with Bennett's squad.

Starting at 0100 the 3d Battalion, 344th CCF Regiment, launched an attack on the southern sector of the perimeter, occupying the knoll on the left flank of the 1st Platoon position within forty minutes.

Acting on McGee's request, Heath obtained Sgt. Kenneth G. Kelly's 3d Squad from the 3d Platoon of Company F. At 0200 Kelly's squad arrived, and Kelly contacted Kluttz. As Kluttz started to take Kelly's squad over to the gap between the 3d and 1st Platoons, two Chinese with burp guns fired at him but missed. Kluttz disposed of them with his M-1. Soon afterward Kluttz returned to McGee and reported that all the men in Kelly's squad were wounded. Kluttz said, "McGee, we have to stop them."

The CCF continued to attack the 3d Platoon. At 0300 the 2d Platoon, which was not under fire, pulled back, thus taking away the machine gun that was supporting the 3d Platoon.

McGee shouted over to Kluttz and asked him if he knew how Bennett's squad was making out. Kluttz replied, "I think three or four are still left."

The Chinese continued to attack. McGee was low on ammunition and Kluttz was having trouble with his machine gun. Growing discouraged, McGee called to Kluttz, "It looks like they have got us." Kluttz called back, "Let's kill as many of these sons of bitches as we can before they get us." At 0245 Kluttz's machine gun jammed and McGee called to him, "Let's try to get out." They threw what grenades they had left and climbed over the crest of the hill. On the reverse slope they joined Bennett, Benoit, and Ziebell. The 3d Platoon survivors then withdrew to the 60mm mortar position.

Lieutenant Haberman, attempting to get reinforcements from Battery B, 503d Field Artillery Battalion, walked into one of their squad tents, which was filled with men. "Hell," he said, "a squad tent won't stop a bullet." He succeeded in persuading five or six men to accompany him. These went outside with Haberman, but none climbed the hill with him.

An estimated four or five Chinese were firing on the 60mm mortar position from the knob on the right flank of the 3d Platoon. Therefore, Haberman moved two guns into a ditch 100 yards back of their position. Four men in the 4th Platoon had been wounded, one by an enemy 60mm mortar round and three by small arms. Most of the enemy mortar rounds were falling on the ridge where the 1st and 3d Platoons formerly were.

Sergeant Schmitt and the twenty men who had been holding the right flank of the 1st Platoon came off the hill at 0300.[16]

Although Company G's main line of resistance had been lost, remnants of the company continued to fight on from rear positions. SFC Warren J. Orr, an eyewitness to the heroism of Pvt. Bruno R. Orig, for which he was awarded the Distinguished Service Cross, provides one description of part of the fighting.

At 0330 hours due to the intensity of enemy fire, which caused numerous casualties, Company G was forced to withdraw about 400 yards. At this time Pvt. Bruno R. Orig, who was returning from laying wire to the OP, noticed a number of his comrades had been wounded. Although under enemy small arms and grenade fire he administered first aid to these men. He then helped carry these men to the comparative safety of the company CP. While returning from one of these trips Private Orig noticed that all except one man on a machine gun had been wounded. Without hesitation he volunteered to man this gun. He remained at this position, placing such effective fire that a platoon was able to withdraw. He remained at this position until overrun by a numerically superior force. The next morning when Company G recaptured the hill Private Orig's body was found dead in his gun emplacement. Around him lay three Chinese dead.[17]

Captain Williamson continues his narrative of the fighting in the southern sector.

Lt. Col. James W. Edwards, commanding the 2d Battalion, ordered Lieutenant Heath to retake the hill. Lieutenant McGee collected Sergeant Kluttz and four men for the forthcoming assault. McGee told Heath, "Get a couple of tanks to help us. We can't do it with what men we have." Eight or ten men from Battery B, 503d Field Artillery Battalion, led by Captain Elledge, joined them. Lieutenant Heady was alerted by Captain Terrell of Company F, who told him to get the rest of his platoon over to Company G, which was being overrun. Heady and his men reached Company G at 0330, and Heady contacted Heath at the bottom of the hill at 0345.

The attacking force was supplemented by a platoon of rangers who arrived at 0400 and five Sherman tanks from the 23d Regimental Tank Company under 1st Lt. Charles W. Hurlburt. Capt. John H. Ramsburg came down from the 2d Battalion staff and took command of the composite group. For the attack, Heady's platoon was on the left, the rangers in the center, and Company G on the right. Ramsburg arranged for a tank to sweep the top of the hill with .50-caliber machine gun fire and for a 60mm mortar to fire a three- to four-minute barrage on the hill. The minute the mortar fire lifted, the attack was to be made.

Heady's platoon lay down a base of fire for the attack using two light .30-caliber machine guns. The enemy replied with fifteen mortar rounds ranging from 60s to 120s, wounding three men, two from McGee's emaciated platoon. McGee now had Kluttz, Martin, and one other man. The rangers succeeded in getting a few men to the top of the hill; however, the superior firepower of the enemy forced them off. The Chinese were effectively using small arms, mortars, grenades, and machine guns. During the action the ranger

platoon leader was killed, and Lieutenant Heath and Captain Ramsburg were wounded. Lieutenant Haberman took over command of
Company G. Heady's platoon had twenty-two wounded and one
missing. Five men were unscathed as the platoon withdrew from the
hill at 0800.

Colonel Freeman then ordered Company B committed to restore
the break in the line caused by Company G's collapse.

On the MSR between Company G and the French Battalion, 1st
Lt. Arthur J. Junot, 1st Platoon commander of the Tank Company,
had three tanks: his, M. Sgt. Andrew Reyna's, and SFC Kenneth P.
Pitlick's. Ten Frenchmen crossed the road after the failure of Ramsburg's force to retake the hill and requested grenades. These Frenchmen then proceeded up the hill supported by the .50-caliber machine
gun on Junot's tank. Twenty yards from the crest, the French got
into a grenade fight with ten Chinese in the old Company G foxholes. Three more Frenchmen and Captain Elledge, carrying a BAR,
arrived. Two enemy machine guns pinned down the French on top
of the hill. The French kept shouting for reinforcements. At about
0820 they were forced to withdraw.

Shortly thereafter Capt. George E. Votom, tank company executive officer, arrived and with Junot made a brief reconnaissance
for the forthcoming Company B attack. They decided that they
would be able to get two tanks up on the ridgeline. Capt. Sherman
Pratt, commanding Company B, and Junot worked out a plan for
the operation of the tanks.

In preparation for supporting the Company B attack, Haberman reorganized Company G. The remainder of the 1st Platoon,
plus the CP group, plus the cooks, amounting to twenty-one men,
went into the line. The 2d Platoon, which had not been hit, added
thirty-one men more. The 3d Platoon now consisted of McGee,
Kluttz, and Martin. In the 4th Platoon, only two mortars were
manned under Cpl. Maurice McCormick. SFC Vernon Eggenburg
acted as mortar observer. Lt. William H. Gibson, the artillery forward observer, and part of Battery B, 503d Field Artillery Battalion,
were with Company G. The battery's guns sat abandoned in a no-
man's-land between Company G and the Chinese. At 1000 Company B jumped off, Company G laying down a base of fire.[18]

The 3d Platoon, Company B, led by 1st Lt. Richard S. Kotite, played a critical role in the ensuing attack. Capt. Sherman W. Pratt, commander of Company B, describes Lieutenant Kotite's actions in his recommendation for award of the Distinguished Service Cross.

At 0245 on 15 February 1951, Company B, 23d Infantry, was assigned the mission of recapturing from the enemy and occupying certain strategic high ground on the south rim of the 23d RCT defense perimeter at Chip'yong-ni. This terrain, essential to the continued successful defense of the perimeter, had been wrestled from friendly units the preceding night, and its occupation by the enemy constituted an actual breach of the positions of the RCT.

The terrain in question was a series of small hills from which the entire perimeter could be seen, and especially all the artillery positions, battalion and regimental trains, and CPs. In addition, by occupying this terrain, the enemy was in a position to deliver close range, flanking fire on friendly units to the right and left, and they were afforded an excellent observation post from which to adjust mortar fire. Chinese Communist infantry were occupying positions on the forward friendly military crest of the hill. When in these positions, they could not be seen from friendly positions, nor could they be fired on by flat trajectory weapons. It was only when individual infantrymen climbed the hill and passed over the topographical crest of the hill that the enemy could be fired upon by friendly troops.

The mission of overcoming enemy resistance on and occupying this hill was assigned to the 3d Platoon, Company B, led by 1st Lt. Richard S. Kotite. With two squads forward and abreast, Lieutenant Kotite began his attack, jumping off at 1000 hours under heavy small arms support and preceded by an air strike and mortar barrage. The platoon worked its way up the hill toward the enemy positions, and as it neared the top, it was suddenly subjected to an intense heavy mortar barrage that killed two of his men, including one squad leader, and wounded five others, including one other squad leader. In addition the fire scattered, disorganized, and bewildered his men to such an extent that Lieutenant Kotite personally defied protection of defilade to quickly organize and encourage his men to continue the attack and move forward out of the dispersion area. Only because of this officer's courageous and forceful leadership was the attack continued.

After reorganizing his troops, Lieutenant Kotite urged them forward and had progressed only eight to ten yards when a heretofore unseen enemy machine gun, located about a hundred yards to the left front, began delivering deadly flanking fire, which killed the platoon sergeant and one other squad leader, leaving Lieutenant Kotite virtually alone to lead his platoon. In spite of this close range machine gun fire, Lieutenant Kotite shouted at his men and led them over the geographical crest of the hill into the point-blank fire of about thirty to forty enemy troops occupying well-dug-in positions. As these enemy troops opened fire at the friendly troops, Lieutenant Kotite rushed at the nearest hole, which contained two Chinese soldiers who were training a light machine gun at his men. Lieutenant Kotite threw a grenade into the hole, which killed one enemy soldier, slightly wounding the other. He then killed the second soldier with his carbine when the enemy opened fire with the machine gun. Lieutenant Kotite then went on to another hole containing two more enemy soldiers, who were firing rifles directly at him, badly ripping and tearing his clothing about the neck and chest, and finally wounding him in the left hip. Disregarding his injury, Lieutenant Kotite continued his heroic and determined attack by killing two more enemy in their holes. As the two enemy threw hand grenades at him that slightly stunned him, he rushed to the side of the hole and shot both of them.

Of the thirty-eight men who began the attack on this position, only fourteen succeeded in getting over the topographical crest and closing with the enemy. Of these fourteen, five were killed. The remaining nine, which included Lieutenant Kotite, killed, wounded, or dispersed the remaining enemy and secured their objective.[19]

The attack of the 3d Platoon, although successful at first, was too weak to hold the ridge. Captain Williamson continues his narrative of the action in the southern sector of the Chip'yong-ni perimeter.

Pratt succeeded in getting his company almost to its objective when heavy small arms and automatic weapons fire from the reverse slope drove them from the hill. Slippery going caused by snow, plus an enemy 75mm recoilless rifle, prevented the tanks from gaining the ridgeline in support of Company B.

At 1715 that evening the 5th Cavalry Regiment entered the perimeter, having broken through the enemy. The enemy immediately withdrew. That night Company G was relieved by Company B, the 2d Platoon being attached to Company F and remaining in position.

In the fighting at Chip'yong-ni, Company G had forty-eight wounded, fourteen killed, and ten missing.[20]

The enemy occupation of the main line of resistance of Company G just before dawn on 15 February was serious. The CCF 3d Battalion, 344th Regiment, was ordered to dig in on the MLR and hold the position in preparation for continuing the attack the night of 15–16 February. Infantry counterattacks and artillery and tank fire during the daylight hours of 15 February were unable to dislodge the enemy. With the commitment of Company B, 23d Infantry, as part of the unsuccessful counterattack effort, the remaining reserve for the Chip'yong-ni defense was now an engineer company. However, the Chinese were not able to launch their attack that night, because an infantry-armor relief force, Task Force Crombez, broke through the Chinese lines, dispersed the attack force that was in position on the southern part of the perimeter, and reinforced the battered 23d Infantry.

Chapter 10

THE RELIEF OF CHIP'YONG-NI

Task Force Crombez

While the fighting continued into the daylight hours of 15 February on the southern section of the 23d Infantry's perimeter, the 5th Cavalry's fight to open the road to Chip'yong-ni began. Officers of the regiment describe the action.

MAJ. ROBERT A. HUMPHREY, S-2 OF THE 5TH CAVALRY: One platoon of Company A, 70th Tank Battalion, was with each infantry battalion, as well as one platoon from Company A, 8th Engineer Combat Battalion. The 61st Field Artillery Battalion (105mm howitzers) was kept under regimental control.

At 0700 hours, 15 February, the 1st Battalion jumped off on foot with the mission of taking the high ground east of the road in the vicinity of Hill 152, about two miles north of the blown bridge at Hup'o-ri. Lead elements of the 1st Battalion encountered an enemy minefield on the road and shoulders near Hill 152. At that time the battalion began receiving small arms fire from the north.

MAJOR GIBSON, EXECUTIVE OFFICER OF THE 1ST BATTALION: The 1st and 4th Platoons, Company A, 70th Tank Battalion, were attached to the 1st Battalion, 5th Cavalry Regiment. At daylight, 15 February, the regiment continued to move in the original order of march. Initial enemy resistance was met at Sangch'ohyon-ni at about 0800, and Company B deployed off the trucks while Company A was ordered forward. With Companies A and B advancing astride the road, Company C was held in battalion reserve. When the 1st Battalion reached solid positions east of the road, the 2d Battalion was committed west of the road and occupied Hill 143. The enemy

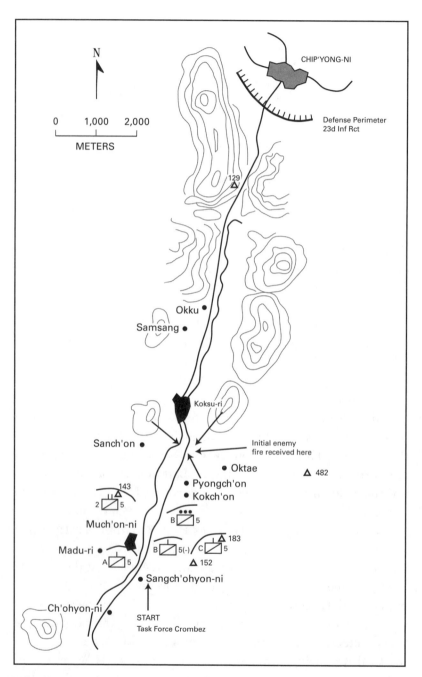

Route of Task Force Crombez, 15 February 1951 (based on maps in CMH Manuscript 8–5.1A BA 29, Task Force Crombez).

held strong positions on both sides of the road, and the 1st and 2d Battalions, making slow progress, continued, heavily engaged.

Lt. Col. Morgan B. Heasley, commanding officer of the 1st Battalion: At 0700, 15 February, the battalion moved out, and at 1100 hours contacted an estimated battalion of enemy dug in on the Hill mass 152. The battalion deployed and moved north. By 1500 hours, Company B had pushed to the vicinity of Kokch'on. Company A was deployed to the left in the vicinity of Much'on-ni, and Company C was deployed in the vicinity of Hills 152 and 183. The 2d Battalion, committed after the initial enemy contact, was located to the left of Hill 143.

Capt. Joe W. Finley, commanding officer, Company F: On the morning of 15 February, the 2d Battalion, 5th Cavalry Regiment, moved to the vicinity of Ch'ohyon-ni, where the companies detrucked. Major Allen, commanding officer of the 2d Battalion, took the company commanders on reconnaissance as far as Sangch'ohyon-ni. Company G then moved up on Hill 143. Company E moved up along the streambed to the right, and Company F moved into Madu-ri, as battalion reserve. Company G worked as far as Sanch'on, and Company E moved a similar distance, when the battalion observation post party on the north edge of Hill 143 noticed heavy enemy activity in the vicinity west and south of Samsang. Company F was then moved along the right edge of Hill 143, and around 1500 occupied the finger ridge just south of Sanch'on, about 1,000 yards from the road to Koksu-ri. From this position I observed great numbers of enemy troops dug in along the road to the north.

Major Humphrey, S-2 of the 5th Cavalry: In the triangular area formed roughly by Kokch'on, Oktae, and Koksu-ri, great numbers of enemy troops were observed by 1st and 2d Battalion troops, artillery liaison planes, division spotting planes, and the Tactical Air Control Party observation planes (T6), which directed air strikes on this terrain. The regimental artillery fired on this area, lifting only for the air strikes. One battery of 155mm self-propelled howitzers also gave support. This fire fell during the morning and early afternoon of 15 February.

In the early afternoon, the 3d Battalion moved up behind the 1st Battalion. Enemy troops were thoroughly entrenched in great numbers on the regimental front and in particular in front of the 1st Battalion, in the Oktae valley. An estimated 2,000 enemy troops were located here. The high Hill mass 482 was of great concern to the regiment because it afforded observation for enemy forces. This area was saturated by artillery and air strikes and kept under close surveillance.[1]

The Formation of Task Force Crombez

Colonel Crombez grew increasingly concerned with the slow progress of the infantry advance in the face of strong enemy opposition. He describes his decision to try a faster method of reaching Chip'yong-ni.

In the morning of 15 February, the 1st Battalion and later the 2d Battalion were committed north toward Koksu-ri. By 1100 hours I realized that the 1st and 2d Battalions were advancing too slowly. I sensed that the enemy offered too much opposition for the infantry battalions to be able to reach Chip'yong-ni by evening. Feeling that the entire route to Chip'yong-ni was heavily defended by enemy forces, I decided that only an armored task force would be able to penetrate the enemy-held territory successfully. I began at that time to plan and organize Task Force Crombez. In addition, I decided that supply trucks and ambulances, which were being organized to accompany the 5th Cavalry Regiment to relieve the 23d Infantry RCT, would not be able to get through.

During the morning Major General Moore [IX Corps commander] visited me at my regimental CP. During the early afternoon, Major General Ruffner from X Corps arrived at the regimental CP and asked me whether I was going to attempt to reach the 23d Infantry RCT that day. I stated that I would do so personally and that I would arrive there before nightfall. Early in the afternoon, Major General Palmer, commanding general, 1st Cavalry Division, arriving by helicopter offered the use of his craft to me, and I made an aerial reconnaissance of the road to Chip'yong-ni.

At 1500 I decided that I would not wait for the supply trucks and the ambulances, which were arriving from the south, but would proceed immediately to Chip'yong-ni with the armored task force.

When the road was clear and suitable for wheeled traffic, I would radio back and have Lieutenant Colonel Treacy, Commanding Officer, 3d Battalion, bring in the supply vehicles and the ambulances.

I composed my task force as follows: A total of twenty-three tanks of Company D, 6th Tank Battalion, and Company A (minus two platoons), 70th Tank Battalion; Company L, 5th Cavalry Regiment. The riflemen of Company L were to ride the tanks, with the exception of the first five, which were to remain bare. They were instructed to remain on the tanks at all times, unless forced off by fire, to protect the tanks from fanatic enemy troops who might attempt to knock out the tanks at very close range. Four engineer troops from Company A, 8th Engineer Combat Battalion, were placed on the second tank in the column for the purpose of lifting possible mine emplacements. The M-46 tanks of the 6th Tank Battalion were placed in the lead because they mounted 90mm guns, because they could turn completely around in place (an important consideration in mountainous terrain traversed by a single narrow road), and because they had better armor protection than the M4A3 tanks of the 70th Tank Battalion, which mounted only 76mm guns and which could not turn completely around in place.

Before the task force departed, I had radio contact with Lieutenant Colonel Chiles, commanding officer, 23d Infantry RCT, and I informed Colonel Chiles that I was coming but without supply trains. Colonel Chiles requested that I come, trains or no trains. I asked for air strikes before my departure, and also that liaison planes cover my advance and maintain contact with the advancing column. At 1545, Task Force Crombez, with me in the fifth tank, departed from the point 500 yards northeast of the road junction in the vicinity of Sangch'ohyon-ni. Major Parziale, operations officer, remained near the point of departure. Lieutenant Colonel Treacy was directed to remain in place so that on personal order from me, he could bring up the supply trucks and ambulances after the road to Chip'yong-ni was cleared.[2]

Major Parziale, regimental S-3, provides more details of the decision making and planning for the task force.
Between 1100 and 1200, 15 February, formation of Task Force

Crombez was started, and during that time Colonel Crombez and I crystallized the plan for the task force operation. The decision to form Task Force Crombez was made because of the following reasons. The infantry was meeting too much opposition, and only an armored column's mobility would be able to make the quick contact with the 23d RCT at Chip'yong-ni that was necessary. Infantry would be needed to accompany the tanks to offer protection from mines and to keep the enemy from climbing on the tanks and using demolition charges. Heavily defended enemy minefields were a calculated risk.

The task force was planned to break open a supply route to the 23d RCT. After considering the advisability of sending the supply column along with the armored column or having it follow the tank column, it was decided to have the supply column leave the regimental area with tank protection and only on Colonel Crombez's personal order at a later time. Lieutenant Colonel Treacy, commanding officer of 3d Battalion, was designated the officer to conduct the supply column to Chip'yong-ni.

At 1200 the task force was formed and ready to move on the order of Colonel Crombez, who had decided that he would personally conduct it into Chip'yong-ni. Orders were given to infantrymen to get off the tanks when the vehicles stopped, cover the tanks and the engineers who might be in the process of mine-lifting, and get back on the tanks when the vehicles started moving again.

At 1500 or thereabouts, when I spoke on the radio with the S-3, 23d RCT, I received the impression that the 23d RCT needed supplies desperately. At this time I was unaware that the 23d RCT had been receiving supplies by airdrop. Yet, the S-3, 23d RCT, wanted Task Force Crombez to come through to Chip'yong-ni with or without supplies. As a result of this, and after some thought, I came to the conclusion that the 23d RCT was in reality most in need of psychological contact with friendly forces, even though the question of evacuating the wounded was certainly an important consideration.[3]

Capt. John C. Barrett, commanding officer, Company L, provides details of the preparations for the infantry company to accompany the armor task force.

At 1100 hours, 15 February, I was informed by Lieutenant

Colonel Treacy that Company L and approximately twenty-five tanks would make up a task force to go to Chip'yong-ni to relieve the 23d Infantry Regiment. The task force was scheduled to depart at 1300 that day. I prepared my company for this mission.

At 1215 hours Lieutenant Colonel Treacy gave me additional information. The mission of the infantry was to protect the tanks against enemy infantry. Whenever the tanks halted, Company L was to dismount and deploy on both sides of the road in order to protect the tanks and the squad of engineer soldiers accompanying the task force. When the tanks were ready to proceed, the infantry was to remount the tanks.

I immediately contacted Captain Hier, commanding officer of Company D, 6th Tank Battalion, and we discussed the employment of the infantry in the task force. It was agreed that if the tanks were halted, the infantry would deploy fifty to seventy-five yards off the road. When the tankers were ready to proceed, they would signal the infantry to remount. Hier would inform the tanks by radio, and the tankers in turn would inform the infantry by voice. It was a natural assumption on my part that the tanks would not be buttoned up because of the infantry riding them.

At 1300 hours Colonel Treacy informed me that the task force would be delayed because the supply vehicles for the 23d Infantry Regiment had not yet arrived. Colonel Treacy further stated that the mission of the task force was to bring supply vehicles into the 23d Infantry Regiment perimeter. The task force would return to the regimental area that same afternoon.

I returned to the company and issued the attack order to the platoon leaders, stating the mission of the task force and the mission of the infantry. I instructed my platoon leaders to exert utmost control over the men in action. Infantrymen who become separated from the tanks were to assemble and make their way back to friendly lines if possible or wait near the road, utilizing the best available defensive positions, for the return of the tanks. They could then rejoin the tanks returning that afternoon from Chip'yong-ni. I had the platoon leaders study the map so they would be oriented on the ground at all times. I also instructed the platoon leaders to select one man per tank to fire the .50-caliber machine gun mounted on the tank.

At approximately 1500 hours, I was told by Colonel Treacy that the task force was ready to depart. Colonel Treacy at that time instructed me to have a two-and-a-half-ton truck follow the rear of the tank column to pick up the wounded, since the task force had no means of medical evacuation. I ordered the Service Company truck assigned to Company L to follow the task force column. I also ordered four ROK soldiers of the 5th Platoon, Company L, to accompany the truck and act as litter bearers.

I mounted the company on the tanks, leaving the first four tanks bare. I rode on the second tank that carried infantry, along with Colonel Treacy and ten enlisted men. The executive officer of the company, Lieutenant Johnson, rode the rear tank. For company communication, Lieutenant Johnson and I each had one SCR 300 radio; also the platoon leaders and I each had an SCR 536 radio.[4]

Task Force Crombez's Advance

Soon after 1530 hours the armor-infantry task force moved north. Colonel Crombez describes the initial action.

The task force, with the tanks at intervals of 50 yards, proceeded 1.8 miles when small arms and automatic weapons fire at long range began to be received from both sides of the road and also from the right rear. About 30 riflemen forced off the tanks took cover in the ditches. I directed the column to continue advancing.

As the lead tanks made the sharp bend into Koksu-ri, enemy fire increased in intensity from the high ground west of the town as well as from the ridges to the east. Enemy personnel could be clearly seen, and machine gun fire and tank shells killed many. Not counting the attacking force against Chip'yong-ni, I estimate that at least 2,000 Chinese were opposing the two infantry battalions of the 5th Cavalry that were attacking the high ridges along the road. Except for die-hard antitank crews, bazooka teams, and satchel and pole charge groups, the enemy was emplaced in the high ridges.

Immediately after the column passed through Koksu-ri, about 100 additional riflemen were forced from the tanks; I felt that the success of the task force depended on the ability of the tanks to keep moving, and I directed the tanks to continue.[5]

Maj. Fred T. Wilson, S-3 of the 1st Battalion, describes his view of the start of Task Force Crombez.

When Task Force Crombez departed the regimental area, I was at an observation post located midway between Sangch'ohyon-ni and Hill 152. Through my field glasses I was able to follow the task force beyond Okku and almost into the pass.

The first enemy fire directed against the task force came from Pyongch'on and the small village beside it to the north. Very few riflemen dismounted until the tank column was just short of the turn into Koksu-ri; I saw twelve to fifteen men lying along the dikes to the left of the road and working their way to the dry streambed.

After the tank column made the turn into Koksu-ri, seven or eight additional riflemen dismounted.

I saw the tanks stop only once, just before entering Koksu-ri. From there to Okku, I could see only the rear of the tank column, which continued without halting.

I saw the tanks receiving small arms fire. I could also distinguish heavy explosive bursts, but it was difficult for me to tell whether those bursts were mortar shells or were from the tank guns.[6]

M. Sgt. Jessie O. Giddens and 1st Lt. William R. Bierwirth, tank platoon leaders in Company D, 6th Tank Battalion, tell of the fighting in and around Koksu-ri.

MASTER SERGEANT GIDDENS: At approximately 1500 hours, the task force moved out, making contact at 1515 hours south of Koksu-ri after moving about 500 yards down the road. My platoon, which was the third in the column, began receiving intense small arms, machine gun, and antitank rifle fire. The infantry platoon leader riding on my tank was wounded along with one other soldier. The column was halted for about five minutes due to a bypass in the town of Koksu-ri. At this time the enemy fire became so intense that all the infantry riding my tank had to dismount to take cover. In so doing, the infantry platoon leader was killed. I had ordered my platoon to lay down as much fire as possible on the high ground and to cover the infantry as much as possible. As the infantry mounted we were ordered to move out and keep going due to the heavy fire coming in on my tanks. We moved out and through the town of Koksu-ri and encountered about two companies of Chinese troops on the high ground to the west and east of the road. In spite of the heavy fire being laid down by the task force, the Chinese made very determined attacks on our tanks with bazooka, pole charges, hand grenades, and what seemed to be bottles of gasoline. My gunner knocked out two men with a bazooka and two with pole charges, and the infantry killed many of the charging enemy. At this time some of the infantry were engaged in hand-to-hand combat in the ditches with the enemy. The task force commander, Colonel Crombez, ordered us to keep moving at all cost. At one point, the column stopped, and the Chinese tried to close in again but were driven off or killed by the heavy fire being laid down by all the infantry and tanks.

LIEUTENANT BIERWIRTH: Task Force Crombez attacked at 1500 hours on 15 February. About 500 yards south of Koksu-ri, the lead element came under heavy rocket, mortar, and automatic weapons fire. Very heavy cannon and machine gun fire was laid down by D Company and the infantrymen of Company L, 5th Cavalry, who were riding the tanks. In Koksu-ri and the high ground just north of it, the enemy resistance became heavier, and most of the infantry were shot off our tanks. The foot soldiers climbed back on the tanks, and the column continued to advance, firing very rapidly and effectively.[7]

Crew members of the tank on which Colonel Crombez rode tell of the experience.

MASTER SERGEANT KIRKLAND, TANK COMMANDER: On 15 February at 1500 hours, Colonel Crombez mounted my tank, which was the fifth tank in the column, and assumed command of the task force. We buttoned up after the first 500 yards. Colonel Crombez directed fire for our gunner and was in complete charge of the task force. If the column slowed down, he would urge them to move on. When the lead tank was slowed and we had no communications with them, Colonel Crombez told the number two tank to close in on it. This kept the lead tank moving and the column continuing toward its objective.

PFC THOMAS BAYES JR., GUNNER: On the 15th of February about

1500 hours, I was informed that Colonel Crombez would ride as my tank commander and that I would receive fire orders from him. We were among the first tanks to fire on the enemy troops. He gave me clear, short fire commands and spotted two or three rocket launcher teams. He was very calm throughout the action and urged the tanks to keep moving through the heavy enemy fire.[8]

The infantrymen of Company L, exposed to fire riding outside the tanks and compelled to dismount and then remount while tanks were moving, had a different perspective of the fighting. Captain Barrett describes his experience.

The task force started from the tank park about 1530. Approximately 1,000 yards from the initial point of departure, the column received the first enemy fire directed against it. This consisted of small arms fire only, increasing in intensity until the column reached Koksu-ri. The column passed through Koksu-ri with the tanks and infantry in good shape. Casualties at this time were extremely light.

Two thousand yards beyond Koksu-ri, the tanks halted for a reason unknown to me. I ordered the infantry to dismount according to instructions. The company deployed along the road with the exception of some wounded who remained on the tanks. The tanks remained halted about eight or ten minutes. The infantry was heavily engaging the enemy in a small arms firefight on both sides of the road when the tanks began moving without notifying the infantrymen.

As soon as I saw the tanks start to move, I ordered the company to load up. Due to the fact that the tanks were seventy-five yards distant from the infantrymen, the tanks were moving at a fast rate of speed when the men were able to reach them. Approximately seventy men of the company were able to rejoin the tanks, including me and one platoon leader, Lieutenant Chastaine.

I was not able to remount the tank I had been on originally because it had moved out rapidly, but I joined the column on the fifth or sixth tank behind my original carrier. Colonel Treacy mounted that tank, but shortly thereafter, he was knocked off due to traverse of the turret. From reports of infantrymen I secured in Chip'yong-ni, I learned that Colonel Treacy rejoined the column on about the twentieth tank. Those in the rear of the column were unable to catch up with the tanks. Some stayed with the wounded.

The men on the ground were organized by Lieutenant Johnson, the executive officer, and Sergeant Jones, and they reached friendly lines later that day. One platoon leader, Lieutenant Lahey, was killed at this time.

According to the mission I received, I felt it was necessary to leave the remainder of the company in command of the executive officer and to proceed with the men able to rejoin the tanks.[9]

Other infantrymen of Company L provide additional details.

M. SGT. LLOYD JONES, 3D PLATOON: Task Force Crombez consisted of twenty-three tanks, the first four and the last four of which were bare, while the others carried approximately ten riflemen each. Just prior to the departure of the task force, the men received information that the task force would break a roadblock and contact the 23d RCT at Chip'yong-ni. Riflemen riding the tanks had the mission of keeping the enemy from destroying the tanks by ground action. They were to dismount when the tanks stopped, give protection by fire, and mount when the tanks were ready to continue. As the men mounted the tanks, they were told that one tanker in each tank would unbutton his vehicle and signal by voice when he was ready to continue.

An air strike directed against the enemy just before the departure of the task force column pointed out the locations of the enemy. The air strike seemed very effective, and the men expected very little enemy fire. Soon after the column got under way, several rounds of 60mm mortar fire fell on the area where the tanks had been assembled, but this was probably not observed fire.

I was riding the fifteenth or sixteenth tank. The lead tanks proceeded around the curve in the road south of Koksu-ri and stopped in the village, where I could not see them. The tank column halted, and heavy small arms fire began to be received from a ridge to the right. The tanks had gone one mile or one and a quarter miles from the point of departure to this first halt.

Two men on my tank were wounded by small arms fire, and I ordered the men to dismount, not so much to protect the tank, but in order for them to take cover themselves. I remained on the tank until the turret, swinging to the right to fire, knocked me off.

Most of the men who had dismounted were taking cover in a culvert or behind an embankment fifteen feet high in a rice field fifty yards to the left of the road. Without warning, the tanks commenced to move forward again, and the dismounted riflemen were unable to get back on the tanks. The tankers gave no indication that they were going to start.

Cpl. Hubert M. Cobb, 4th Platoon: When I mounted the nineteenth tank in the column, I knew only that the men of Company L were going to ride the tanks. I was instructed to get off when my tank stopped, take cover, and remount when the tank was rolling again. I did not carry my 57mm recoilless rifle, and before I mounted the tank I traded my .45-caliber pistol with a South Korean for an M-1 rifle.

After proceeding a very short way, 200 or 300 yards, my tank halted, and I dismounted and took cover against enemy fire. I was unable to see very much. As the tank started to move, I remounted, together with about one-third of the personnel who had originally been on the tank. It was almost impossible to get back on a tank once it had started to move.

Soon after the column crossed the river, my tank halted again in the middle of town [Koksu-ri]. Another man and I helped a wounded soldier off the tank and placed him under a burned truck. I remounted the tank while the other man remained to guard the wounded man. From there to Chip'yong-ni the column halted several times but only for very short intervals.

I fired my weapon all the way to Chip'yong-ni. I fired about 350 rounds. At times I was able to see the enemy I fired on. I saw three enemy machine guns, several Bren guns, bazookas, grenades thrown, and pole charges attempted.

PFC Donald F. Russell, 4th Platoon: I rode on the nineteenth tank in the column. The tank halted almost immediately, and the seven or eight men on my tank dismounted, then remounted. Between this time and the second tank halt, several men riding the vehicles were wounded by enemy fire. I jumped off and took cover in the ditch, where I met Corporal Cobb. After talking about whether we should remain in the ditch or continue with the column, we decided to remount the tanks. Cobb mounted one tank, and as I was running alongside, I received a mortar fragment in my hand. I passed up my carbine to Cobb so he might get on the tank more easily, and he fell in the road. He got on the next tank. When the column halted again, I jumped off my tank and ran up to get back my weapon from Cobb.

I fired my weapon when I could see the targets, but it was very difficult to hit anything because of the movement of the tanks. I saw enemy machine guns and some bazooka teams. Mortar rounds were hitting on the shoulders of the road.

PFC HOMER BASSFORD AND CPL. GEORGE E. REED, 1ST PLATOON: We were informed just prior to the departure of Task Force Crombez that we were to ride tanks to break through an enemy roadblock and make contact with the 23d RCT in Chip'yong-ni. The instructions we received from the noncommissioned officers of the company were that we mount the tanks, dismount when the tanks stopped, cover the tank, and mount again when the tanks were ready to start. We followed instructions, but by the time we had gotten off the tanks, the tanks had started up again, and there was no way to get back on. We were both riding on the fifth tank, the first one to have troops on it. There was firing from enemy forces when the tank we were riding first stopped. We were able to see the enemy as we were pinned down with several others in a rice paddy beside the road that afforded little protection. Machine gun and mortar fire fell in the near area.

CPL. PAUL CAMPBELL, 2D PLATOON: When nine others and I mounted the sixth tank in the column, I had no clear idea of the mission of that force. The riflemen were instructed to dismount when the tanks halted, advance fifty yards, and cover the tanks until the vehicles were able to advance again, and then to remount. At the first enemy resistance, the platoon sergeant on my tank ordered the men to dismount with the exception of me. I was directed to man the .50-caliber machine gun mounted on the tank. The men on my tank had carried a .30-caliber light machine gun with them, and they proceeded to set up the weapon on the ground, but just as the gun was ready to operate, the tanks moved on. By the time the machine gun was disassembled, it was too late for the men to regain the tank. Some mounted other tanks.

I fired the machine gun all the way into Chip'yong-ni. I saw enemy crews with satchel and pole charge, but I saw no bazooka team. I fired at a range between 50 and 200 yards. When the tank gun fired to the right, I fired to the left, covering the blind side of the tank. The enemy was using burp guns, Bren guns, heavy and light machine guns, and small arms against the tank column.

CPL. WAYNE O. KEMP, 1ST PLATOON: When I mounted the eighteenth tank of the column as a gunner of a .30-caliber machine gun, I was instructed as follows: as soon as enemy resistance was encountered, some men were to dismount to the left, and some to the right in order to cover the tanks from ground action; when the tanks started, the men were to remount.

About one-half mile from the start, everyone on my tank dismounted on order of the platoon sergeant when the tank halted. Enemy fire was being received. When the tank commenced moving, I was told to run alongside the tank. I did so, and as I was running, I was wounded in the arm. No one was able to get aboard the tank because by this time it was going too fast.[10]

As the tank column neared Chip'yong-ni, it entered perhaps the most difficult section of the road. A blockage here would halt the column and allow the enemy to close on the tanks and knock them out. Colonel Crombez and several tankers describe the fighting here.

COLONEL CROMBEZ: North of Koksu-ri the road passed through the valley, following the hillside on the left closely, until the high ground or summit when the road then followed along the hills on the east. As the tanks approached the summit in the pass near Benchmark 129, close teamwork among the tanks was particularly necessary since the enemy was located at the top of the cliffs, directly overlooking the task force column. Enemy fire intensified, and bazooka and satchel charges were thrown from the heights. At the summit of the pass, 5.25 miles from the start, the lead tank was hit but not disabled by a bazooka rocket; all members in the fighting compartment of the tank were wounded. The fourth tank [immediately in front of Colonel Crombez] was struck in the turret by a bazooka round, and the rocket exploded the ammunition in the ready racks within the tank and set the tank on fire. Captain Hier, commanding officer of Company D, 6th Tank Battalion, and the men in the fighting compartment of the tank were burned to death. The driver of the tank gunned the motor and got the tank off the road in order to keep from impeding the progress of the following tanks. Lieutenant Bierwirth assumed command of Company D.

LIEUTENANT BIERWIRTH: Going through the cut about 2,000 yards south of Chip'yong-ni, the enemy, in great strength, attacked from above with antitank rockets, antitank rifles, pole charges, and satchel charges with intense small arms fire. The lead tank, commanded by Lieutenant De Schweinitz, was penetrated through the tip of the turret, and several of the crew were wounded. The company commander, Captain Hier, his gunner, and loader were killed when a rocket penetrated the left side of their tank, exploding the ammunition in the ready racks. Although severely burned, Corporal Calhoun, the driver of the tank, drove the vehicle through the pass and off the road, thus permitting the column to continue its advance without interruption. During the entire action, Colonel Crombez was directing the column and picking out targets for the tankers.

MASTER SERGEANT GIDDENS: As the column approached a point 3,000 yards from the town of Chip'yong-ni, we entered a pass with high ground on both sides and hundreds of small troop dugouts. Here we came under the most intense fire. Both tanks and infantry were putting out as much fire as possible, but the lead tank was hit.

The fourth tank, with Captain Hier, entered the pass, and his tank was hit by bazooka fire on the left side of the turret, killing him, his gunner, and loader, and severely wounding the driver and bow-gunner. The driver, seriously wounded, pulled the tank off the side of the road, and Colonel Crombez ordered the other tanks to move faster. As my platoon entered the pass, a bazooka hit the top of my turret, but failed to explode.

SFC JAMES MAXWELL: When we were about 2,000 yards from Chip'yong-ni, I spotted a bazooka man moving over a hill of a pass in which we had to go. I called 1st Lieutenant De Schweinitz, my platoon leader, who was the point tank, but I was too late with my call. The lieutenant's tank was hit through the top of the turret, wounding Lieutenant De Schweinitz; Cpl. Donald P. Harrell, the gunner; and Pvt. Joseph Garland, the loader. Lieutenant De Schweinitz's radio was put out of order and no one could contact him. I was in the second tank. As I came through the pass my tank was hit in two road wheels, one on each side of the tank. I started taking the call from Colonel Crombez, the task force commander.[11]

Arrival At Chip'yong-ni

While the 5th Cavalry and Task Force Crombez fought their way north toward Chip'yong-ni, the 23d Infantry inside the beleaguered defensive perimeter had been fighting to recover lost ground, particularly in the south, where the Company G and an artillery position had been overrun. Although the approach of the task force had been observed since 1630 hours, tanks from the 23d Infantry were the first to encounter the relief column. The meeting is described by Sergeant 1st Class Maxwell, the tank commander at the head of the task force.

About 500 yards from where I started taking the calls [at the north end of the pass], we spotted tanks down the road. I started to fire on them, but the lead tank turned its turret, and I recognized it as one of our friendly forces. We came up to a halt and both just sat for a while. We had no radio contact with each other, so I dismounted from my tank and went forward on foot and made contact with the lead tank from the 23d Infantry Regiment. I told him to pull back so we could get on through. When we entered Chip'yong-ni, some of the men of the 23d Infantry and some of the French troops came out and kissed my tank.[12]

Colonel Crombez describes the arrival at Chip'yong-ni and the decisions he made.

Shortly before 1700, the task force had almost reached the defense perimeter of the 23d Infantry RCT. Stopping in the vicinity of the road junction near Masan, the tanks cleared out the area to the right of the road by heavy and concentrated fire. Enemy troops attempting to escape up the draws bunched up in groups of as many as 50 to 100 men and were destroyed by the tank 90mm guns firing HE. This fire hit the enemy on his flank as the enemy was making an attack on Chip'yong-ni.

The task force so demoralized the enemy that his positions disintegrated. It struck the Chinese forces attacking the 23d Infantry RCT at the most psychological moment, while they were progressing in their attack against the 23d Infantry RCT. The 23d Infantry RCT was at that moment making a counterattack to regain a 155mm howitzer battery position that had been overrun. A platoon of tanks of the 23d Infantry RCT met the lead tanks of Task Force Crombez at the 23d Infantry RCT perimeter. Shortly after 1700 hours, Task Force Crombez entered the defense perimeter of the 23d Infantry, 6.2 miles from the start of the operation. I made contact with Colonel Chiles, who stated that he had been flown in to assume command of the 23d Infantry when Colonel Freeman, former commanding officer of the 23d, was evacuated by air after being wounded two days previously.

When Task Force Crombez entered Chip'yong-ni, twenty-three infantrymen and the four engineer troops were still aboard the tanks. Of these, thirteen were lightly wounded, and one died of wounds that evening. The infantrymen forced from the tanks before reaching Chip'yong-ni made their way to the regiment, about a hundred returning to the original point of departure that night.

At 1730 I decided to spend the night at Chip'yong-ni. My reasons were as follows: one hour of daylight remained, and in the event that enemy opposition was encountered on the return trip, it might be dark before contact could be made with the regiment. Tanks unprotected by infantrymen and operating in darkness could be ambushed by enemy crews or destroyed by mines. But also I thought that the firepower of the task force had effectively destroyed the capability of the enemy to attack Chip'yong-ni that night. In view of the fact that the enemy had attacked the 23d Infantry RCT on the two previous nights, and because ammunition supplies of the 23d Infantry RCT were dangerously low, this decision was a calculated risk. Colonel Chiles anticipated a night attack, and I agreed to use some of my tanks on the defense perimeter of Chip'yong-ni. Most of these tanks were placed along the two valley routes to guard the north and west approaches to the town. The enemy did not attack that night.[13]

Captain Barrett, commander of Company L, describes the situation of the infantry of Task Force Crombez upon arrival at Chip'yong-ni, and also provides some observations about the effectiveness of the infantry in their role with the armor task force.

The column advanced about 1,500 yards [beyond the pass] receiving enemy small arms and mortar fire. There the tanks halted because they had met tanks of the 23d Infantry Regiment.

I again ordered the infantry to dismount, deploy, and protect the tank column. At this time, about thirty men of Company L remained with the task force. The others had been wounded or killed or had fallen off the tanks, including Lieutenant Chastaine, who was killed before this halt.

When the road was cleared, the task force proceeded to Chip'yong-ni. Again no signal was given by the tankers when the tanks were ready to move. However, the tanks moved out so slowly that it was comparatively easy to get on them. There was no shooting at this time.

At Chip'yong-ni I was informed by Colonel Crombez that the task force would not return to the regimental area that evening, although the infantrymen who were not wounded volunteered to a man to return on the tanks.

The infantry fired from the moving tanks, engaging the enemy at fifty or sixty yards. This fire was not effective unless the tanks were moving slowly. Just before the second halt, as the tanks were moving slowly, I shot and killed at a distance of fifty yards three enemy soldiers who were carrying a bangalore torpedo as they trotted across a rice field toward the tanks. My control by radio of the company was hindered by the tank radios, which completely obliterated all company channels.

The two-and-a-half-ton truck with a load of wounded followed the column to the pass within sight of the 23d RCT perimeter. The next day I learned what happened to the truck by talking with a wounded man of Company L who had spent the night on the truck. This man told me that after the driver of the truck was wounded,

Sergeant Kerzan, although wounded himself, drove the truck to the pass. At this time, since the tanks had departed, the Chinese closed in on the road and took all who were able to walk prisoner, including Colonel Treacy.[14]

The Escape of the Company L Infantrymen

Many of the infantrymen farther to the south, who were left behind by the task force, fared better. Several soldiers describe their experiences after the column moved on. Some made it back to the 5th Cavalry positions; others who were wounded were picked up by the two-and-a-half-ton truck and managed to make it to Chip'yong-ni.

CORPORAL KEMP, 1ST PLATOON, SOUTH OF KOKSU-RI: I was armed only with a .45-caliber pistol and took cover in a ditch with a group of others. Some men fired into the village ahead from where it was thought enemy fire was coming.

Following the tanks of Task Force Crombez, a two-and-a-half-ton Service Company truck came along with a driver and several ROK litter bearers. The truck stopped and picked up me, Sergeant Mogue, the platoon sergeant, and Sergeant Kerzan, the squad leader.

Continuing behind the tanks, the truck picked up three wounded men of the 4th Platoon who were lying in the ditch. As he was picking up the wounded, the driver of the truck was hit. Sergeant Kerzan drove the truck, and although he was wounded again, he continued driving. All along the way, the truck and its occupants were subject to enemy fire. The truck managed to reach the pass south of Chip'yong-ni, where it was knocked out. Some of the wounded, including me, were carried from the truck and placed on a tank, which carried us into Chip'yong-ni.

MASTER SERGEANT JONES, 3D PLATOON, SOUTH OF KOKSU-RI: A two-and-a-half-ton truck following Task Force Crombez picked up three wounded men from the 1st Platoon who were lying on the road. Although I had two wounded men with me, I deemed it inadvisable to place them on the truck because of the heavy small arms fire directed against the truck.

I sent a man back to the regimental area to ask that litters be brought to the men in the rice field or that more tanks be sent to

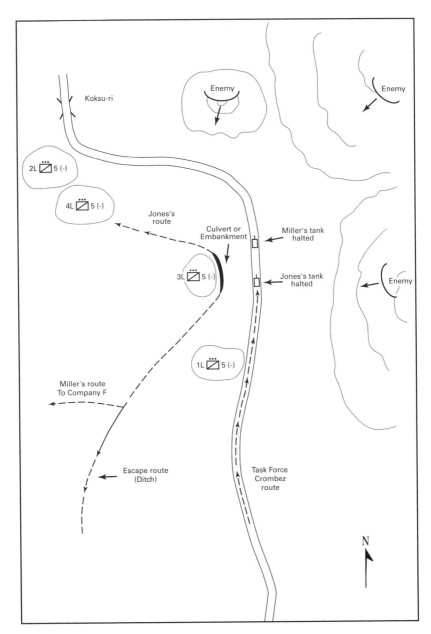

Escape of Company L soldiers south of Koksu-ri, 15 February 1951 (based on maps in CMH Manuscript 8–5.1A BA 29, Task Force Crombez).

cover the high ground on the right of the road from which enemy fire was being received.

About 300 or 500 yards to the northwest (see map, page 279), men from the 2d and 4th Platoons were taking cover in a ditch. I organized the men of my platoon to take up firing positions on the culvert, while I went to the other groups to order them to withdraw to the culvert before making it back to the original regimental positions.

While the sergeants of the 2d and 4th Platoons were organizing the men for the move to the culvert, the enemy took positions on a ridge to the front. Machine gun fire from this position made the culvert untenable. At about this time, eight mortar rounds fell near the culvert, one round wounding Lieutenant Lahey, already wounded, quite badly. Lieutenant Johnson, executive officer, Company L, who had by this time organized about three-quarters of the men in the field under his control, was also wounded by the mortar fire. I then ordered the men to cease fire and withdraw along the ditch.

SERGEANT 1ST CLASS MILLER, 3D PLATOON, SOUTH OF KOKSU-RI: When my tank halted I helped a man who had a broken leg off the tank. When the tank started moving without warning, the riflemen under enemy fire were forced to take cover behind the culvert. While Sergeant Jones moved to the men of the 2d and 4th Platoons, the men at the culvert had to cut out steps with their shovels because of the ice and snow on the ground and the steepness of the embankment, so that we could take up firing positions.

As the group of about fifty men in the field began to withdraw, I suggested and received permission from Lieutenant Johnson to move westward about 2,000 yards to Company F, which was in position on a hill from where it could observe what was taking place out of range of its weapons. I reached Company F, contacted a platoon leader, and requested that tanks and medical aid men be sent to cover and evacuate the men in the field.

MASTER SERGEANT JONES, 3D PLATOON: As the men were withdrawing, tanks came up the road from the regimental area and fired against enemy positions on the ridges to the right, but not against the enemy forces who had occupied the knoll to the front. The tanks started picking up wounded. These tanks went to within 500 or 600 yards short of Koksu-ri. The tanks made two trips in this fashion. The men of all the platoons under me withdrew safely along the ditch and reached Company A after dark.[15]

The Relief of Chip'yong-ni

Overnight, recognizing that the tide had turned against them, the Chinese began to withdraw from the area around Chip'yong-ni. Colonel Crombez describes the relief activities on the following day.

At 0900 hours on 16 February, the scheduled time for the return to the regiment, I informed my assembled task force that the return trip would be postponed because of the weather. A light snow was falling, and visibility was less than one hundred yards. Air cover was therefore out of the question. The weather cleared at 1100 hours, and the task force was reassembled. I informed the infantrymen that only volunteers would ride the tanks back, but none volunteered.

At 1215 hours, twenty-two tanks of Task Force Crombez started back. Two questions were in my mind: Would the enemy remain in position? And had the enemy placed mines on the road? I had asked Colonel Chiles to place a heavy 4.2-inch mortar concentration on the pass as the task force approached, and this was done. On the return voyage not a single enemy was seen nor a single shot fired. The task force reached the 1st and 2d Battalions of the 5th Cavalry at 1245.

Supply trucks and ambulances were quickly assembled and started back to Chip'yong-ni. Since the previously designated commander of this column, Lieutenant Colonel Treacy, had been captured by the Chinese, Capt. Keith M. Stewart, the assistant S-3 of the 5th Cavalry, was put in charge. Captain Stewart describes the return of the relief column.

At 1200 hours on 16 February, I was designated as commander of a task force that had the mission of moving supplies and ambulances to the 23d RCT at Chip'yong-ni. Although the 23d RCT was not so much concerned with supplies because of the airdrops it had received, it was vitally concerned with evacuating about 200 wounded. Only the very serious cases had been flown out of Chip'yong-ni by helicopter.

Supply trucks had been coming in to the regimental area in piecemeal fashion, and by noon twenty-eight two-and-a-half-ton trucks, most of them filled with ammunition, and nineteen ambulances were ready. The vehicles assembled at 1430 and were placed in the following order of march: one platoon, Company D, 6th Tank Battalion (five tanks); twenty-eight trucks; two tanks Company A, 70th Tank Battalion; nineteen ambulances with four tanks interspersed; one wrecker; and two tanks of Company A, 70th Tank Battalion. Vehicles that broke down or were knocked out were to be pushed or pulled off the road, and the column was to continue without halting. Infantrymen of a platoon of Company I, 5th Cavalry Regiment, rode on the trucks, and they were instructed to get on another truck, if the one they rode was disabled. The column departed at 1500 hours; I was in the third tank.

I worried about receiving enemy mortar fire along the route, but no enemy contact was made. The column arrived at Chip'yong-ni without incident at 1545 hours, making contact with the 23d RCT in the pass south of the town. One wounded man was picked up along the way. The wrecker picked up the truck that had been knocked out on the previous day in the pass south of Chip'yong-ni and also the wrecked tank of Captain Hier.

The ambulances and about seven trucks were loaded with wounded, and the vehicles departed Chip'yong-ni at 1715 with tanks in front, in the middle, and in the rear of the column, and arrived in the regimental area without incident about 1815.[16]

Captain Barrett, not waiting for the return of the large relief column, had personally checked to see if any men of Company L were still scattered along the route. He tells what he found.

The task force returned the next day [from Chip'yong-ni to the 5th Cavalry area] without the infantry because Colonel Crombez had given the men a choice of volunteering or not. I ordered the men not to volunteer. However, I returned with the task force to the regimental area because I wanted to find out what had happened to the remainder of my company.

Upon my return to the regimental area, I secured a company jeep and with the jeep driver immediately returned over the same route to Chip'yong-ni, picking up wounded men who were still lying alongside the road. I picked up four men. As I reached the truck in the pass near the 23d RCT perimeter, the task force of tanks, ambulances, and supply vehicles arrived on its way to Chip'yong-ni. I stopped the ambulances and put the wounded inside. The truck had not been disabled, but it did have a flat tire. It was driven off within an hour by members of the 23d Infantry Regiment.

Company L casualties were extremely heavy due to the intense small arms fire, which could not be avoided as long as the men remained on the tanks. Approximate casualty figures, as I remember them, were twenty killed in action, including four Koreans, forty wounded in action, and twenty missing in action.[17]

An Assessment

There were hearty congratulations from all for the success of Task Force Crombez. Colonel Crombez received the Distinguished Service Cross, and Company L of the 5th Cavalry Regiment was awarded the Presidential Unit Citation. However, there were many lessons to be learned from Task Force Crombez. Captain Barrett of Company L and Lt. Col. George B. Pickett, the IX Corps Armor officer, explain.

CAPTAIN BARRETT: If a task force is contemplated where movement will be a continuous dash through enemy territory, I recommend that no infantry be employed for these reasons: (1) tanks can provide their own protection, for the tank behind can cover the one ahead; (2) if infantry is not allowed to deploy and maneuver against the enemy, the infantrymen riding the tanks are in effect sitting ducks silhouetted against the sky, ideal targets for enemy fire.

Some type of outside communications should be placed on Patton tanks. Some type of elevated rack should be devised so that infantrymen may ride the back deck of the Patton tanks. Although the weather on 15 February was quite cold, the deck of the Patton tank was too hot to stand on for any length of time. As an example, one man on my tank was wounded seriously by a bullet in the head, which knocked him unconscious. Because of the intensity of the enemy fire, it was not more than five minutes before the wounded man could be attended to. In that short time, his clothing caught on fire, and the man undoubtedly suffered severe burns.

I recommend that tanks not be permitted to traverse their turrets and fire their 90mm guns while the infantrymen are on the tank. The concussion of the blast will knock men off the tank. Guns can be fired straight ahead or at a slight angle of traverse without knocking riders off, provided the infantrymen have sufficient warning so they can crouch behind the turret for protection against the blast.

LIEUTENANT COLONEL PICKETT: My remarks are not intended as criticism but as an evaluation of an armored action that had to be performed without the proper equipment, which was not available. Colonel Crombez did a magnificent job with what he had. A capable commander, who realized the urgency of the situation, Colonel Crombez appreciated the shock effect of an armored formation on the enemy.

In general, infantry divisions do not utilize the tank battalion headquarters as it was intended to be used when a special tank mission has to be performed. In this case, Colonel Crombez had no tank battalion headquarters, and he did the next best thing. Within the limitations of equipment available to him, Colonel Crombez had the best task force organization possible, and therefore the correct one.

The entire evaluation for the point of view of armor hinged on the fact that tank-borne infantry could not be expected to do the job of armored infantry. This proved without doubt the necessity of having in Korea an armored division or at the bare minimum an armored group with a tank battalion, an armored infantry battalion, an armored field artillery battalion (105mm), and a reconnaissance company. The Chip'yong-ni action was definitely a mission for a combat command or an armored group. If Colonel Crombez had had to fight in Chip'yong-ni, he would have needed his infantry. An armored infantry company mounted in armored personnel carriers would have arrived in Chip'yong-ni ready to fight. Infantry losses would have been reduced by 80 percent.

The relief of the 23d Infantry was an ideal job for a reinforced tank battalion with armored infantry in support, and it proved false the generalization that Korea is not tank country. A combat command or an armored group with a reinforced tank battalion (containing a minimum of one company of armored infantry) in the lead, followed by a reinforced armored infantry battalion (containing at least one tank company) could have done the job with only a small fraction of the loss and would have been able to continue the attack in the Chip'yong-ni area after arriving.

Communication, maintenance, and resupply facilities in the average infantry regiment are not adequate to support for continuous operation the number of tanks the 5th Cavalry Regiment had at the time. The operation at Chip'yong-ni was successful because the unit that arrived had a protected perimeter to move into. It could not have protected itself or established a perimeter of its own.

The following information indicates the speed with which Task Force Crombez was organized. When Major General Moore sent Colonel Crombez to the relief of Chip'yong-ni, the 5th Cavalry had Company A, 70th Tank Battalion, attached. Company D, 6th Tank Battalion, was located at Changhowan-ni in corps reserve. The remainder of the 6th Tank Battalion was in 24th Infantry Division reserve at Taepyong-ni, seven miles from Company D. General Moore at 1700 hours requested me to move Company D out to join Colonel Crombez immediately. My reaction was that the entire 6th Tank Battalion ought to be sent. But General Moore had already notified either General Palmer or Colonel Crombez that he would secure Company D immediately, and General Moore would not discuss any changes in the plan at that time. General Moore instructed me to have the company move in thirty minutes; Company D moved in twenty-eight minutes, and the first sergeant with the kitchen and administrative sections moved an hour later. Company D was commanded by Captain Hier, one of the outstanding tank company commanders in Korea. His loss in the task force operation was a severe loss to the service.

Colonel Crombez was handicapped by the absence of a tank battalion headquarters, for such a headquarters would have contained all the specialist personnel and equipment necessary for an armor action.

Some armored personnel carriers, organic to armored field artillery battalions and used by them as ammunition carriers, could have been made available to Task Force Crombez if the operation had not been conceived and executed so quickly. Twelve hours would have been necessary to make these carriers available. They could also have served to evacuate the wounded.

Radio or visual signals should have been arranged between the infantrymen and the tankers for coordination, but the rush-job aspects of this operation made impossible adequate arrangements.

It is difficult to fire from the back deck of a tank, which was not intended for that purpose. Tanks carrying infantrymen through enemy territory where the riflemen must fight is not an assault formation. In this case, however, Colonel Crombez had no alternative, because he lacked armored personnel carriers.

A tank dozer should have been a part of the task force for use against physical obstructions or roadblocks, but, again, one was not available to Colonel Crombez for use.

The people who formed Task Force Crombez knew what they needed, but what they needed was not available.[18]

A combat historian, 1st Lt. Martin Blumenson, who interviewed many of the participants soon after the battle and prepared a report of the action, summarized the operation.

This action illustrates some of the difficulties that arise when riflemen ride tanks through territory defended by the enemy. The riflemen had difficulty firing small arms effectively from moving tanks. They dismounted in order to be effective, and once dismounted, they had difficulty in determining when the tank column was ready to move. Thus, in certain cases, infantrymen who had dismounted to take cover and fire effectively against the enemy were not able to rejoin the tank column and were therefore lost to the task force. Getting aboard a moving tank was not easy. Swinging turrets added another hazard.

The task force plan lacked provision for evacuation of casualties. The decision by an unauthorized officer to send a two-and-a-half-ton truck to follow the tank column was no solution since the personnel in the truck became casualties, the truck was lost, and no evacuation resulted. The expedient of sending tanks forward to cover and evacuate casualties succeeded, even though armored personnel carriers could have been utilized to transport wounded with greater effectiveness.

The importance of this action, in addition to its tactical success, lies in the particular problems posed by the mission to be carried out over difficult terrain heavily defended. Only one very narrow road could be utilized by the 5th Cavalry Regiment, and this was a valley route under constant enemy observation and subject to enemy fire from well-prepared positions on the heights. A further possibility existed that the enemy had laid and was strongly defending minefields, which, by disabling one of the lead tanks in the column, might have thereby obstructed the route for those following. The decision to attempt an armored breakthrough in the face of these calculations was reached because of the necessity to effect a rapid relief of the encircled 23d Infantry RCT.

The importance of this aggressive task force was its destruction of enemy forces surrounding Chip'yong-ni defenders and isolating them from friendly troops. The action of Task Force Crombez forced the enemy to withdraw his forces, and made possible the retention of Chip'yong-ni by friendly elements.[19]

The successful defense of Chip'yong-ni and Wonju boosted the morale of Eighth Army. General Ridgway regarded the actions as turning points: Chip'yong-ni and Wonju demonstrated defensive strength, and Task Force Crombez showed offensive power. There was now a widespread belief in the UN forces that the Chinese could be defeated. With the enemy bloodied by their losses and in retreat in the central sector, Ridgway ordered the advance to continue to the Han River and beyond.

CONCLUSION

The contrast between the situation in Korea in late December 1950 and that which existed two months later is striking. When General Ridgway arrived to take command, it was unclear whether UN forces would be able to remain on the peninsula. Ridgway quickly discovered that the only military plans that existed at Eighth Army called for a withdrawal to Pusan and evacuation by sea. The confidence in victory at all levels in October 1950 had turned to deep pessimism. Disdain for the military capabilities of the Chinese Communists in October had changed at first to cautious respect followed by an overestimation of their potential, tinged in some cases with fear that the enemy could not be stopped. Because of the demonstrated enemy expertise in infiltrating into rear areas to cut supply lines and maul retreating units, some commanders seemed more focused on preventing a disaster than they were on inflicting punishment on the enemy.

Low morale and uncertainty had spread throughout the command, the result of the defeat in the far reaches of North Korea and the subsequent hasty withdrawal to the south, combined with rumors of further retreat. Problems of cohesion and training remained in many American units; these forces had deployed from Japan and the United States after being hastily brought up to strength and had not yet had time to assimilate replacements. South Korean units, a significant portion of the UN paper strength and a favorite target of enemy attacks, faced even greater challenges in overcoming problems of leadership, training, morale, and cohesion. Most military experts who surveyed the condition of the UN forces in Korea at the end of 1950, knowing that the Chinese were rapidly concentrating for a major attack that would not allow any time for Ridgway's troops to recover, would have concluded that the chances for UN success were doubtful.

By mid-February 1951 a fundamental change had occurred. There was a renewed fighting spirit among UN forces. Gone was the talk of retreat. Commanders were confident and worked on plans for punishing the enemy while moving back into North Korea. Morale was solid despite the harsh weather and terrain. Soldiers knew that they could win and that the enemy could be defeated.

The tactical success during January and February 1951 in stopping the Chinese offensive and regaining the initiative by pushing the enemy back had an impact far beyond the rugged, wintry battlefields of Korea. At the operational level, consistent battlefield success in stopping the enemy and undertaking limited offensive actions meant that planners could begin developing ways to continue the advance, to keep the enemy off balance, and to defeat him when he regained strength and attacked again. Seizing the initiative would gain time to make needed improvements in American and ROK forces. At the strategic level, the possibility of a successful defense of South Korea and the defeat of future Chinese attacks would allow the reinforcement of Europe to continue, while at the same time, those divisions in the United States that had been stripped to rush troops to Korea during the summer of 1950 were rebuilt and newly mobilized divisions were trained.

A quick victory over North Korea in late September and October 1950 had been an enticing strategic goal, but now the realism of what could be accomplished with limited resources in the presence of strong opponents had taken hold. Washington planners believed that the Cold War was global in extent, and priorities had to be set. South Korea, despite the mobilization of the Free World to fight aggression under the auspices of the United Nations, was considered of less importance than the overall security of the United States and Europe. Only so much could be done to stop the Chinese in Korea, and the limits of personnel and materiel allocated to the fighting there were rapidly approaching. But the battlefield success in January and February pointed to a more promising future. Perhaps victory in more narrowly defined terms could be achieved in Korea.

In some respects, the reasons for the turnaround in Korea are easily identified; however, a different combination among the elements at play might instead have led to disaster. The outcome was by no means certain.

Without a doubt, a major factor was the fresh perspective and strong leadership provided by General Ridgway. Coming from his Pentagon job, he knew what was at stake and what had to be done. The solution did not involve more men, weapons, munitions, and equipment. Success required something else: a change in attitude, a demonstration that UN forces were superior to the enemy, a restoration of confidence in their own strengths and abilities. These are the intangibles of leadership that build morale and winning units, and Ridgway was well suited for the task. He was positive, aggressive, and demanding. Adept at exploiting the fighting strengths of the UN forces, he seemed to know instinctively exactly what had to be done. Publicly he exuded confidence; privately he had doubts about some of his subordinates. He had no misgivings about the basic fighting qualities of the American soldier.

Among Ridgway's subordinates, General Almond of X Corps stands out in the narrative of events covered in this volume. Also a strong, aggressive leader, Almond seemed to complement Ridgway in advancing his goal of instilling a new attitude within Eighth Army. Examples of this are seen in Almond's efforts to stop the withdrawal of the 2d Infantry Division from the key town of Wonju in early January and in the fight to regain the heights above the town later in the month. Eventually Almond fired the division commander and installed his own handpicked replacement. Almond believed that strong leadership was the key to mission success and could overcome significant obstacles. But Almond also overestimated the capabilities of American and ROK forces, frequently placing them in untenable positions. In addition Almond continued to underestimate the enemy, just as he had in North Korea in late November and early December. He disregarded the proven enemy ability to move around open flanks and to infiltrate into rear areas to cut supply lines and to ambush and destroy units.

Almond's overconfidence led to Operation Roundup, an ill-conceived attempt to improve the fighting efficiency of the ROK soldiers, which nearly led to disaster. Ignored by Almond, intelligence reports of a massive Chinese buildup to the front were proved correct. In the ensuing attack, the South Korean units collapsed, and the American support units were cut off. Almond's complex and unworkable command and communication arrangement failed. Almond's headquarters attempted to retain control, but their orders only worsened the situation. Eventually control was restored to the local commander, Colonel Coughlin of the 38th Infantry Regiment, and he executed a fighting retreat of all of his units to safety.

Almond was not alone in overestimating the capabilities of his own forces or in underestimating the enemy. Ridgway also fell prey to this when he ordered the 23d Infantry to remain at Chip'yong-ni to face an overwhelming enemy force. Ridgway considered it an acceptable risk, believing that air power could keep the Chinese from overwhelming the 23d Infantry and that UN forces would be able to break through to relieve the unit, if the situation deteriorated. Using the night to negate UN air power, the Chinese hit the 23d Infantry hard, and casualties mounted. Ridgway monitored the situation closely and quickly recognized that Almond's X Corps did not have the strength to penetrate the enemy cordon to relieve Chip'yong-ni. He shifted the 27th British Commonwealth Brigade and the 5th Cavalry Regiment from IX Corps, but their attacks stalled in the face of strong Chinese forces on the roads south of Chip'yong-ni. An armored task force was hastily assembled by Colonel Crombez to break through, but this was a gamble. The road was narrow, running through a valley covered by Chinese fire. Disaster might ensue if the road was mined or blocked. Fortunately the route was clear, and Task Force Crombez reached Chip'yong-ni in time to disperse a Chinese force already inside the outer perimeter and preparing to continue its attack under the cover of darkness. The defense and relief of Chip'yong-ni were successful, but the whole affair might easily have been a costly failure.

Strong leadership was a key factor, but not the only factor in UN success in January and February. UN forces also relied on firepower, in particular, air power, which kept the Chinese on a short logistic shoestring, ensuring that their offensive operations would not be sustained over a long time. Close air support was a key aspect of the successes around Wonju and at Hill 312, Twin Tunnels, and Chip'yong-ni. The Air Force even began to take the cover of night away from the enemy. But the Air Force could not seal the battlefield or destroy the enemy; ground forces were still needed for this.

Persistent problems remained, some lingering from World War II. The inadequacy of U.S. Army cold weather gear had been recognized after the winter of 1944–1945 along the German frontier, but six years later American soldiers still fought in the cold and wet with footgear that did little to protect them, and in many cases contributed to producing cold weather casualties. The inadequacy of infantry-tank training and the need for a means of communication between soldiers on the ground and crewmen inside their tanks were revealed during the fighting in the hedgerow country of Normandy in the summer of 1944; yet Task Force Crombez encountered the same problems, with disastrous results for many of the infantrymen riding the tanks to the relief of Chip'yong-ni.

Nevertheless, American soldiers and Marines overcame harsh weather, rugged terrain, poor training, leadership failures extending to the highest levels of the government, and a formidable enemy to find battlefield success. For the heroes that were recognized by award of the Medal of Honor and other decorations, there were many more, unnamed and unrewarded, who did what was required to overcome all obstacles, hold positions, take objectives, fight, and win. They provided the example and the spark needed by others on many small battlegrounds scattered across the Korean peninsula. Together, they changed Eighth Army from a dejected force, low in spirits and self-confidence, to a determined group, intent on staying the course and overcoming the enemy as they pushed forward, back into North Korea.

NOTES

1. War Comes to Korea

1. For the initial North Korean attacks, see Roy E. Appleman, *South to the Naktong, North to the Yalu* (Washington, D.C.: Center of Military History, 1961), pp. 19–35, and Robert K. Sawyer, *Military Advisors in Korea: KMAG in Peace and War* (Washington, D.C.: Center of Military History, 1988), pp. 114–139. There are a number of different interpretations on the causes and other background issues of the Korean War; in this overview chapter only the main sources are cited. For a summary of the main arguments, see Steven Hugh Lee, *Seminar Studies in History: The Korean War* (London: Longman, 2001), and Allan R. Millett, "The Korean War: A 50-Year Critical Historiography," *Journal of Strategic Studies* 24 (March 2001), pp. 188–224. A valuable recent work on the war's background is Allan R. Millett, *The War for Korea, 1945–1950: A House Burning* (Lawrence: University Press of Kansas, 2005).

2. On the question of surprise, see Rod Paschall, *Witness to War: Korea* (New York: Berkley Publishing Group, 1995), pp. 21–24. For North Korean strength, see Appleman, *South to the Naktong, North to the Yalu,* pp. 7–12.

3. On South Korean forces, see Appleman, *South to the Naktong, North to the Yalu,* pp. 12–18. See Robert K. Sawyer, *KMAG in Peace and War,* pp. 27–113, for efforts to develop the ROK army.

4. James F. Schnabel, *Policy and Direction: The First Year* (Washington, D.C.: Center of Military History, 1972), pp. 49–52.

5. Stephen E. Ambrose, *Rise to Globalism* (New York: Penguin, 1976), pp. 188–197, and David T. Fautua, "The 'Long Pull' Army: NSC 68, the Korean War, and the Creation of the Cold War U.S.

Army," *Journal of Military History* 61 (January 1997), pp. 93–120. The security review was N.S.C. 68.

6. On the Army situation at the beginning of the Korean War, see Schnabel, *Policy and Direction: The First Year,* pp. 41–60; William T. Bowers, William M. Hammond, and George L. MacGarrigle, *Black Soldier, White Army: The 24th Infantry Regiment in Korea* (Washington, D.C.: Center of Military History, 1996), pp. 27–68; and William W. Epley, *America's First Cold War Army, 1945–1950,* Association of the U.S. Army, Land Warfare Paper No. 15, August 1993. The exceptions to the organization reductions in Japan were the 24th Infantry Regiment, which had three battalions, and the 159th Field Artillery Battalion, which had three firing batteries; both were segregated units.

7. Church's quote is from Appleman, *South to the Naktong, North to the Yalu,* p. 61.

8. On Task Force Smith, see Appleman, *South to the Naktong, North to the Yalu,* pp. 59–76; Roy K. Flint, "Task Force Smith and the 24th Division: Delay and Withdrawal, 5–19 July 1950," in Charles E. Heller and William A. Stofft, eds., *America's First Battles, 1776–1965* (Lawrence: University Press of Kansas, 1986), pp. 266–299.

9. On the retreat of the 24th Infantry Division, see Appleman, *South to the Naktong, North to the Yalu,* pp. 77–181, and Heller and Stofft, *America's First Battles,* pp. 282–299.

10. The Army Field Forces observer report is quoted in Bowers et al., *Black Soldier, White Army,* pp. 122–123.

11. On the retreat of Eighth Army to the Pusan Perimeter, see Appleman, *South to the Naktong, North to the Yalu,* pp. 182–234.

12. On the Pusan Perimeter fight, see Appleman, *South to the Naktong, North to the Yalu,* pp. 235–487; for American policy during this period, see Schnabel, *Policy and Direction,* pp. 115–138.

13. On the collapse of North Korea, see Appleman, *South to the Naktong, North to the Yalu,* pp. 488–666; for U.S. policy, see Schnabel, *Policy and Direction,* pp. 173–232.

14. The quote of the Chinese evaluation of American troops is from Appleman, *South to the Naktong, North to the Yalu,* p. 720.

15. On the initial Chinese intervention, see Appleman, *South to the Naktong, North to the Yalu,* pp. 667–778. On the late November Chinese attack, see Billy C. Mossman, *Ebb and Flow* (Washington, D.C.: Center of Military History, 1990), pp. 1–176.

16. On the changed situation, see Mossman, *Ebb and Flow,* pp. 177–184, and Schnabel, *Policy and Direction,* pp. 274–314.

2. Retreat to Wonju

1. 2d Infantry Division, Command Report, December 50, Narrative Summary, G-1 Section, Operations Section, Record Group 407, Entry 429, Box 2476, National Archives. Hereafter Record Group is abbreviated RG and the National Archives is NA.

2. 23d Infantry Regiment, Command Report, December 50, Narrative and Operations Sections, RG 407, Entry 429, Box 2473; 23d Infantry Regiment, Command Report, January 51, Narrative and Operations Sections, RG 407, Entry 429, Box 2695; both NA.

3. Award Case File, Junior D. Edwards, Medal of Honor (Posthumous), RG 500, Eighth Army, Box 1385, NA.

4. Interview 33, 1st Lt. Jerrell F. Wilson with 1st Lt. Martin Blumenson, 22–23 January 51, Manuscript 8–5.1A BA 31, Action at Wonju, Center of Military History. Hereafter manuscript is abbreviated Ms. and the Center of Military History is CMH. With first use, the complete manuscript number will be cited; subsequent citations will use an abbreviated manuscript number (BA 31 or Ms. 31).

5. 23d Infantry Regiment, Command Report, January 51, p. 4, RG 407, Entry 429, Box 2695, NA.

6. Interview 6, SFC Raymond Lott Jr. with 1st Lt. Martin Blumenson, 6 February 51, Ms. 8–5.1A BA 31, Action at Wonju, CMH.

7. 38th Infantry Regiment, Command Report, January 51, pp. 4–7, RG 407, Entry 429, Box 2704, NA.

3. Action at Wonju

1. Interview 27, Col. Paul L. Freeman with Capt. Edward C. Williamson, 23 February 1951, Ms. 8–5.1A BA 31, Action at Wonju, CMH.

2. Interview 35, 1st Lt. John H. Heath with 1st Lt. John Mewha, 23 February 1951, and Interview 33, 1st Lt. Wilson; both in Ms. 8–5.1A BA 31, Action at Wonju, CMH.

3. Interview 17, Sgt. Raul Villarreal with 1st Lt. Martin Blumenson, 26 January 1951, Ms. 8–5.1A BA 31, Action at Wonju, CMH.

4. Interviews 33, 1st Lt. Wilson and #35, 1st Lt. Heath; both Ms. 31.

5. Interview 9, Sgt. Richard W. Carey with 1st Lt. John Mewha, 7–8 February 1951, Ms. 8–5.1A BA 31, Action at Wonju, CMH.

6. Interview 8, PFC Herbert D. Wiggins with Capt. Edward C. Williamson, 22 January 1951, Ms. 8–5.1A BA 31, Action at Wonju, CMH.

7. Interview 11, M. Sgt. Olen McGregor with 1st Lt. John Mewha, 2 February 1951, Ms. 8–5.1A BA 31, Action at Wonju, CMH.

8. Interview 17, Sgt. Villarreal, Ms. 31.

9. Interview 20, Maj. John Lapotka with 1st Lt. John Mewha, 21 February 1951, Ms. 8–5.1A BA 31, Action at Wonju, CMH.

10. Interview 21, Capt. Michael Swatko with Capt. Edward C. Williamson, 10 February 1951, Ms. 8–5.1A BA 31, Action at Wonju, CMH.

11. Interview 4, 2d Lt. David Brisbane with 1st Lt. Martin Blumenson, 21 February 1951, Ms. 8–5.1A BA 31, Action at Wonju, CMH.

12. Narrative of the Action at Wonju and Vicinity, 5 to 20 January 1951, pp. 6–7, Ms. 8–5.1A BA 31, Action at Wonju, CMH.

13. Interview 5, 1st Lt. Walter Hurtt with Capt. Edward C. Williamson, 6 January [February] 1951, Ms. 8–5.1A BA 31, Action at Wonju, CMH.

4. Return to Wonju

1. 2d Infantry Division, Command Report, January 1951, p.7, RG 407, Entry 429, Box 2695, NA.

2. 23d Infantry Regiment, S-3 Journal, 071630 to 081630 January 51, 0800 Summary, RG 407, Entry 429, Box 2695, NA.

3. Interview 33, 1st Lt. Wilson, Ms. 31.

4. Interview 31, Cpl. Julius L. Stephens with 1st Lt. John Mewha, February 1951, Ms. 8–5.1A BA 31, Action at Wonju, CMH.

5. Interview 11, M. Sgt. McGregor, Ms. 31.

6. Interview 10, 1st Lt. Frank J. Barnes with 1st Lt. John Mewha, 24–25 January 1951, Ms. 8–5.1A BA 31, Action at Wonju, CMH.

7. Interview 18, Sgt. Rena F. Lattorre-Lopez with 1st Lt. John Mewha, 22 January 1951, Ms. 8–5.1A BA 31, Action at Wonju, CMH.

8. Interview 14, Sgt. Frank J. Monte with Capt. Edward C. Williamson, 30 January 1951, Ms. 8–5.1A BA 31, Action at Wonju, CMH.

9. Interview 7, SFC Peter H. Palamidy with 1st Lt. John Mewha, 26 January 1951, Ms. 8–5.1A BA 31, Action at Wonju, CMH.

10. Interview 9, Sgt. Carey, Ms. 31.

11. Interview 17, Sgt. Raul Villarreal with 1st Lt. Martin Blumenson, 26 January 1951, Ms. 8–5.1A BA 31, Action at Wonju, CMH.

12. Interview 33, 1st Lt. Wilson, Ms. 31

13. Interview 36, Cpl. John J. Breslin with 1st Lt. Martin Blumenson, 22 January 1951, Ms. 8–5.1A BA 31, Action at Wonju, CMH.

14. Narrative of the Action at Wonju and Vicinity, pp. 13–14.

15. Interview 35, 1st Lt. Heath, Ms. 31.

16. Interview 30, Sgt. Willard S. White with 1st Lt. Martin Blumenson, 23 February 1951, Ms. 8–5.1A BA 31, Action at Wonju, CMH.

17. 23d Infantry Regiment, Periodic Operations Report 118, 041200 to 111200 January 1951, RG 407, Entry 429, Box 2695, NA.

18. Interview 9, Sgt. Carey, Ms. 31.

19. Interview 10, 1st Lt. Barnes, Ms. 31.

20. Interview 11, M. Sgt. McGregor, Ms. 31.

21. 23d Infantry Regiment, Command Report, January 1951, pp. 5, 12.

22. Interview 30, Sgt. White, Ms. 31.

23. Interview 35, 1st Lt. Heath, Ms. 31.

24. Interview 7, SFC Palamidy, Ms. 31.

25. Award Case File, PFC Elmer D. Lewellyn, Distinguished Service Cross (Posthumous), RG 500, Eighth Army, Box 1261, NA.

26. Interview 9, Sgt. Carey, Ms. 31.

27. Interview 10, 1st Lt. Barnes, Ms. 31.

28. Interview 5, 1st Lt. Hurtt, Ms. 31.

29. Command Report, 9th Infantry Regiment, January 1951, pp. 4–5, RG 407, Entry 429, Box 2688, NA.

30. Interview 48, Sgt. James L. Hadley with Capt. Edward C. Williamson, 22–23 January 1951, Ms. 8–5.1A BA 31, Action at Wonju, CMH.

31. Interview 49, Sgt. William R. Shockey with Capt. Edward C. Williamson, 26 January 1951, Ms. 8–5.1A BA 31, Action at Wonju, CMH.

32. Interview 42, PFC Willie Johnson with Capt. Edward C. Williamson, 22 January 1951, Ms. 8–5.1A BA 31, Action at Wonju, CMH.

33. Interview 48, Sgt. Hadley, Ms. 31.

34. Interview 49, Sgt. Shockey, Ms. 31.

35. Interview 53, 1st Lt. Angelo J. Balafas with Capt. Edward C. Williamson, 8 February 1951, Ms. No. 8–5.1A BA 31, Action at Wonju, CMH.

36. Interview 27, Col. Paul L. Freeman, Ms. 31.

37. Interview 46, 1st Lt. Philip Mallory with Capt. Edward C. Williamson, 16 February 1951, Ms. 8–5.1A BA 31, Action at Wonju, CMH.

5. Hill 312

1. Interview 2, Maj. James M. Gibson with 1st Lt. Martin Blumenson, 3 April 1951, Ms. 8–5.1A BA 32, Hill 312, CMH.

2. Resume of Action, 1st Lt. Martin Blumenson, Hill 312, Ms. 8–5.1A BA 32, Hill 312, CMH.

3. Interview 13, Sgt. Hal B. Mason and M. Sgt. James Chikahisa with 1st Lt. Martin Blumenson, 2 April 1951, Ms. 8–5.1A BA 32, Hill 312, CMH.

4. Interview 14, SFC Virgil M. Atwood and SFC John W. Hudson

with 1st Lt. Martin Blumenson, 2 April 1951, Ms. 8–5.1A BA 32, Hill 312, CMH.

5. Interview 9, M. Sgt. Morgan H. Clark with 1st Lt. Martin Blumenson, 3 April 1951, Ms. 8–5.1A BA 32, Hill 312, CMH.

6. Interview 10, SFC Joseph Manfredi with 1st Lt. Martin Blumenson, 2 April 1951, Ms. 8–5.1A BA 32, Hill 312, CMH.

7. Operations Log, 1st Bn., 5th Cav. Rgt., entry 0900 hours 29 January 1951, in Ms. 8–5.1A BA 32, Hill 312, CMH.

8. Interview 3, Capt. Marvin J. Rezac with 1st Lt. Martin Blumenson, 2 April 1951, Ms. 8–5.1A BA 32, Hill 312, CMH.

9. Award Case File, 2d Lt. Green B. Mayo, RG 500, Eighth Army, Box 1264, NA.

10. Interview 3, Capt. Rezac, Ms. 32.

11. Interview 4, 1st Lt. James F. Eismann with 1st Lt. Martin Blumenson, 3 April 1951, Ms. 8–5.1A BA 32, Hill 312, CMH.

12. Interview 3, Capt. Rezac, Ms. 32.

13. Interview 2, Maj. Gibson, Ms. 32.

14. Interview 21, Capt. Keith M. Stewart with 1st Lt. Martin Blumenson, 3 April 1951, Ms. 8–5.1A BA 32, Hill 312, CMH.

15. Interview 2, Maj. Gibson, Ms. 32.

16. Report of Operation, 1st Bn., 5th Cav. Rgt., Maj. James M. Gibson, Executive Officer, Assault on Hill 312, dated 3 February 1951, in Ms 8–5.1A BA 32, Hill 312, CMH.

17. Interview 12, 1st Lt. George A. Bailey with 1st Lt. Martin Blumenson, 2 April 1951, Ms 8–5.1A BA 32, Hill 312, CMH.

18. Interview 11, Capt. William C. Dobson Jr. with 1st Lt. Martin Blumenson, 2 April 1951, Ms 8–5.1A BA 32, Hill 312, CMH.

19. Interview 16, PFC Ellsworth E. Brown with 1st Lt. Martin Blumenson, 2 April 1951, Ms 8–5.1A BA 32, Hill 312, CMH.

20. Interview 15, 2d Lt. Robert E. Bundy with 1st Lt. Martin Blumenson, 2 April 1951, Ms 8–5.1A BA 32, Hill 312, CMH.

21. Interview 14, SFC Atwood and SFC Hudson, Ms. 32.

22. Interview 13, Sgt. Mason and M. Sgt. Chikahisa, Ms. 32.

23. Report of Operation, 1st Bn., 5th Cav. Rgt., Assault on Hill 312, dated 3 February 1951.

24. Interview 17, 1st Lt. John Kader with 1st Lt. Martin Blumenson, 2 April 1951, Ms. 8–5.1A BA 32, Hill 312, CMH.

25. Award Case File, 1st Lt. Robert M. McGovern, RG 500, Box 1385, NA.

26. Ibid.

27. Ibid.

28. Interview 5, SFC Leonard J. Ford with 1st Lt. Martin Blumenson, 3 April 1951, Ms. 8–5.1A BA 32, Hill 312, CMH.

29. Interview 20, M. Sgt. Fred L. Poe with 1st Lt. Martin Blumenson, 2 April 1951, Ms. 8–5.1A BA 32, Hill 312, CMH.

30. Interview 17, 1st Lt. Kader, Ms. 32.

31. Report of Operation, 1st Bn., 5th Cav. Rgt., Assault on Hill 312, dated 3 February 1951.

32. Interview 12, 1st Lt. Bailey, Ms. 32.

33. Interview 14, SFC Atwood and SFC Hudson, Ms. 32.

34. Interview 11, Capt. William C. Dobson Jr., Ms. 32.

6. Twin Tunnels

1. The following account is based on Twin Tunnels, Ms. 8–5.1A BA 84, CMH. See also Special Report, 23d Infantry Regiment, Battle for the Tunnels Area, 30 January–1 February 1951, RG 407, Entry 429, Box 2494, NA; and Eighth Army Unit Award Case Files, French Battalion and 3d Battalion, 23d Infantry, RG 500, Boxes 1182 and 1183, NA. The 29 January 1951 patrol action is described in detail in Russell A. Gugeler, *Combat Actions in Korea* (Washington, D.C.: U.S. Army Center of Military History, 1987), pp. 80–99.

7. Operation Roundup: Supporting the ROK Troops

1. Narrative Summary, Command Report, 1–28 February 1951, 2d Inf. Div., pp. 3–8, RG 407, Entry 429, Box 2495, NA.

2. Letter, Lt. Col. William P. Keleher to Commander, 38th Infantry Regiment, 14 February 1951, sub: Summation of Action of the 1st Bn., 38th Inf. during the Period 11–12 February 1951, pp. 1–2, in Ms. 8–5.1A BA 83, Ch'angbong-ni to Hoengsong, CMH.

3. Interview, Capt. Chester B. Searls with 1st Lt. John Mewha, 12 April 1951, Ms. 8–5.1A BA 83, Ch'angbong-ni to Hoengsong, CMH.

4. Interview, SFC Floyd W. Frazier with 1st Lt. John Mewha, 12 April 1951, Ms. 8–5.1A BA 83, Ch'angbong-nito Hoengsong, CMH.

5. Interview, SFC Robert P. Major with 1st Lt. John Mewha, 12 April 1951, Ms. 8–5.1A BA 83, Ch'angbong-ni to Hoengsong, CMH.

6. Letter, Lt. Col. Keleher, Ms. 83.

7. Interview 1st Lt. George W. Gardner with 1st Lt. John Mewha, 12 April 1951, Ms. 8–5.1A BA 83, Ch'angbong-ni to Hoengsong, CMH.

8. Interview, 1st Lt. Duncan A. MacLeod and 1st Sgt. Morton L. Copenhaver with 1st Lt. John Mewha, 12 April 1951, Ms. 8–5.1A BA 83, Ch'angbong-ni to Hoengsong, CMH.

9. Interview, Maj. Jack W. Rodearme with 1st Lt. John Mewha, 13 April 1951, Ms. 8–5.1A BA 83, Ch'angbong-ni to Hoengsong, CMH.

10. Interview, Maj. [then Capt.] Leonard Lowry with 1st Lt. John Mewha, 12 April 1951, Ms. 8–5.1A BA 83, Ch'angbong-ni to Hoengsong, CMH.

11. Interviews, 1st Lt. Earle M. Welch, 2d Lt. Mark W. Mairich, 1st Sgt. Billy J. Wallace, and Sgt. James E. Hays with 1st Lt. John Mewha, 13 April 1951, Ms. 8–5.1A BA 83, Ch'angbong-ni to Hoengsong, CMH.

12. Interviews, Capt. Searls and SFC Major, both Ms. 83.

13. Letter, Lt. Col. Keleher, Ms. 83.

14. Ibid.; interviews, Capt. Searls and SFC Major, both Ms. 83; interview Capt. [then 1st Lt.] James H. Jacobs with 1st Lt. John Mewha, 13 April 1951, Ms. 8–5.1A BA 83, Ch'angbong-ni to Hoengsong, CMH.

8. Operation Roundup: Escaping the Trap

1. Interview, Capt. Tate with Capt. Valentine, no date, Ms. 8–5.1A BA 83, Ch'angbong-ni to Hoengsong, CMH.

2. Award Case File, Sgt. Charles R. Long, RG 500, Eighth Army, Box 1385, NA.

3. Interview, Capt. Tate, no date, Ms. 83.

4. War Diary, Tank Company, 38th Inf. Rgt., 11–13 February 1951, Ms. 8–5.1A BA 83, Ch'angbong-ni to Hoengsong, CMH.

5. Interview, Cpl. James J. Lee with Capt. Valentine, 4 April 1951, Special Report on Hoengsong Action.

6. Interviews, 1st Lt. Gardner, 1st Sgt. Copenhaver, 1st Lt. MacLeod, Capt. Searls, SFC Major, Capt. Lowry, 1st Lt. Jacobs, 1st Lt. Welch, PFC Reed, all Ms. 83.

7. Interview, Maj. Rodearme, Ms. 83.

8. Interviews, Capt. Lowry, 1st Lt. Welch, 1st Lt. Jacobs, PFC Reed, all Ms. 83.

9. Interviews, Capt. Searls and SFC Major, both Ms. 83.

10. Interview, Capt. Searls, Ms. 83.

11. Interviews, 1st Lt. Gardner and 1st Lt. MacLeod, both Ms. 83.

12. Interviews, 1st Sgt. Copenhaver and Maj. Rodearme, both Ms. 83.

13. Letter, 1st Lt. George W. Gardner to Commanding Officer, 1st Bn., 38th Inf., 16 February 1951, subj.: Summary of Combat Action of Company A, 38th Inf., During 11–12 February 1951; Ms. 8–5.1A BA 83, Changbong-ni to Hoengsong, CMH.

14. Ibid.

15. Interview, Capt. Tate, Ms. 83.

16. Interviews, 1st Lt. Jacobs, PFC Reed, 1st Lt. Welch, all Ms. 83.

17. War Diary, Tank Company, 38th Inf., Ms. 83.

18. Interviews, Lt. Col. Keleher, Maj. Rodearme, Capt. Tate, 1st Lt. Gardner, Capt. Searles, and 1st Lt. Welch, all Ms. 83.

19. Interview, Capt. Tate; Letter, 1st Lt. Paul L. Meyer to Commanding Officer, 1st Bn., 38th Inf., 17 February 1951, subj.: Account of Roadblock on 12 February 1951; both Ms. 83.

20. Unit Award Case File, Task Force White, RG 500, Eighth Army, Box 1183, NA. The recommendation for award of the Presidential Unit Citation to the units of Task Force White was disapproved by Eighth Army.

21. Unit Award Case File, Netherlands Detachment, RG 500, Eighth Army, Box 1182, NA. Award of the PUC to the Netherlands Detachment included their action at Hoengsong and their defense of Wonju a few days later.

9. Holding the Chinese

1. After Action Report, 23d Regimental Combat Team, 29 January–16 February 1951, pp. 4–5, in Unit Award Case File, 23d Inf. Rgt., RG 500, Eighth Army, Box 1182, NA.

2. Capt. Williamson was unable to conduct the interviews for this action until October 1951. By that time many of the participants of the action were unavailable, including Lt. Heath, the Company G commander, killed in action on 22 September.

3. Narrative Report, Capt. Edward C. Williamson, Ms. 8–5.1A BA 74, Chip'yong-ni: Defense of the South Sector of the 23d Regimental Combat Team Perimeter by Company G, 13–15 February 1951, CMH. The actions in the southern sector of the perimeter are described in much more detail in Russell A. Gugeler, *Combat Actions in Korea* (Washington, D.C.: Center of Military History, 1954), pp. 100–125.

4. Narrative Summary, Command Report, 1–28 February 1951, 2d Inf. Div., pp. 10–11, RG 407, Entry 429, Box 2495, NA.

5. Command Report, February 51, 38th Inf. Regt., p. 9, RG 407, Entry 429, Box 2705, NA.

6. Unit Award Case File, Company E, 187th Airborne Infantry, RG 500, Eighth Army, Box 1183, NA.

7. Ibid.

8. Unit Award Case File, Netherlands Detachment, RG 500, Eighth Army, Box 1182, NA.

9. Command Report, February 1951, 2d Inf. Div., pp. 11–12, NA.

10. Unit Award Case File, Netherlands Detachment, NA.

11. Interview, Col. Marcel G. Crombez with 1st Lt. Martin Blumenson, 26 March 1951, Ms. 8–5.1A BA 29, Task Force Crombez, CMH.

12. Interview, Maj. James M. Gibson with 1st Lt. Martin Blumenson, 27 March 1951, Ms. 8–5.1A BA 29, Task Force Crombez, CMH.

13. After Action Report, 23d Regimental Combat Team, 29 January–16 February 51, pp. 5, in Unit Award Case File, 23d Inf. Rgt., RG 500, Eighth Army, Box 1182, NA.

14. Award Case File, SFC William S. Sitman, MOH, RG 500, Eighth Army, Box 1386, NA.

15. After Action Report, 23d Regimental Combat Team, 29 January–16 February 1951, pp. 5–6, in Unit Award Case File, 23d Inf. Rgt., RG 500, Eighth Army, Box 1182, NA.

16. Narrative Report, Capt. Edward C. Williamson, Ms. 8–5.1A BA 74, Chip'yong-ni: Defense of the South Sector of the 23d Regimental Combat Team Perimeter by Company G, 13–15 February 1951, CMH.

17. Award Case File, Pvt. Bruno R. Orig, DSC, RG 500, Eighth Army, Box 1271, NA.

18. Narrative Report, Capt. Edward C. Williamson, Ms. 8–5.1A BA 74, Chip'yong-ni: Defense of the South Sector of the 23d Regimental Combat Team Perimeter by Company G, 13–15 February 1951, CMH.

19. Award Case File, 1st Lt. Richard S. Kotite, DSC, RG 500, Eighth Army, Box 1260, NA.

20. Narrative Report, Capt. Edward C. Williamson, Ms. 8–5.1A BA 74, Chip'yong-ni: Defense of the South Sector of the 23d Regimental Combat Team Perimeter by Company G, 13–15 February 1951, CMH.

10. The Relief of Chip'yong-ni

1. Interviews, Maj. Robert A. Humphrey with 1st Lt. Martin Blumenson, 27 March 1951; Maj. Gibson with 1st Lt. Blumenson; Lt. Col. Morgan B. Heasley with 1st Lt. Martin Blumenson, 28 March 1951; Capt. Joe W. Finley with 1st Lt. Martin Blumenson, 28 March 1951; all in Ms. 8–5.1A BA 29, Task Force Crombez, CMH.

2. Interview, Col. Crombez, Ms. 29.

3. Interview, Maj. Charles J. Parziale with 1st Lt. Martin Blumenson, 27 March 1951, Ms. 8–5.1A BA 29, Task Force Crombez, CMH.

4. Interview, Capt. John C. Barrett with 1st Lt. Martin Blumenson, 26 April 1951, Ms. 8–5.1A BA 29, Task Force Crombez, CMH.

5. Interview, Col. Crombez, Ms. 29.

6. Interview, Maj. Fred T. Wilson with 1st Lt. Martin Blumenson, 28 March 1951, Ms. 8–5.1A BA 29, Task Force Crombez, CMH.

7. Statements, M. Sgt. Jessie O. Giddens, 21 February 1951, and 1st Lt. William R. Bierwirth, no date, both in Ms. 8–5.1A BA 29, Task Force Crombez, CMH.

8. Statements, M. Sgt. Joe Kirkland, no date, and PFC Thomas Bayes Jr., no date, both Ms. 8–5.1A BA 29, Task Force Crombez, CMH.

9. Interview, Capt. Barrett, Ms. 29.

10. Interviews, M. Sgt. Lloyd L. Jones with 1st Lt. Martin Blumenson, 28 March 1951; Cpl. Hubert M. Cobb with 1st Lt. Martin Blumenson, 27 March 51; PFC Donald F. Russell with 1st Lt. Martin Blumenson, 27 March 1951; PFC Homer Bassford and Cpl. George E. Reed with 1st Lt. Martin Blumenson, 28 March 1951; Cpl. Paul Campbell with 1st Lt. Martin Blumenson, 27 March 1951; and Cpl. Wayne O. Kemp with 1st Lt. Martin Blumenson, 27 March 1951; all Ms. 8–5.1A BA 29, Task Force Crombez, CMH.

11. Interview, Col. Crombez; statements, 1st Lt. Bierwirth, M. Sgt. Giddens, SFC Maxwell; all Ms. 8–5.1A BA 29, Task Force Crombez, CMH.

12. Statement, SFC Maxwell, Ms. 29.

13. Interview, Col. Crombez, Ms. 29.

14. Interview, Capt. Barrett, Ms. 29.

15. Interviews, Cpl. Kemp, M. Sgt. Jones, SFC Miller, all Ms. 29.

16. Interview, Capt. Keith M. Stewart with 1st Lt. Martin Blumenson, 27 March 1951, Ms. 8–5.1A BA 29, Task Force Crombez, CMH.

17. Interview, Capt. Barrett, Ms. 29.

18. Interviews, Capt. Barrett and Lt. Col. George B. Pickett with 1st Lt. Martin Blumenson, 1 April 1951, both Ms. 8–5.1A BA 29, Task Force Crombez, CMH.

19. Resume of Action: Task Force Crombez, 5th Cavalry Regiment: 15 February 1951, 1st Lt. Martin Blumenson, Ms. 8–5.1A BA 29, Task Force Crombez, CMH.

BIBLIOGRAPHICAL ESSAY

This work is based primarily on interviews conducted by U.S. Army military historians during the Korean War. Copies of the interviews are held by the U.S. Army Center of Military History at Fort McNair in Washington, D.C. Other primary sources supplement the interviews. These sources include unit historical files from Record Group 407 and award case files from Record Group 500, all held by the National Archives at College Park, Maryland. Other primary sources are noted in the chapter endnotes.

There is a substantial and growing body of secondary material on the Korean War. Only a few of the major titles are noted here as a starting point for those readers who desire to explore additional material about this conflict. For an introduction to the historiography of the war and bibliography, see Allan R. Millett, "The Korean War: A 50-Year Critical Historiography," *Journal of Strategic Studies* 24 (March 2001), pp. 188–224, and Allan R. Millett, *The Korean War: The Essential Bibliography* (Dulles, Va.: Potomac Books, 2007). Millett should also be consulted on the background of the war; see Allan R. Millett, *The War for Korea, 1945–1950: A House Burning* (Lawrence: University Press of Kansas, 2005). For information on the U.S. Army in the years between the conclusion of World War II and the beginning of the Korean War, see William W. Epley, *America's First Cold War Army, 1945–1950* (Association of the U.S. Army, Land Warfare Paper No. 15, 1993).

Military operations are covered in a number of official histories published by the U.S. Army. These include the series United States Army in the Korean War, consisting of the following volumes: Roy E. Appleman, *South to the Naktong, North to the Yalu* (Washington,

D.C.: Center of Military History, 1961); James F. Schnabel, *Policy and Direction: The First Year* (Washington, D.C.: Center of Military History, 1972); Billy C. Mossman, *Ebb and Flow* (Washington, D.C.: Center of Military History, 1990); and Walter G. Hermes, *Truce Tent and Fighting Front* (Washington, D.C.: Center of Military History, 1992).

The U.S. Army also published a number of monographs on the Korean War. Of special interest for small unit combat actions is Russell A. Gugeler, *Combat Actions in Korea* (Washington, D.C.: Center of Military History, 1987). A work covering the background on the U.S. Army in Japan before the war and the experiences in the war of one regiment, the 24th Infantry, the last segregated infantry regiment in the U.S. Army, is William T. Bowers, William M. Hammond, and George L. MacGarrigle, *Black Soldier, White Army: The 24th Infantry Regiment in Korea* (Washington, D.C.: Center of Military History, 1996). For an outline of efforts to develop the South Korean army, see Robert K. Sawyer, *Military Advisors in Korea: KMAG in Peace and War* (Washington, D.C.: Center of Military History, 1988).

The U.S. Marine Corps official history is covered in Lynn Montross et al., *History of U.S. Marine Operations in Korea, 1950–1953*, 5 vols. (Washington, D.C.: Marine Corps Historical Branch, 1954–1972). The other services published one-volume histories of their service during the Korean War; see James A. Field Jr., *History of United States Naval Operations in Korea* (Washington, D.C.: Director of Naval History, 1962), and Robert F. Futrell, *The United States Air Force in Korea, 1950–1953*, rev. ed. (Washington, D.C.: Office of the Chief of Air Force History, 1983).

Among the plentiful secondary works covering the military aspects of the war that are not part of the official histories, of note are Roy E. Appleman, *Ridgway Duels for Korea* (College Station: Texas A&M University Press, 1990), which provides considerable detail on the period covered by the combat interviews in this work, and Clay Blair, *The Forgotten War: America in Korea* (New York: Times Books, 1987), which is based on numerous interviews with commanders at regimental level and above and provides a unique view of the war from those levels. Other works drawn largely from personal accounts of the war include Rod Paschall, *Witness to War: Korea* (New York: Berkley Publishing Group, 1995), and Allan R. Millett, *Their War for Korea: American, Asian, and European Combatants and Civilians, 1945–53* (Dulles, Va.: Brassey's, Inc., 2002).

Works covering the South Korean perspective of the war include the volumes published by the Korea national defense ministry, Institute of Military History, *The Korean War,* 3 vols. (Lincoln: University of Nebraska Press, 2000–2001), and the memoirs of a South Korean general, Gen. Paik Sun-Yup, *From Pusan to Panmunjom* (Dulles, Va.: Brassey's, 1992). The story of the war from the view of North Korea and her allies is gradually becoming more complete, but there is still much that remains unclear. Much of the material is from the Chinese perspective; see for example, Sergei N. Goncharov, John W. Lewis, and Xue Litai, *Uncertain Partners: Stalin, Mao and the Korean War* (Stanford, Calif.: Stanford University Press, 1993); Xiaoming Zhang, *Red Wings Over the Yalu: China, the Soviet Union, and the Air War in Korea* (College Station: Texas A&M University Press, 2002); Xiaobing Li, *A History of the Modern Chinese Army* (Lexington: University Press of Kentucky, 2007); and Xiaobing Li, Allan R. Millett, and Bin Yu, translators and editors, *Mao's Generals Remember Korea* (Lawrence: University Press of Kansas, 2001).

INDEX